IMAGES
of America

AROUND LAKE CUMBERLAND

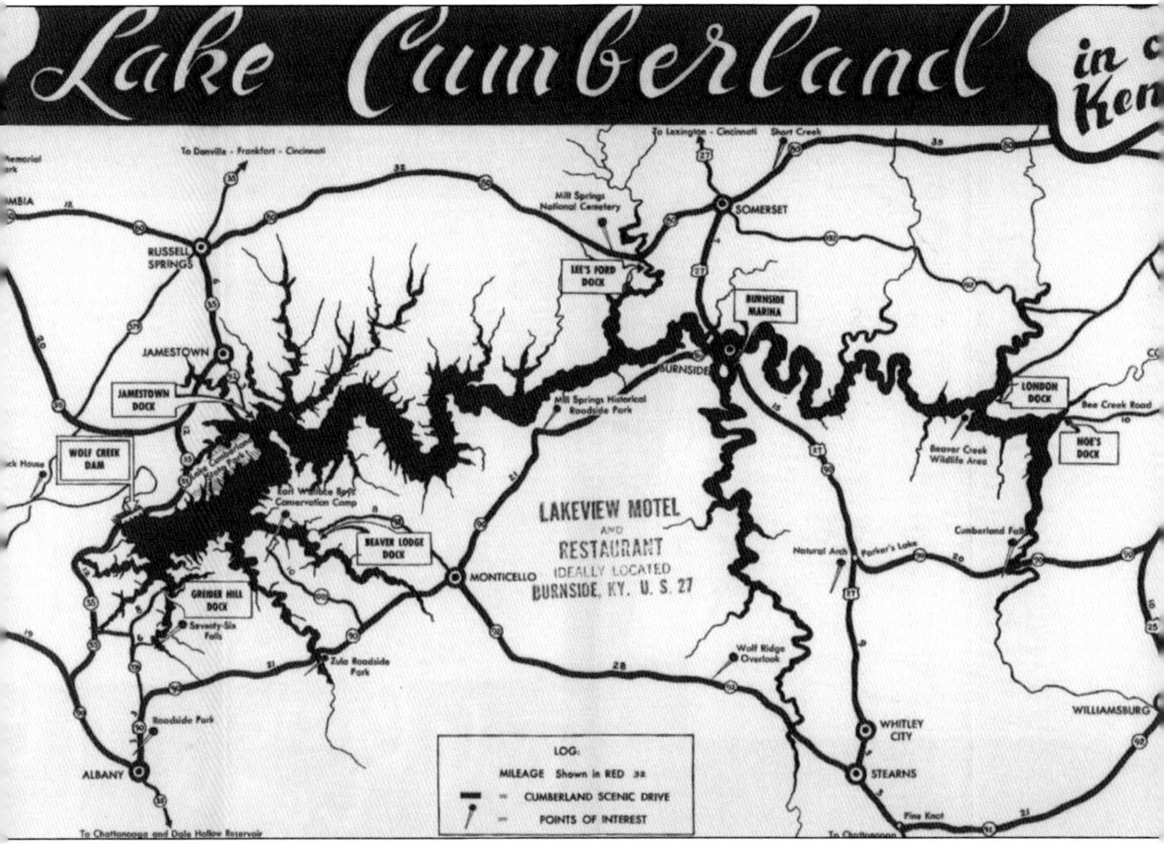

This map of south-central Kentucky shows Lake Cumberland in the late 1950s. Notice the absence of the two main roadways in the area—Interstate 75 (started in 1960 and completed in 1970) and the Cumberland Parkway (built in 1972). The Cumberland Parkway is now known as the Louie B. Nunn Parkway. This map was available to visitors of the Lakeview Motel and Restaurant in Burnside, Kentucky. The motel was razed in the late 1990s to make room for the widening of U.S. Highway 27, but the restaurant was unharmed. Although the name of the restaurant has changed several times over the years, the picturesque views remain. (Courtesy of Phil Ruchka.)

ON THE COVER: From left to right, Jean Greene, Allese Criswell, Inez Criswell, and Annetha Walters pose for a photograph while enjoying a day of frolicking, sunbathing, and swimming. This photograph was taken at Burnside Beach in Burnside, Kentucky, in the mid-1940s. The Cumberland River was a vital part of everyday life for residents in south-central Kentucky. She was known for her beauty as well as her wild and wicked ways. (Courtesy of Jim Fitzgerald.)

IMAGES of America

AROUND LAKE CUMBERLAND

Kris Applegate and Jarenda Miller

ARCADIA PUBLISHING

ISBN 978-0-7385-6819-5

Published by Arcadia Publishing
Charleston, South Carolina

Printed in the United States of America

Library of Congress Control Number: 2009925188

For all general information contact Arcadia Publishing at:
Telephone 843-853-2070
Fax 843-853-0044
E-mail sales@arcadiapublishing.com
For customer service and orders:
Toll-Free 1-888-313-2665

Visit us on the Internet at www.arcadiapublishing.com

*This book is dedicated to our children
and to the loving memory of father, grandfather,
and friend Adeline Miller.*

Contents

ACKNOWLEDGMENTS

This book would not be possible if it had not been for the generosity of the following: the Pulaski County Historical Society (PCHS); Thomas (Tom) Moody; Debbie Lake; John T. Carter; Laura Lee Smith Butler and her father, Randolph Smith; Jim Fitzgerald; Carole Tupman; Judith Waddell; Phil Ruchka; Brian King and Grider Hill Dock; Ron Halcomb; Carol Ann Lewis Lovell; Dudley Bryant; James Lawrence; James Sears and Lake Cumberland State Dock; Don O'Brien; Jonathan Goforth; Dawn Garvan and the Kentucky Department of Parks; Marge Bateman and the Kentucky Department of Travel; the Varland family; Sarah-Jane Poindexter and the Filson Historical Society; Tabitha Crawford; Paul Shepherd and the Cumberland Valley Manor; Margo Fransworth and the Cumberland River Compact; Pat Howard and Carolyn Mounce from the Somerset-Pulaski Convention and Visitor's Bureau; Judy and Floyd at the Cookery; Bryan E. Bihl and Gone Fishing Guide Service; the Lakes Community; the "Mayor" of Marrowbone; and Rogers Photography.

Personal thanks go to the following for their moral and mental support in this endeavor: Todd, Adeline, Weston, and Samuel; our families; Becky and Rod; Elizabeth and Tom; Ali; Roger; the members of the DePauw Memorial United Methodist Church; Timothy Reed; and Luke Cunningham.

INTRODUCTION

Nearly seven million recreation and relaxation seekers alike flock to the rocky shores of Lake Cumberland each year. The tourist season officially opens Memorial Day weekend and extends well into October. In 1999, an average of 250,000 people per month visited Lake Cumberland's shore.

Located in south-central Kentucky, Lake Cumberland is one of the largest man-made lakes east of the Mississippi River. The lake covers 65,530 acres and spreads over the counties of Clinton, Laurel, McCreary, Pulaski, Russell, and Wayne.

Lake Cumberland boasts an impressive 1,255 miles of federally protected shoreline. To put this in perspective, the coastline of Florida is 770 miles in length. The total Atlantic coastline (Maine to Florida) is 2,069 miles, and the total Pacific coastline (California, Oregon, and Washington) is 1,293 miles in length.

The main body of Lake Cumberland is 101 miles long and supplies drinking water to more than 200,000 people. With its tributaries and numerous coves, Lake Cumberland is a tourist's ideal destination.

Lake Cumberland is actually a reservoir for Wolf Creek Dam and ranks ninth in the United States in size with a capacity of 6.1 million acre-feet of water—roughly 1.9 trillion gallons of water. That is enough water to cover the entire state of Kentucky to a depth of 3 inches.

But Lake Cumberland has not always been the houseboat capital of the world, as it is now. Lake Cumberland was born after Wolf Creek Dam was built by the U.S. Army Corps of Engineers. It was constructed mainly for flood control and for hydroelectric power.

The story of Lake Cumberland actually begins with the Cumberland River. Byrd Douglas, author of *Steamboatin' on the Cumberland*, said, "The area was one of the last frontiers in the Eastern United States, unexcelled in beauty and unadorned by any semblance of modern improvements. Rich in raw materials, peopled by the finest stock of pioneers and unperturbed by advancing civilization all around it, here was a prize that caused many steamboat captains to gasp for breath."

The Cumberland River formed near Harlan, Kentucky, and flowed through south-central Kentucky down to Nashville, Tennessee. In Nashville, the river curves back northward into western Kentucky before draining into the Ohio River at Smithland, Kentucky, for a total of 687 miles.

The Cumberland River was a vital waterway in the lives of Kentuckians. It was first used as a travel passage for hunters and settlers. As the population increased, floating stores and shops appeared on the river. Entrepreneurs, including blacksmiths and dry-goods merchants, often traveled in flatboats along the river looking for business. The river later supported steamboat trade, which settlers depended upon. Towns and villages grew along her banks from Burkesville to Burnside.

Burnside was the head of navigation on the Cumberland. Navigation above Burnside was impossible because of shoals or sandbanks and mountainous terrain. Steep cliffs sometimes rose 300 to 500 feet above the river. However, the 325 miles of terrain between Burnside and Nashville was more suited to travel. The river alternated between high rocky hills and fertile floodplain.

With the growth of river traffic, bandits and river pirates occasionally preyed on river travelers. "Boatwreckers" offered to help navigate a stranded boat across a shoal. They would then deliberately wreck the boat and help themselves to the cargo as it was "salvaged."

Many travelers relied on the safety of steamboats. Steamboats were a common sight on the Cumberland River by the mid-1840s. There were 12 principal river landings and towns on the Cumberland River. Upstream from Nashville were Martinsburg, McMillin's Landing, Black's Ferry, Cloyd's Landing, Burkesville, Bakerton, Albany Landing, Creelsboro, Rowena (Wild Goose), Mill Springs, Waitsboro, and Burnside.

Minor docking points included Marrow's Landing, Dunbar's Landing, Rankin Landing, Eads Landing, and Robertsport—which currently sits under Conley Bottom Resort in Wayne County.

Creelsboro was a prominent river landing and at one point was the largest town in Russell County. Thomas Elijah and William Jackman were the first settlers in the area. William Campbell opened a ferry business in 1814. Near this ferry was an established tavern and trading post owned by Elijah and Elza Creel. On January 29, 1836, Creelsboro was incorporated. There were only about 50 residents in the 1840s, but it was considered a major trading center on the Cumberland.

Although Creelsboro was small, it had a constable, a post office, a tavern, a store, a hotel, a Union Church, a tanyard, doctors, and a school. The first bank opened in 1808. The bank was robbed on July 14, 1932, by Forest Bradshaw, Mark Weams, and Clinton Turnham. The robbers were caught later that day and given prison terms.

Long Bottom was a small community between Rowena and Kendal, Kentucky. Long Bottom was in the southern part of Russell County and followed along the flat land of the Cumberland River. It was an open area with the river on one side and a steep hill on the other side. Established in 1822, Long Bottom had the first post office in the area.

River travel was only possible during the rainy seasons until the U.S. Army Corps of Engineers created a series of locks and dams along the river. From 1888 to 1928, a total of 15 dams and locks were built along the Cumberland River to aid in navigation during low river levels. Even though this system of locks and dams was almost obsolete as soon as it was completed, these locks were, and are, an important part of the history of the Cumberland River.

Trade was increasing alongside the river as the railroad entered south-central Kentucky. The Southern Railway was completed, and the first freight train arrived in Burnside in February 1880.

Automobiles and trucks were becoming commonplace in the 1930s. The good roads movement was under way, and the area was thriving.

One thing that was not improving in the area was the threat of floods. With the Flood Act of 1939, plans were put into the works to build Wolf Creek Dam. That is when the entire region changed forever.

One

Life along the Cumberland

In 1750, an explorer named Dr. Thomas Walker led an expedition across the Appalachian Mountains to the western wilderness of "Kanta-Ke." Walker happened upon a waterway, which he named the Cumberland River in honor of Prince William, Duke of Cumberland. Prior to Walker's trip, the Cumberland River was called "Warioto" (beautiful) by Native Americans and "Shauvanon" (River of the Shawnees) by French traders.

Despite suitable conditions for settlement, growth and development along the Cumberland River was sluggish until the mid-1800s. The Great Western Movement brought an influx of pioneers into Kentucky. As people forded the Cumberland River, they found the land hospitable with rich soil and an abundance of fish and wildlife. Many families ended their journey west to settle along the banks of the Cumberland. They cleared timber, opened trails, hunted game, fished the Cumberland, farmed the land, and established small communities.

The river was the main artery for trade in south-central Kentucky in the mid-1800s. It was also the center of recreation with swimming, fishing, and picnicking.

Just as the river was mesmerizing and ever flowing, she was equally erratic and volatile with sudden flooding of her banks. Residents living in the floodplain grew to expect being awakened by the ringing of church bells warning of rising water. Townspeople rushed to help their neighbors move precious possessions to higher ground.

Morning light revealed buildings, houses, and outbuildings underwater. Boats soon appeared floating over flooded streets. As the river subsided, residents shoveled the mud and muck from their homes and businesses. Floods, although often devastating, were a way of life for residents along the Cumberland.

In spite of floods, communities along the Cumberland River such as Burnside, Creelsboro, Albany, and Burkesville continued to grow and thrive.

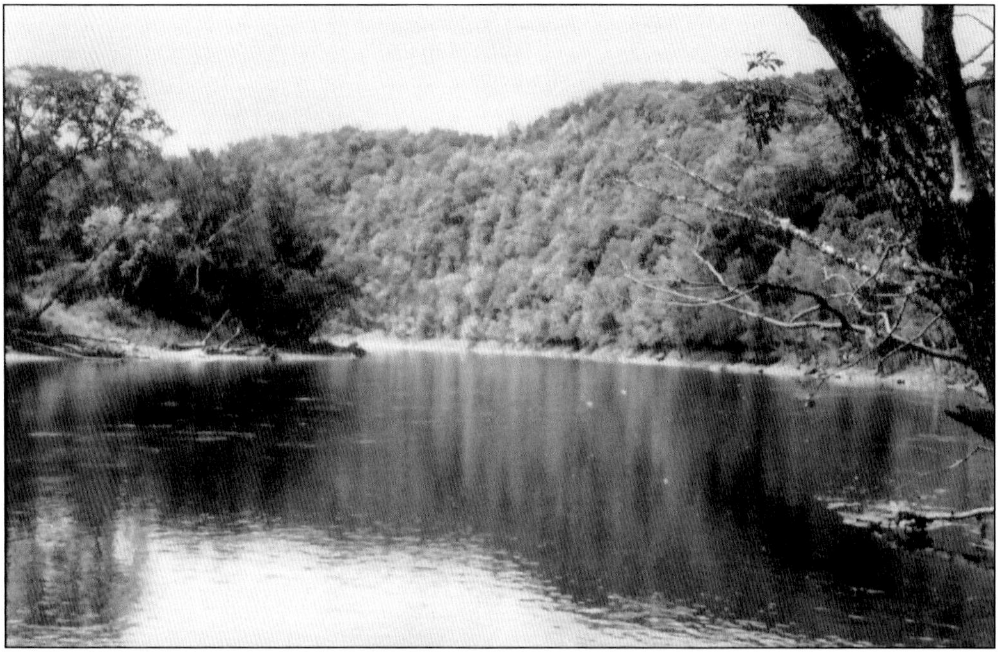

Dr. Thomas Walker discovered and named the Cumberland River in 1752, forty-two years before Kentucky became a state. Walker initially started his expedition in Virginia in 1748 with five men, seven horses, and an assortment of dogs to find and claim land suitable for settlement. (Courtesy of Carole Tupman.)

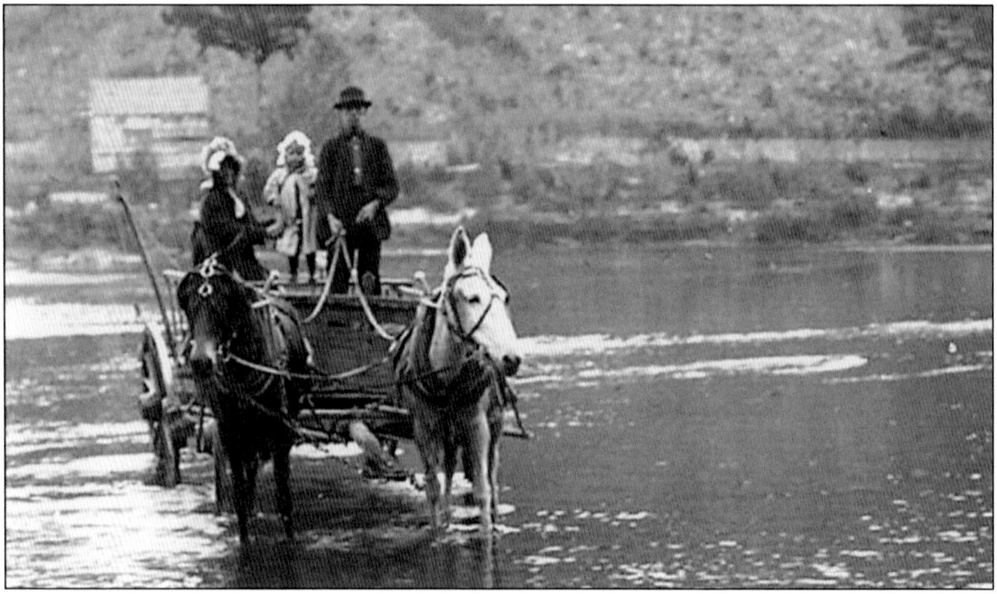

The Owens family stopped shortly after making their way across the Cumberland River because Nancy Owens was in labor. An elderly Native American woman happened upon the family, delivered the baby girl, and named her Rowena. The family settled there, and the new community was established as Rowena, Kentucky, on May 14, 1847. Although this photograph does not show the Owens family, it depicts an early family crossing the Cumberland River. (Courtesy of the PCHS.)

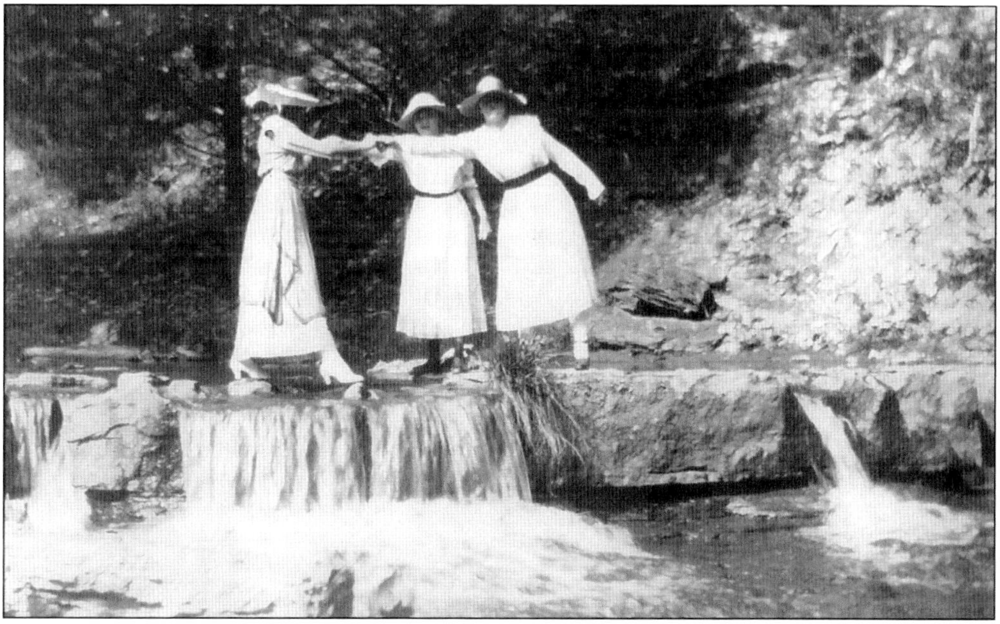

Shown in this photograph are three young ladies carefully navigating across a stream on their way to a Sunday picnic. Sundays were the only socially acceptable day for courting. Suitable forms of courting were sitting on the porch talking, walking home from church, or attending a church picnic. Dating was almost always conducted under the watchful eye of a chaperone. (Courtesy of Randolph Smith.)

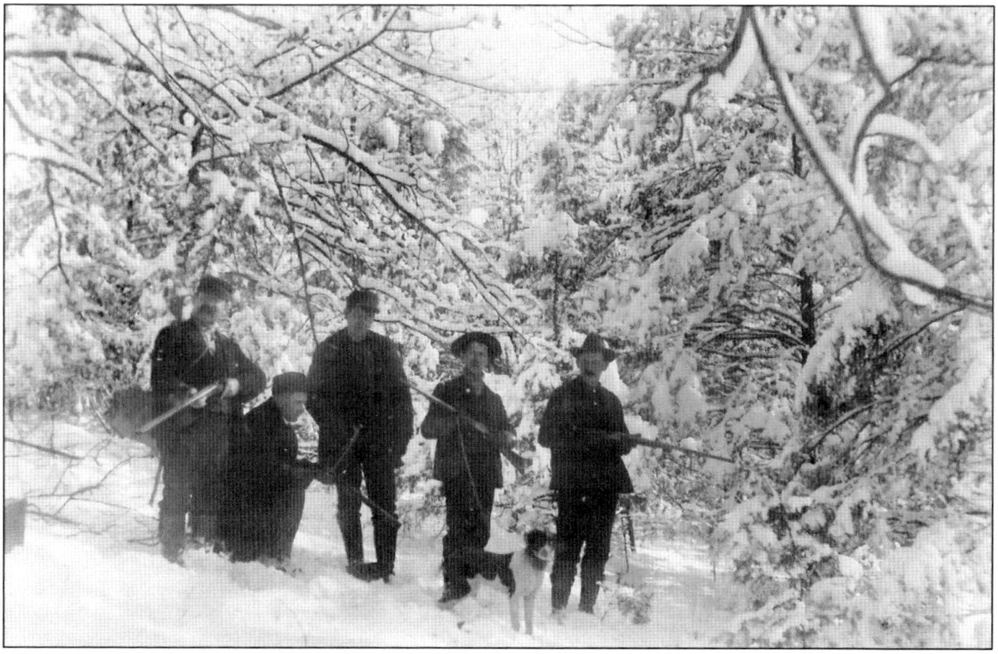

The Cumberland River basin was often referred to as one of the finest game preserves in North America. Deer, buffalo, bear, fox, elk, wild turkey, quail, and pheasant were found in abundance in the rich forests surrounding the river. To feed their families, men had to hunt in all weather conditions. (Courtesy of the PCHS.)

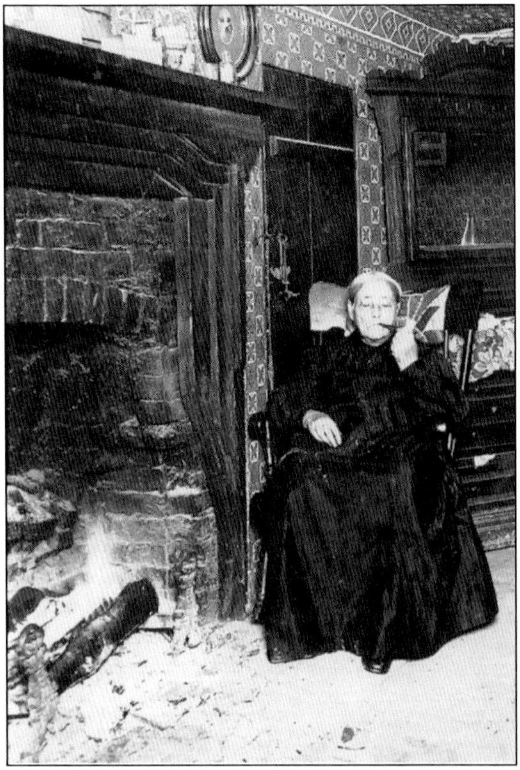

Mary Elizabeth "Betty" Barnes Fitzgerald enjoys her pipe after a long day of hard work in the late 1800s. Betty was the mother of John Morgan Fitzgerald, who was killed on the banks of the Cumberland River in Burnside in 1913. (Courtesy of Judith Waddell.)

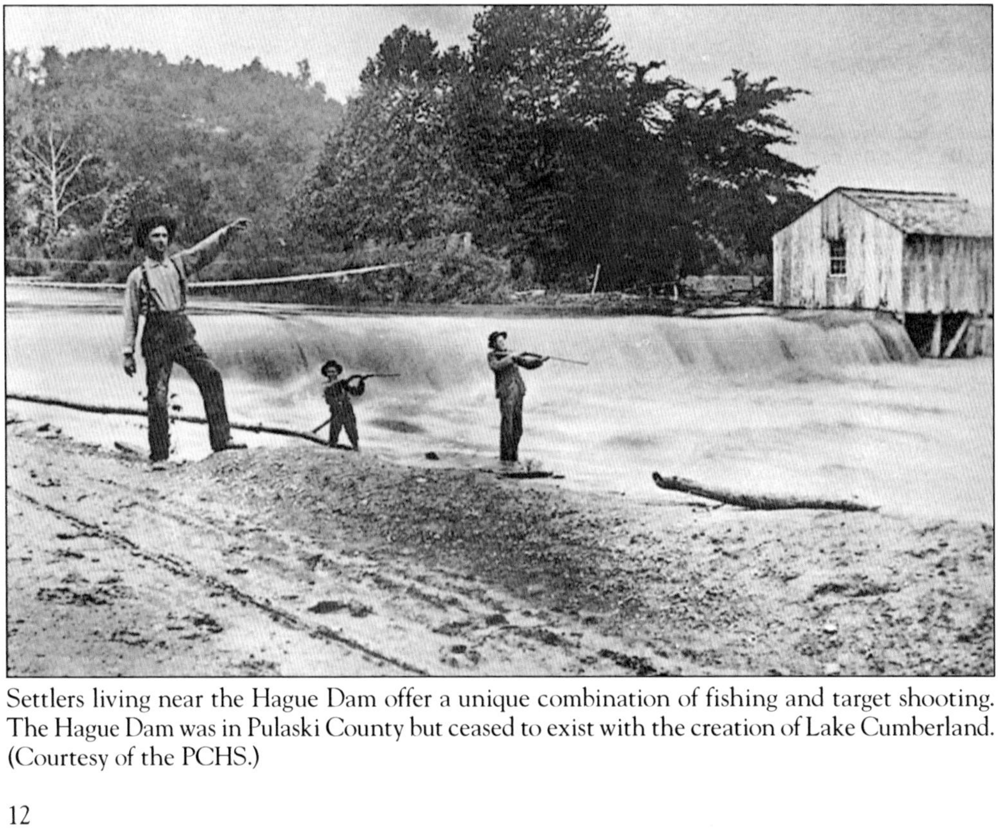

Settlers living near the Hague Dam offer a unique combination of fishing and target shooting. The Hague Dam was in Pulaski County but ceased to exist with the creation of Lake Cumberland. (Courtesy of the PCHS.)

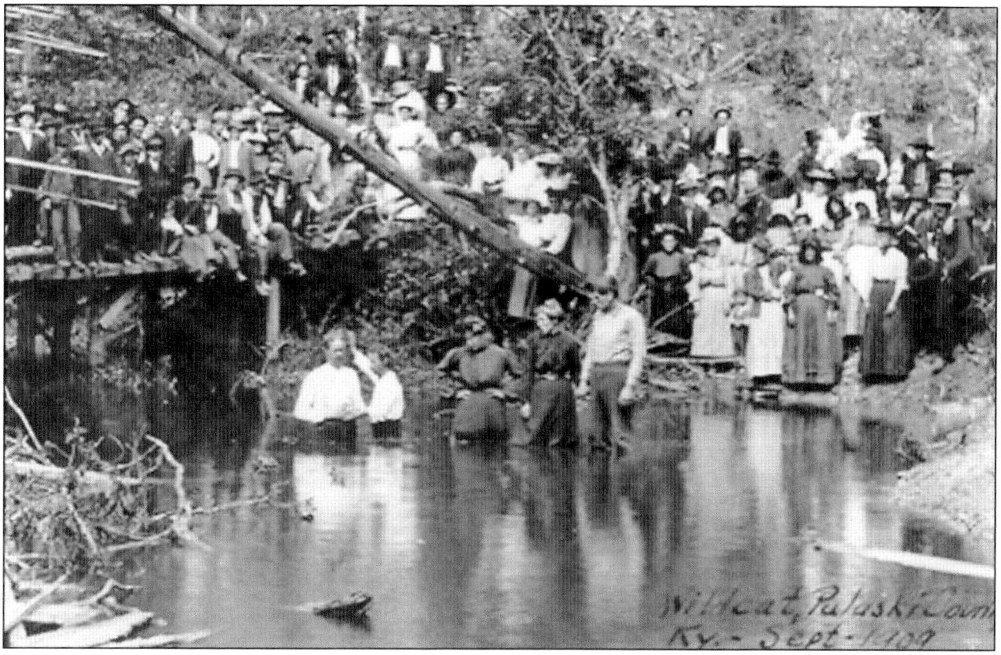

Full submersion baptisms in ponds, creeks, and the Cumberland River were popular among early Christian settlers. As a prerequisite to baptism, a person had to publicly declare their experience of salvation in front of the congregation. This photograph shows a baptism in Pulaski County in September 1909. (Courtesy of John T. Carter.)

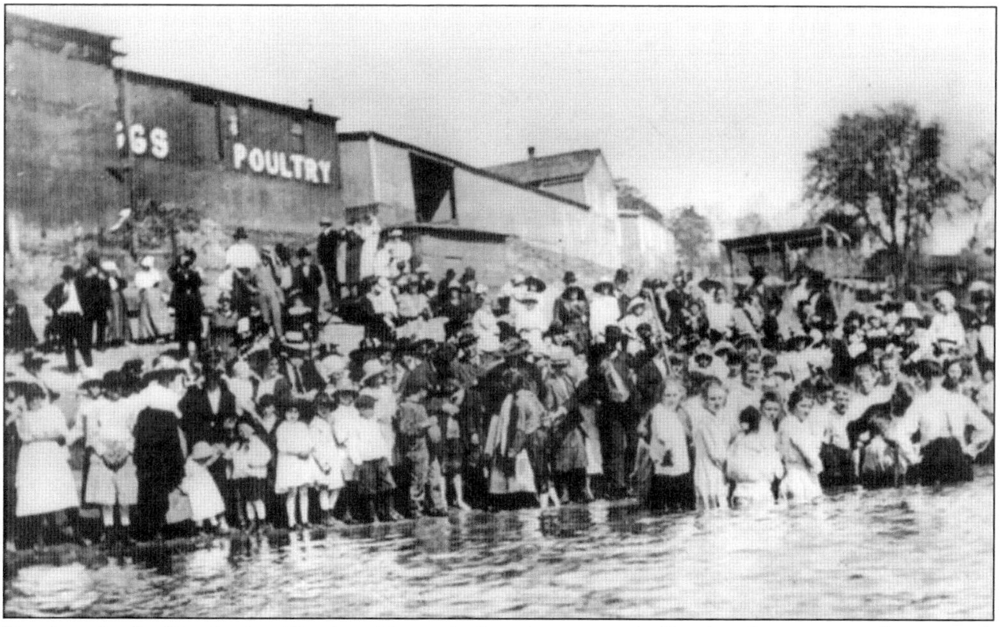

Baptisms in the Cumberland River at Burnside drew large crowds. Outdoor baptism is still practiced, although most churches now have built-in baptismal pools. Some people disagree over which is more appropriate. One Pulaski County church split over the issue, resulting in two separate churches, one called "Hot Water Baptists" and the other "Cold Water Baptists." (Courtesy of Rogers Photography.)

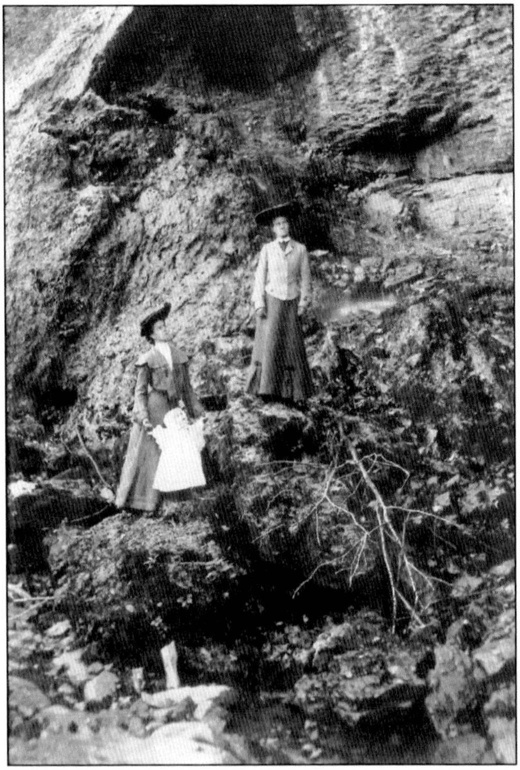

Cora Babbs (left), her son, Maynard, and sister, Edna Plump, look up to the top of a steep cliff. A section of land along the river near Burnside was called "Rock City" because of its steep cliffs, caves, and rock formations. Some cliffs were between 300 and 500 feet high. It was a popular spot for the locals as well as visitors. This photograph was taken in 1904. (Courtesy of the PCHS.)

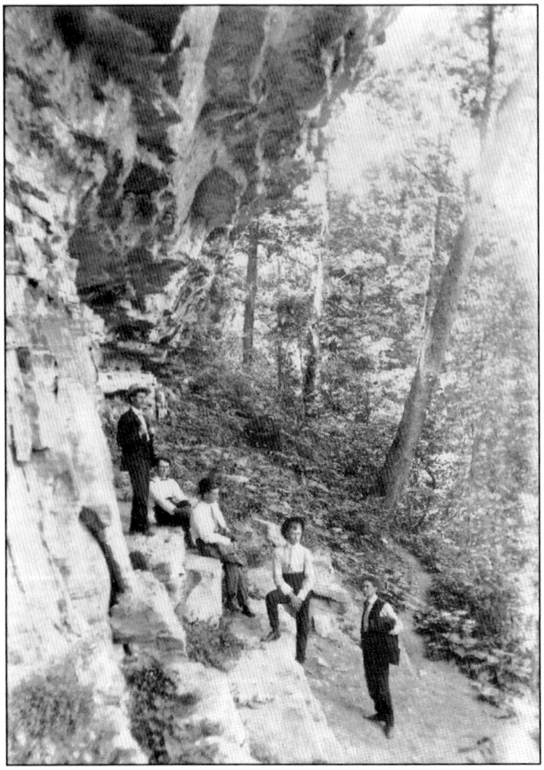

From left to right, David Spoonman, Lee Kessler, Harry Rankin, Tom Rankin, and John Allgeyr stand in front of an entrance to Newell Cave at "Rock City." Gentleman enjoyed the rugged terrain, and ladies enjoyed the beautiful scenic surroundings of Rock City. (Courtesy of the PCHS.)

Diddle Ville School was a one-room schoolhouse in Russell County. One-room schools were common in the area until the 1950s. Historian David Tyack has said these schools were antiquated with poorly trained teachers and inadequate buildings. They were often poorly attended. Consolidation of one-room schools into larger schools was possible mainly because of modern transportation. (Courtesy of Debbie Lake.)

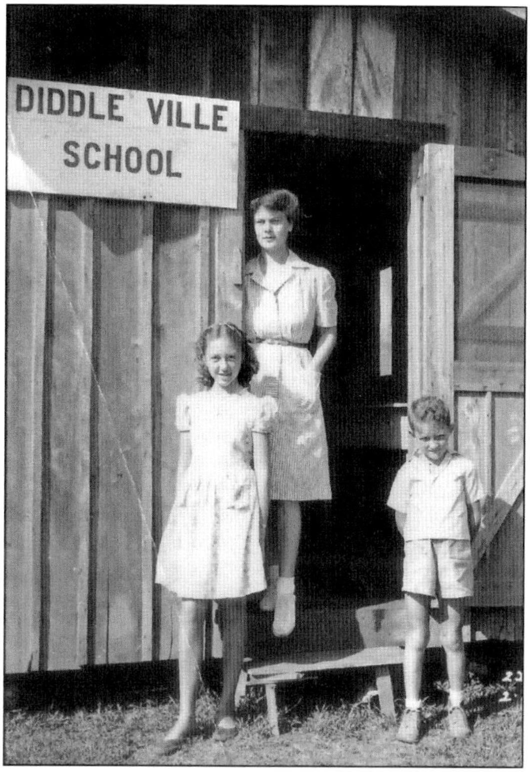

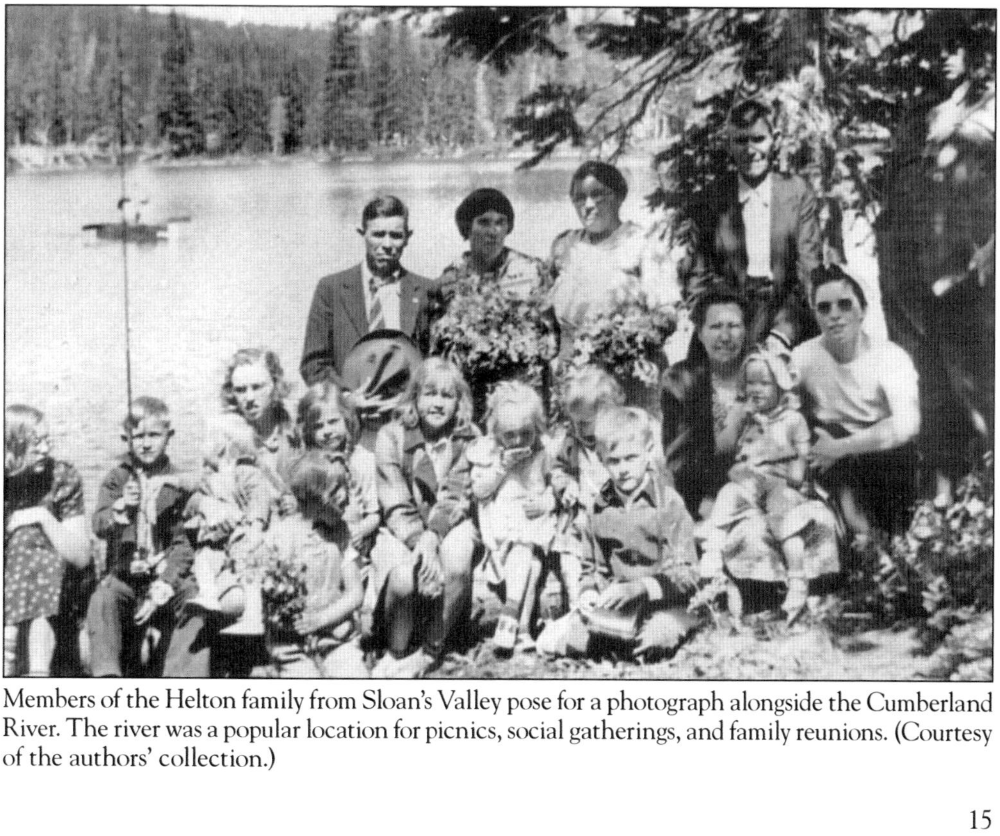

Members of the Helton family from Sloan's Valley pose for a photograph alongside the Cumberland River. The river was a popular location for picnics, social gatherings, and family reunions. (Courtesy of the authors' collection.)

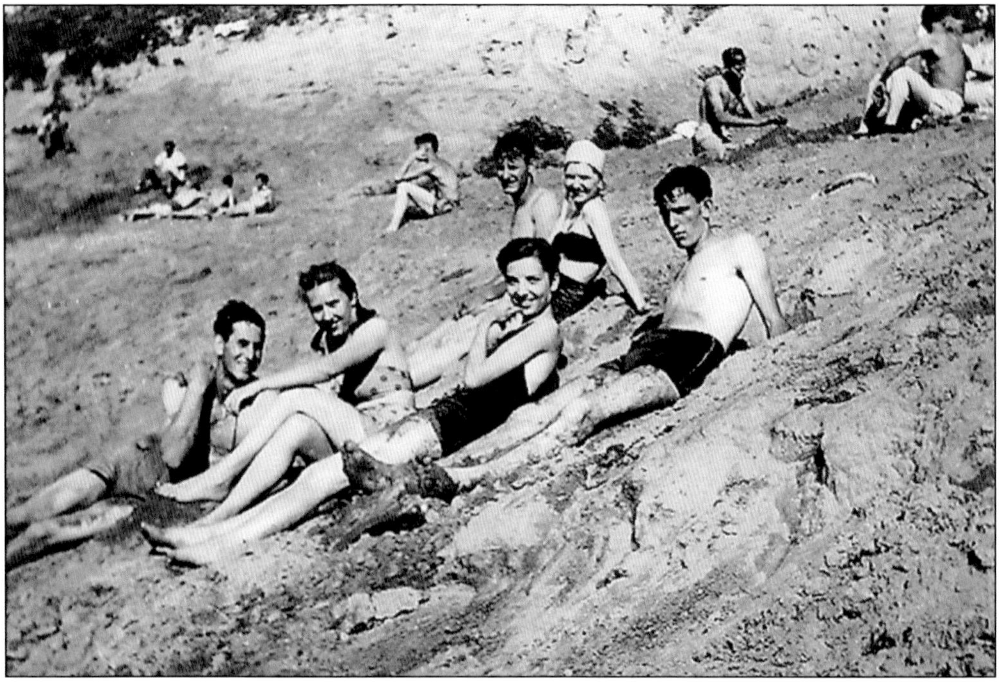

Burnside Beach was an extremely popular place for teenagers and young adults to enjoy a sunny summer afternoon along the warm waters of the Cumberland River. Beachgoers enjoyed sunbathing, swimming, and playing in the river. (Courtesy of Judith Waddell.)

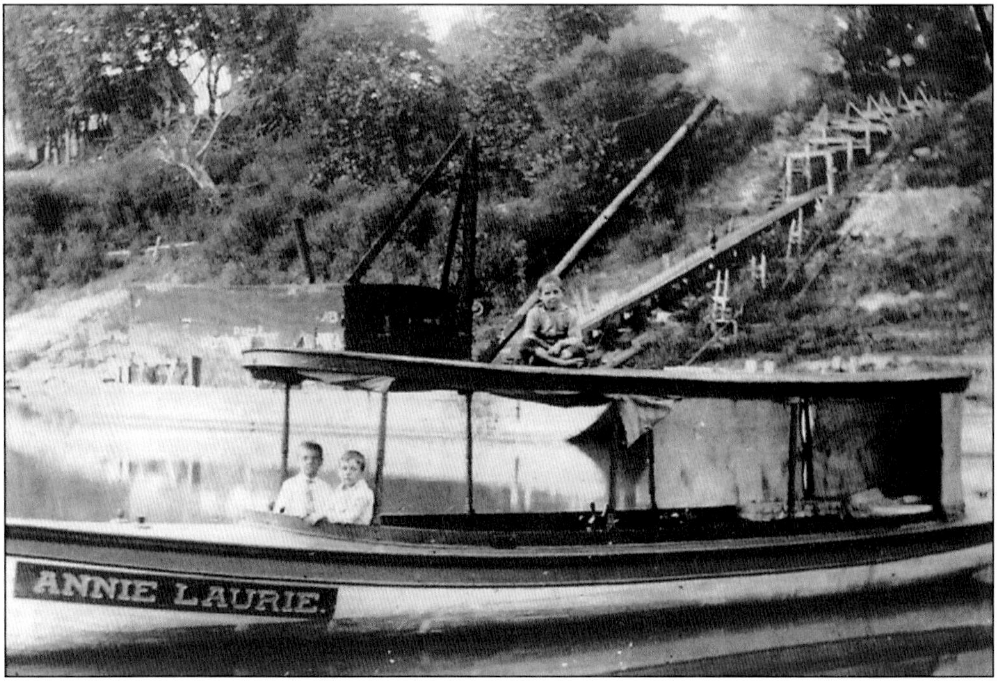

The *Annie Laurie* was crafted by John Morgan Fitzgerald for one of his daughters. The photograph was taken on the Big South Fork in Burnside in 1913, the same year John Morgan Fitzgerald was shot and killed. (Courtesy of Judith Waddell and John T. Carter.)

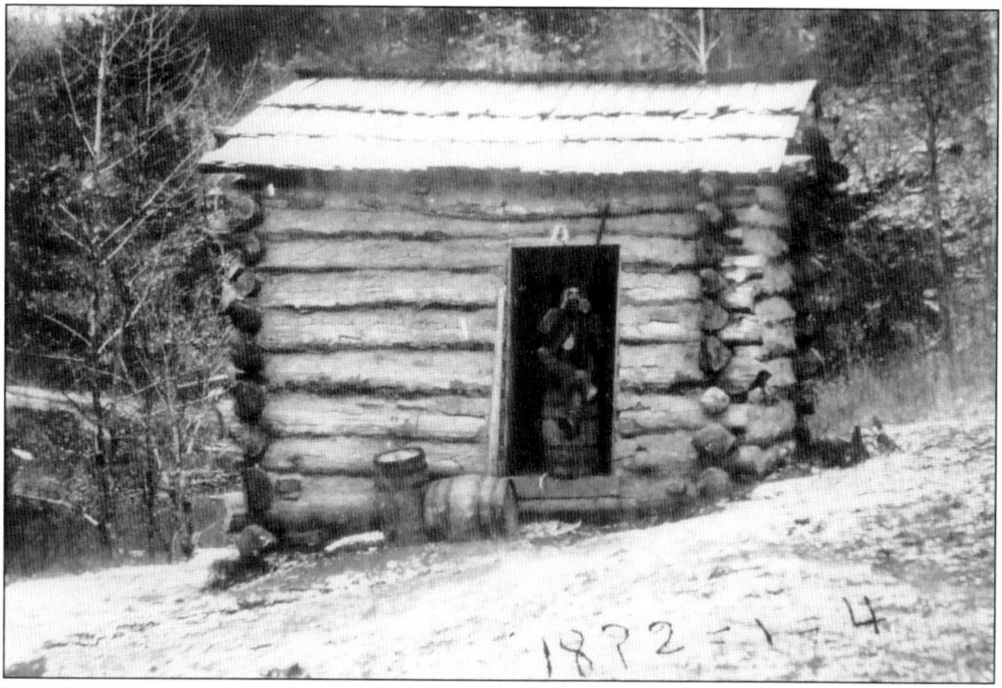

James VanHoozer sits armed with a shotgun in the doorway of the barrel house. The barrel house was near the old still on Tommie Simpson's farm. This photograph was taken in the early winter of 1872. (Courtesy of the PCHS.)

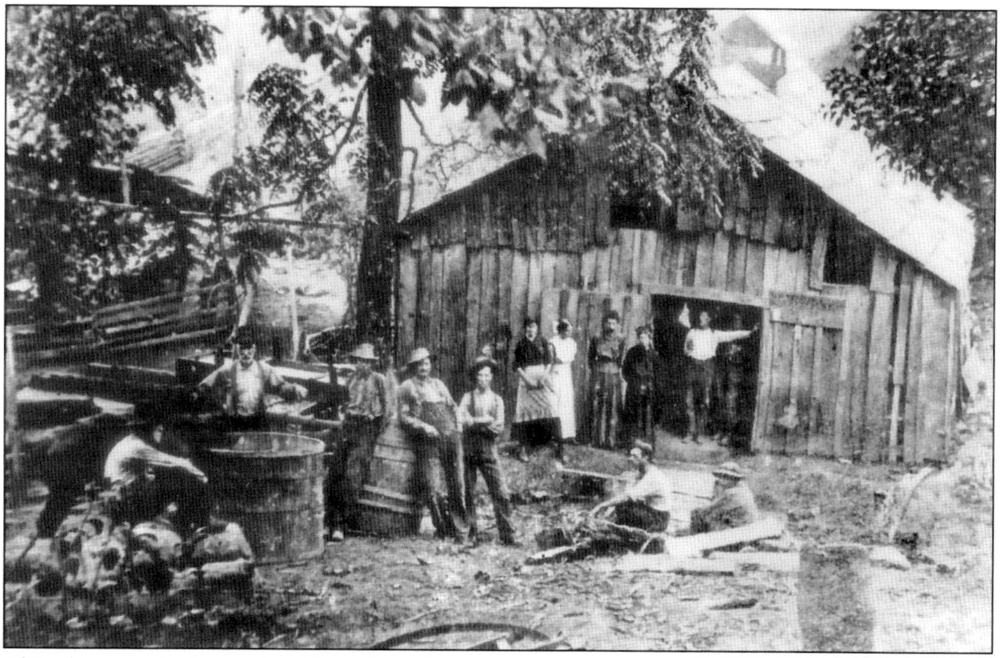

This photograph shows a legal brandy mill near Jamestown in the late 1800s. The brandy mill was licensed and taxed by the State of Kentucky, which made it legal. The production of distilled liquor without a license was called moonshining, while selling illegal alcohol was called bootlegging. (Courtesy of Carole Tupman.)

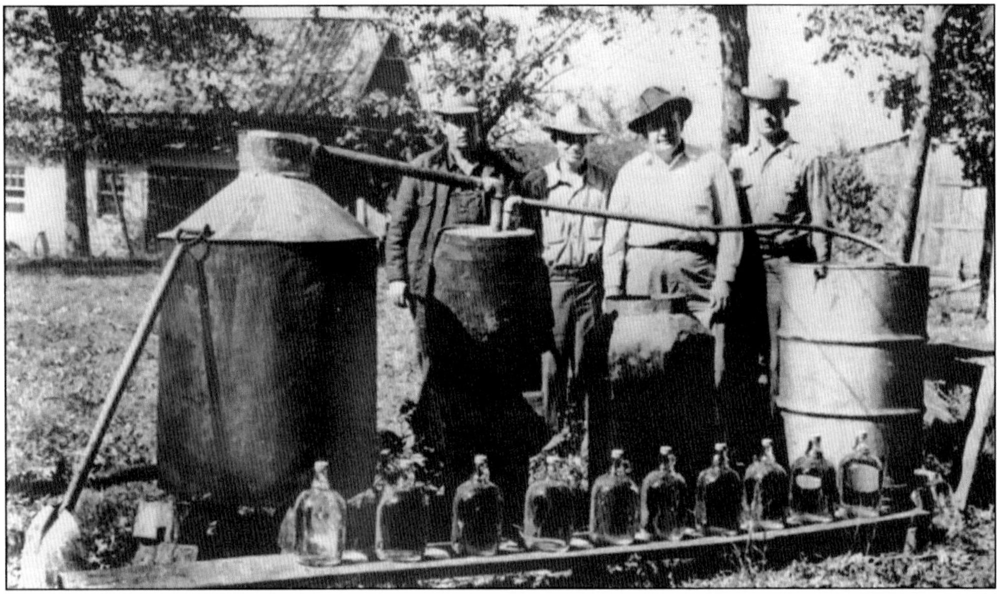

Basic moonshine ingredients were universal—cornmeal, water, malt, sugar, and yeast. This mixture, called mash, was allowed to ferment before it was added to the copper pot stills where it was heated. A cap was placed over the pot to collect and drain the vapor into a container. As the vapor cooled, it condensed into alcohol. Other names for moonshine were corn liquor, skull cracker, sugar whiskey, rotgut, ruckus juice, happy Sally, hillbilly pop, and white lightning. (Courtesy of Rogers Photography.)

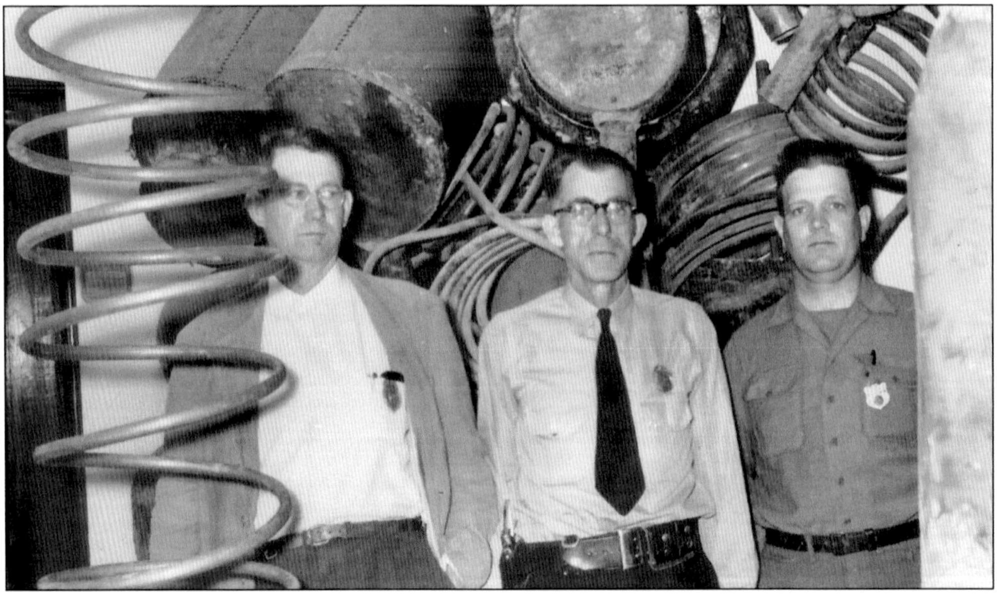

Authorities are shown with confiscated stills in this photograph. Most communities remained "dry" after Prohibition, meaning no alcohol was legally sold. However, in 2004, Burnside residents voted on the issue. In 2005, seventy years after Probation, Burnside became a "moist" town, meaning restaurants selling alcohol must obtain at least 70 percent of their net sales from food. Beer, wine, and spirits are not permitted to be sold through any other establishments. (Courtesy of Randolph Smith.)

The Cumberland Falls are 68 feet high, average a water flow of 3,600 cubic feet per second, and are referred to as the "Niagara of the South." The falls have always been a popular tourist spot. A rare phenomenon called a "moonbow," or lunar rainbow, only occurs at the Cumberland Falls and Victoria Falls in Africa. This photograph was taken in the late 1800s. (Courtesy of Carole Tupman.)

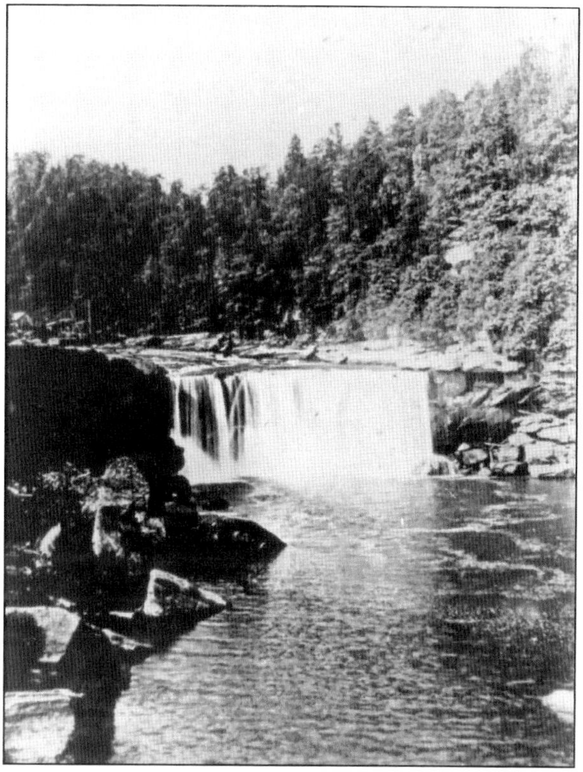

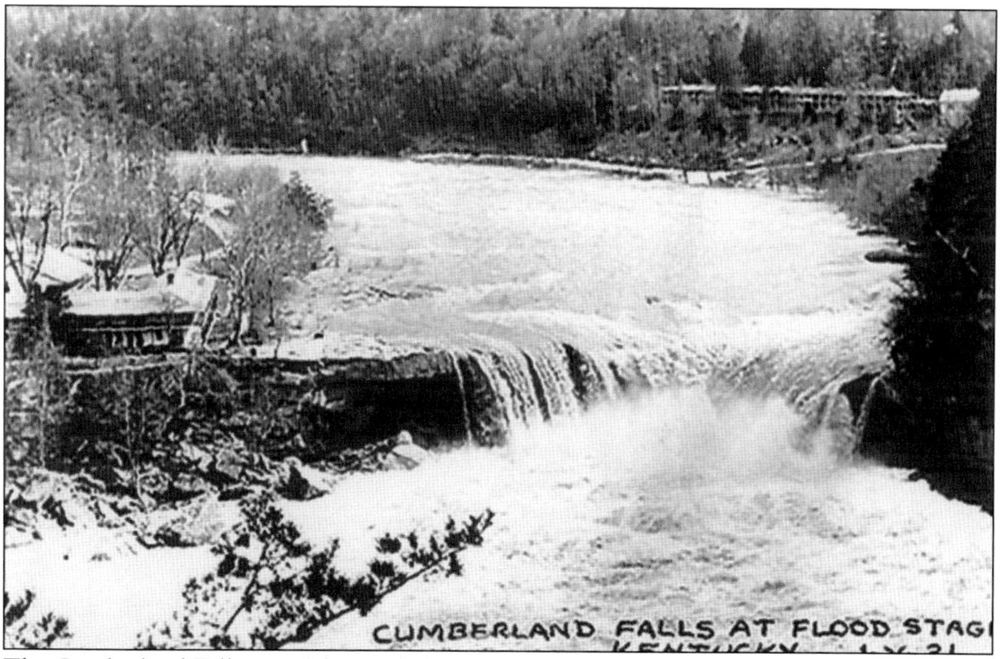

The Cumberland Falls is 125 feet wide but can quickly expand to 300 feet wide during flood stage. The Cumberland Falls Inn (upper right) was destroyed by fire in 1947, and the Moonbow Inn (left) burned in 1949. Neither of the hotels were rebuilt on the properties. (Courtesy of John T. Carter.)

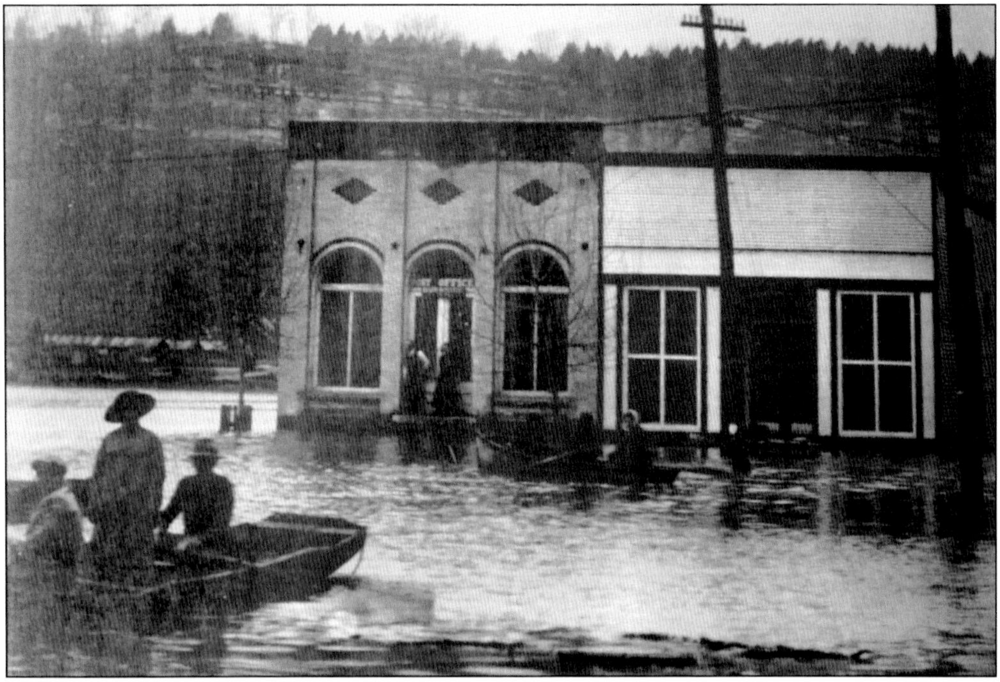

This photograph shows the old post office in Burnside in 1902 when the flooded Cumberland River reached 64.4 feet. Soon after this photograph was taken, the post office was moved to a building on higher ground to escape further flooding. (Courtesy of Dudley Bryant.)

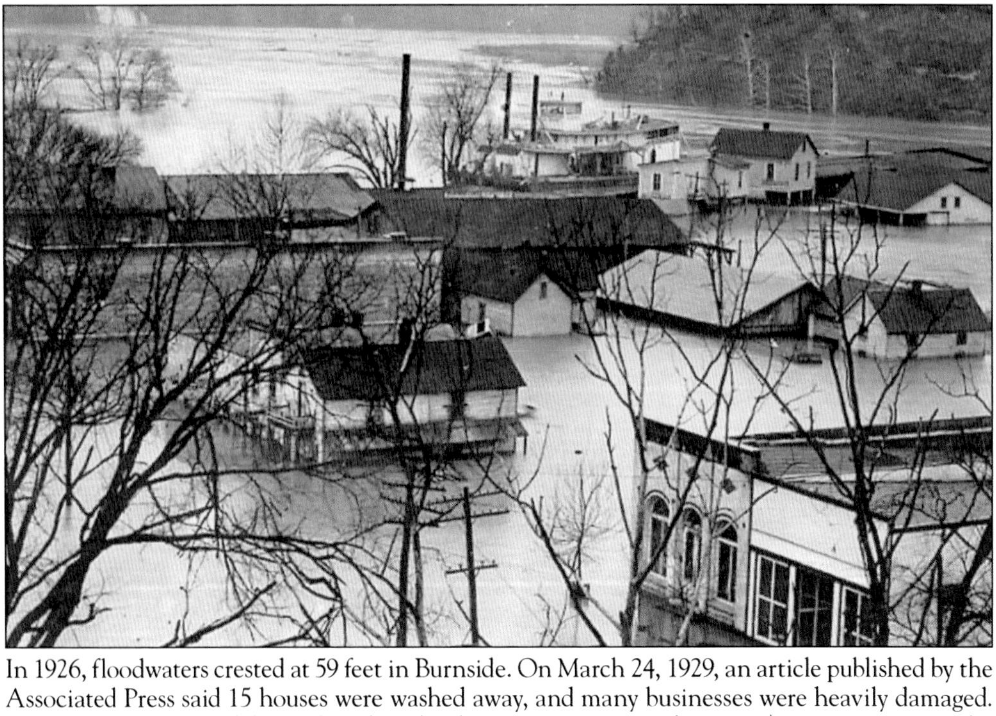

In 1926, floodwaters crested at 59 feet in Burnside. On March 24, 1929, an article published by the Associated Press said 15 houses were washed away, and many businesses were heavily damaged. The article read, "No life was lost, but the damages are expected to cost $200,000." Notice the *Rowena* in the upper section of the photograph. (Courtesy of the PCHS.)

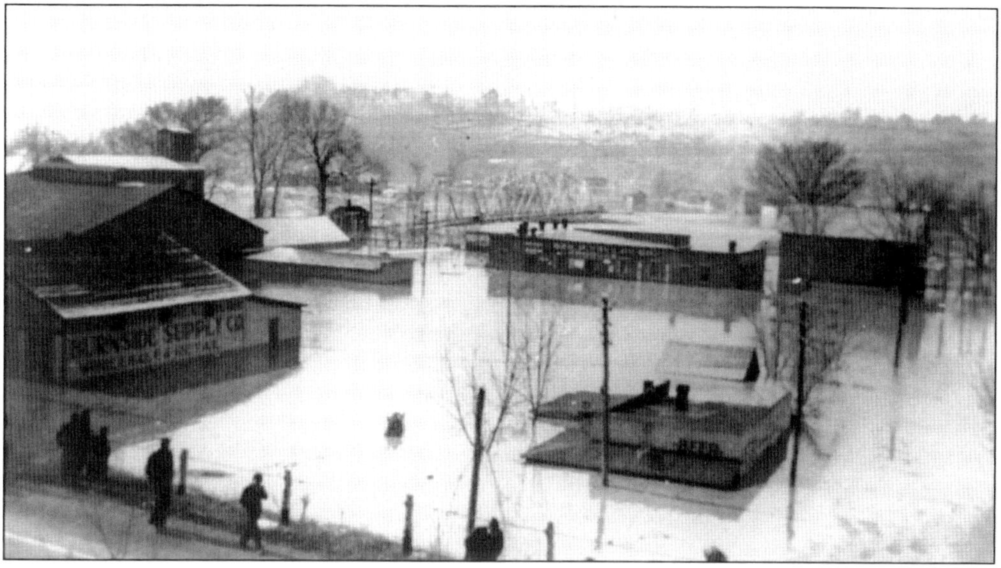

In 1929, muddy waters covered Fanny Brown's restaurant. Brown was one of Burnside's most infamous residents—not for her restaurant's good food, but for her antics. Fanny had an artificial leg made of cork, and each night, she hid her money in her leg. One night, her home was burglarized and her leg was stolen. The police found her leg, but the money was gone. Fanny also had a tendency to drink hard liquor and received the nickname "Happy Sal" from locals. After an evening of imbibing, she loved to play "Hell Broke Loose in Georgia" on the phonograph. (Courtesy of the authors' collection.)

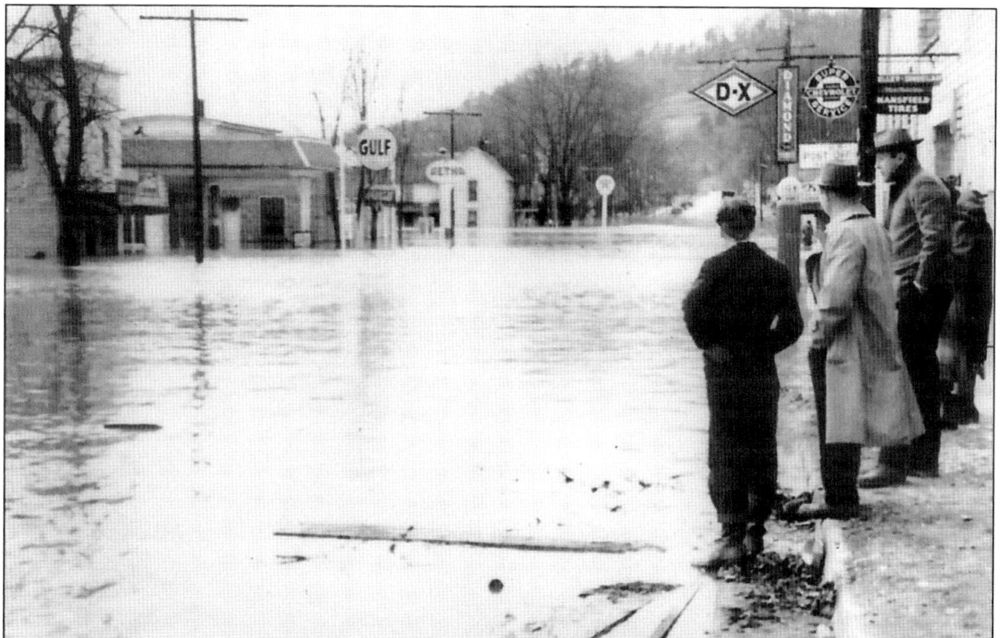

The photograph shows high water covering a street in Burkesville, Kentucky, in the mid-1940s. The city of Burkesville was incorporated in 1846 and was named after Isham Burke, a prominent citizen leader at the time. People of all ages often walked to the edge of the floodwater to see well-known landmarks underwater. (Courtesy of Randolph Smith.)

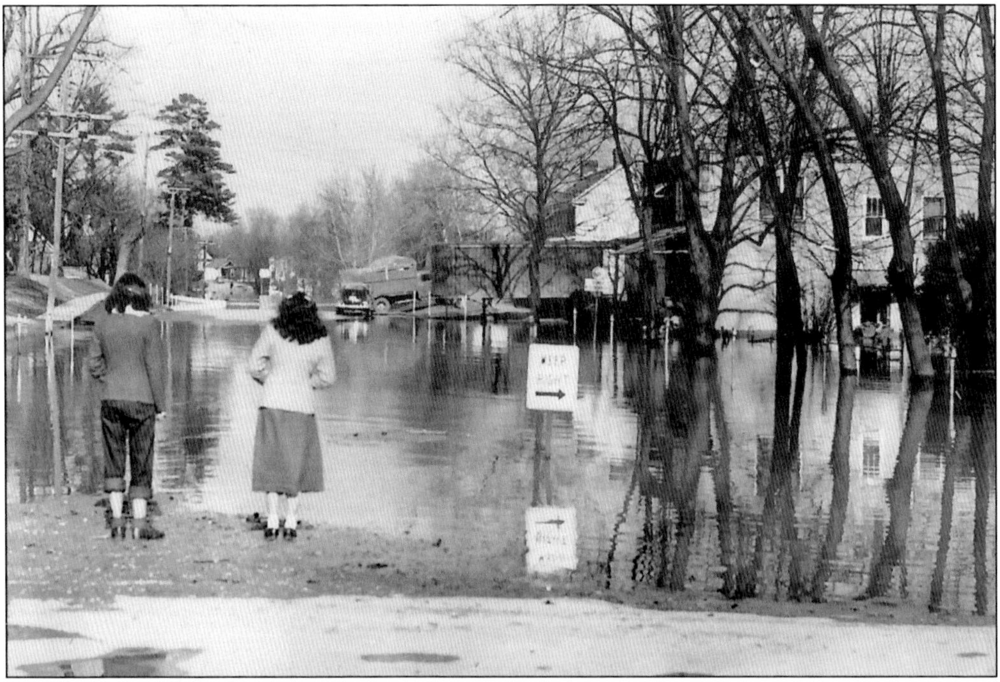

As floodwater recedes after the flood of 1946, two young ladies stand at the water's edge to marvel at the water level and compare it to past floods. It was not uncommon for the Red Cross to send in supplies for flood victims. (Courtesy of Randolph Smith.)

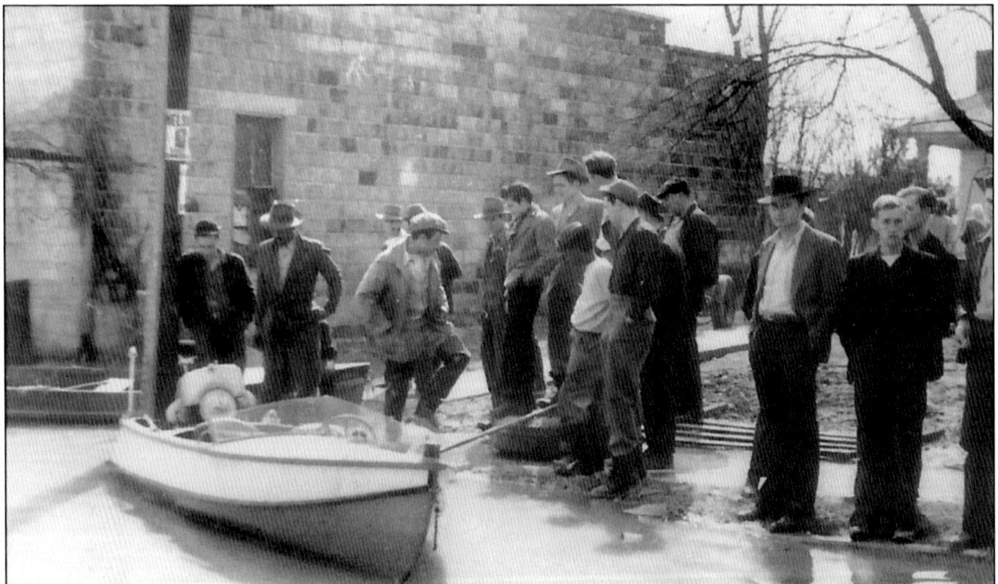

Oftentimes boats were needed to maneuver though town after the Cumberland flooded her banks. This photograph shows townspeople congregating at the floodwater's edge, ready to take their turn in rescue efforts in Burkesville. (Courtesy of Randolph Smith.)

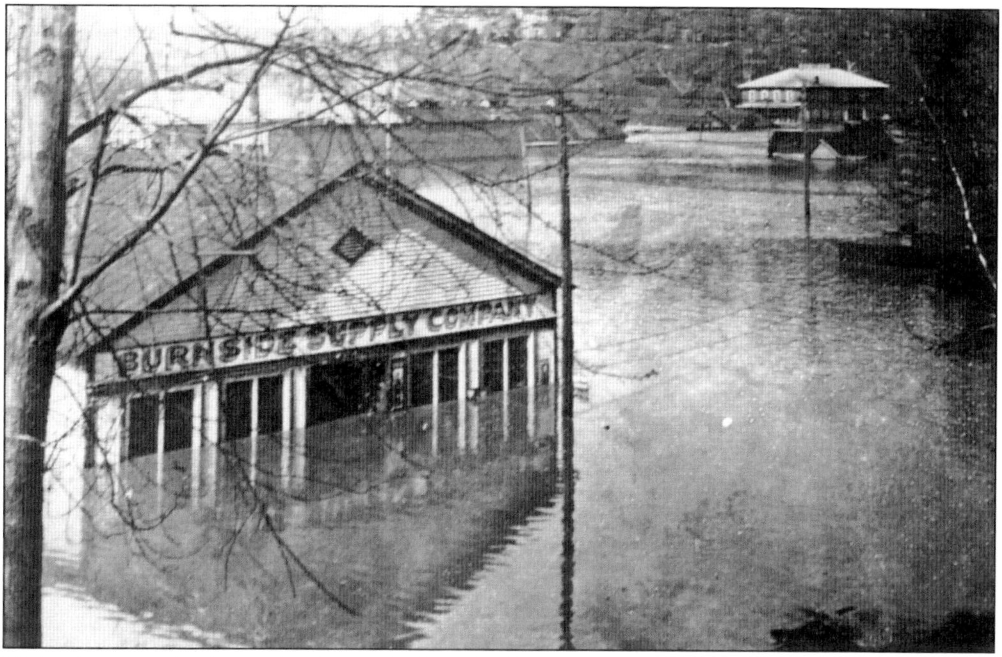

This photograph shows the Burnside Supply Company in 1929, two years after it opened. Unfortunately, the Cumberland River crested at 69.2 feet in 1929, destroying much of the store's merchandise. However, the greatest flood ever recorded in Burnside crested at 73.4 feet in 1882. (Courtesy of Dudley Bryant.)

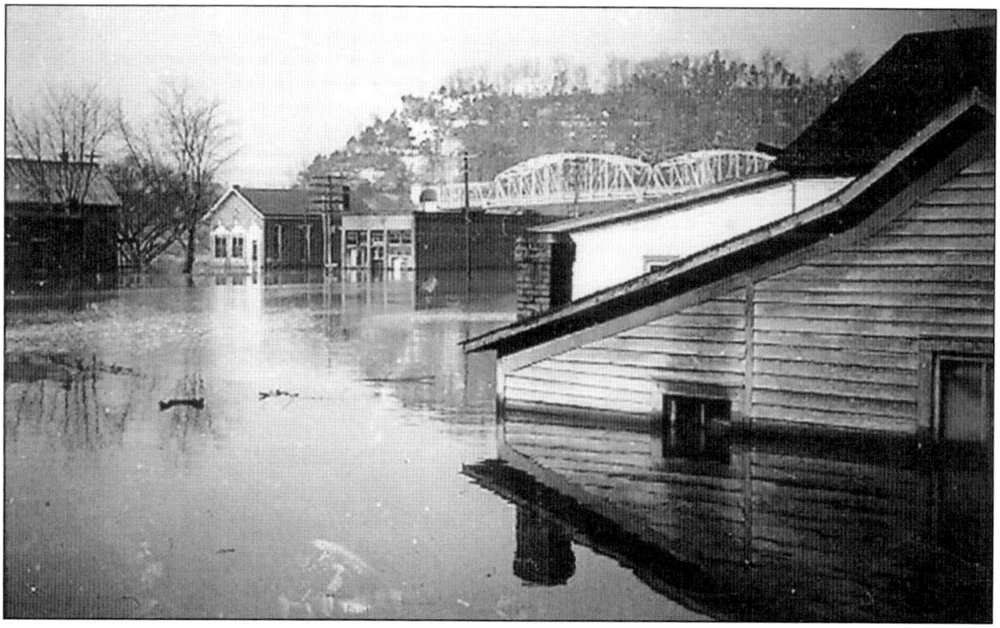

On February 4, 1939, the Cumberland River crested at 65.2 feet. The First National Bank in Burnside (second building from the left) barely escaped the floodwater. The bank opened in 1900. Flood gauges were painted on the side of the bank so residents could read the height of the water. Other significant floods were 72.4 feet in 1826, 61.4 feet in 1886, 64.4 feet in 1902, 70 feet in 1918, 59 feet in 1926, 54.3 feet in 1928, 64 feet in 1943, and 66 feet in 1946. (Courtesy of the PCHS.)

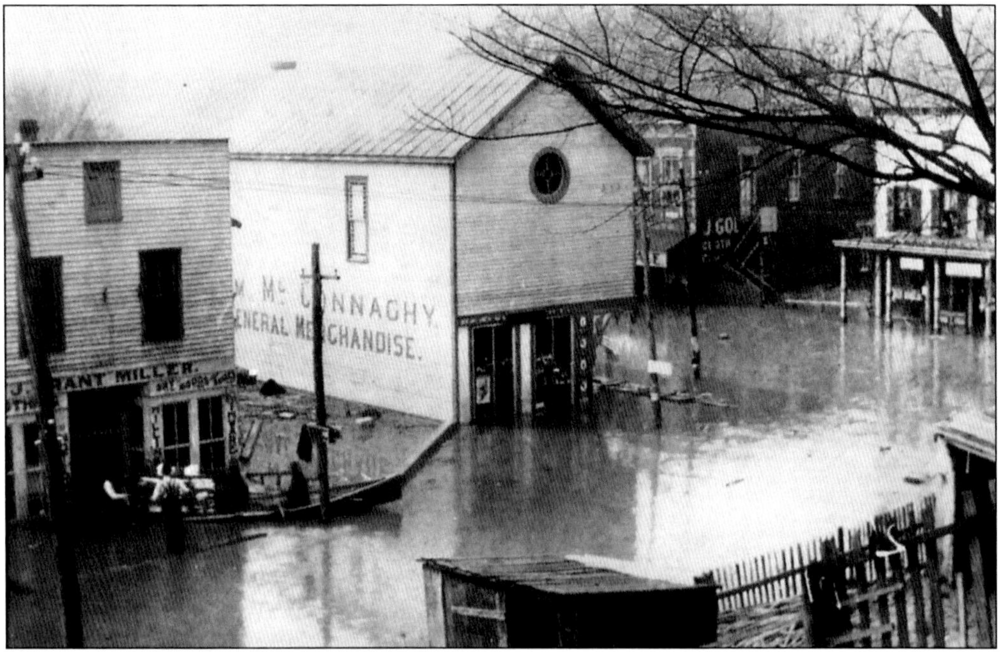

This photograph shows merchandise being salvaged from the J. Grant Miller Dry Goods Store in Burnside. Notice the fence in the foreground of the photograph. Livestock could wander freely around town until 1920, when fences became mandatory. Residents often had to watch their step—especially at night—since gas lamps were sparse. (Courtesy of the PCHS.)

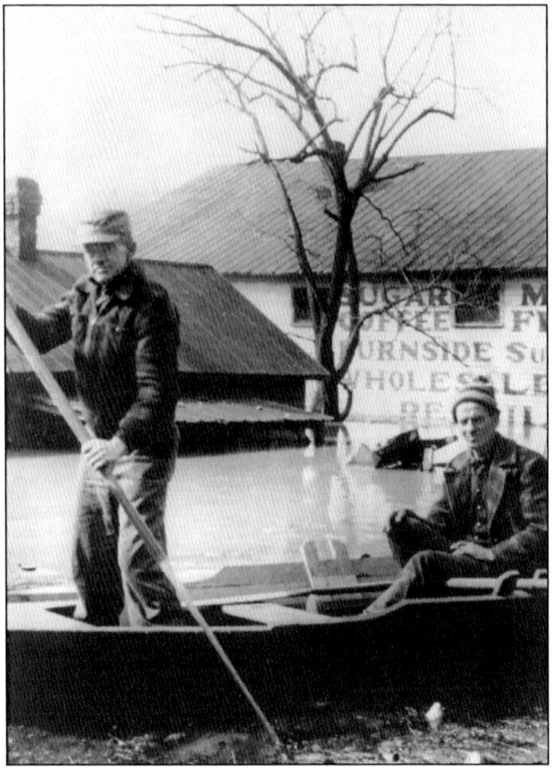

Residents were accustomed to floods along the Cumberland River, and neighbors were quick to help one another. This photograph shows men rowing a boat through Burnside, ready to help store owners salvage their items. (Courtesy of Rogers Photography.)

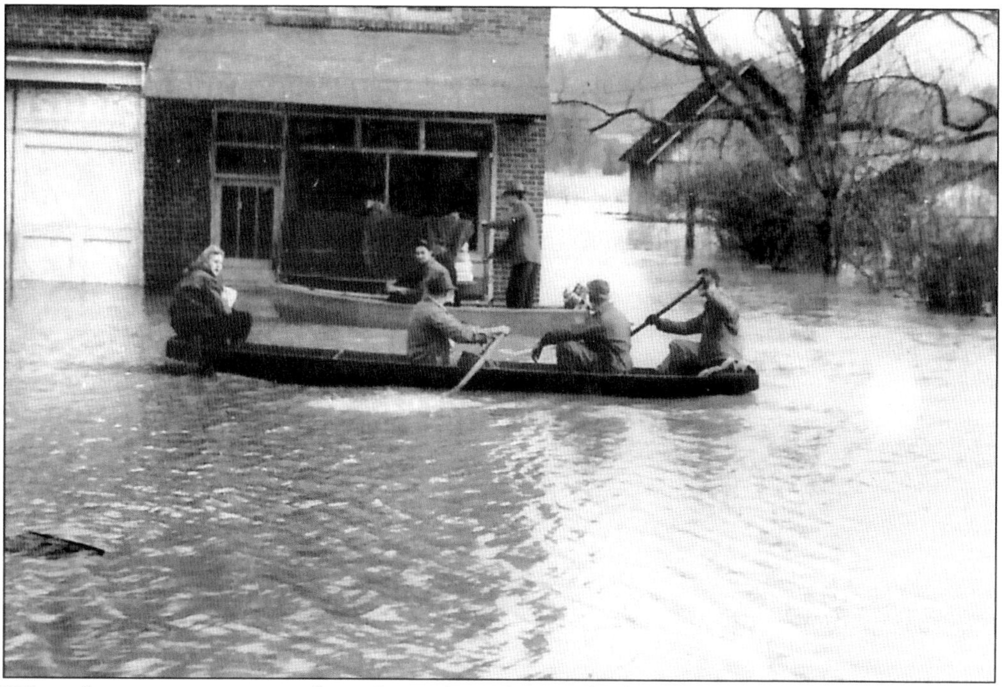

When the rainy season arrived, residents along the Cumberland River never knew what Mother Nature had in store for them. It was often necessary to communicate with contacts upriver to calculate how deep the water would be by the time it arrived in town. (Courtesy of Randolph Smith.)

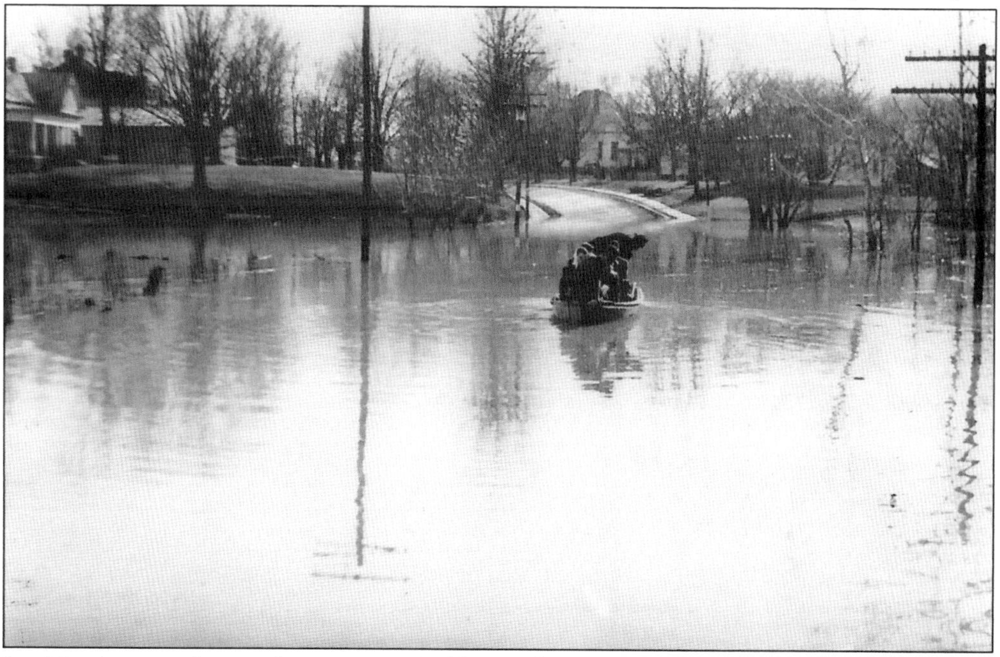

In this photograph, people are evacuated by rowboat to escape rising water in Burkesville. Burkesville became a busy river port during the latter part of the 1800s, when water transportation was the only feasible way to move large quantities of goods in and out of the town. (Courtesy of Randolph Smith.)

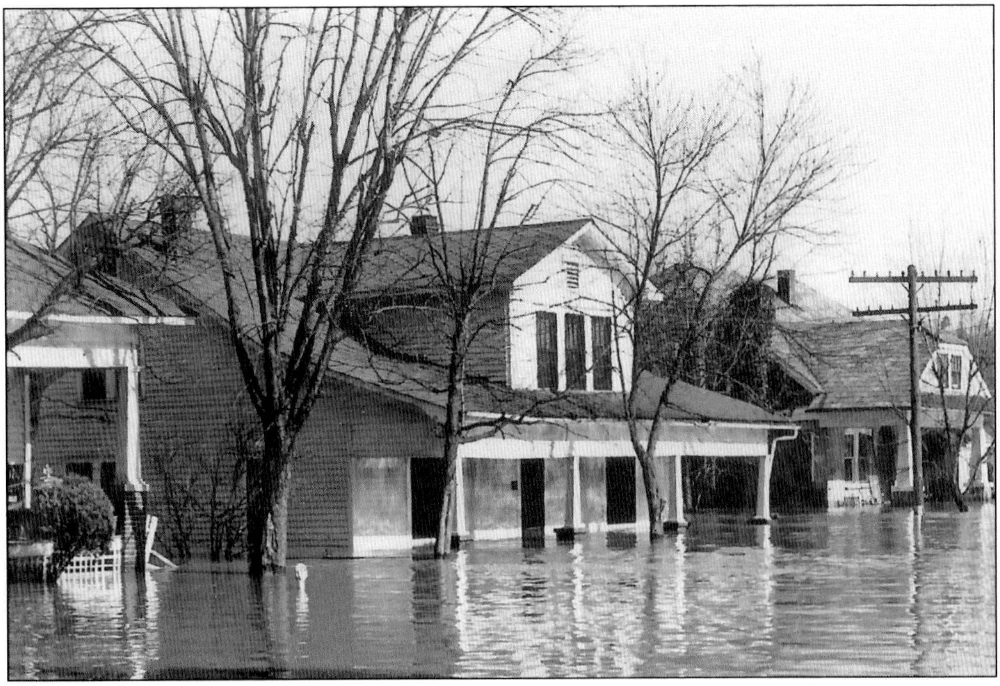

Residents living in homes along River Street were the most susceptible to flooding in Burkesville. This photograph shows three flooded houses on River Street in the flood of 1946. (Courtesy of Randolph Smith.)

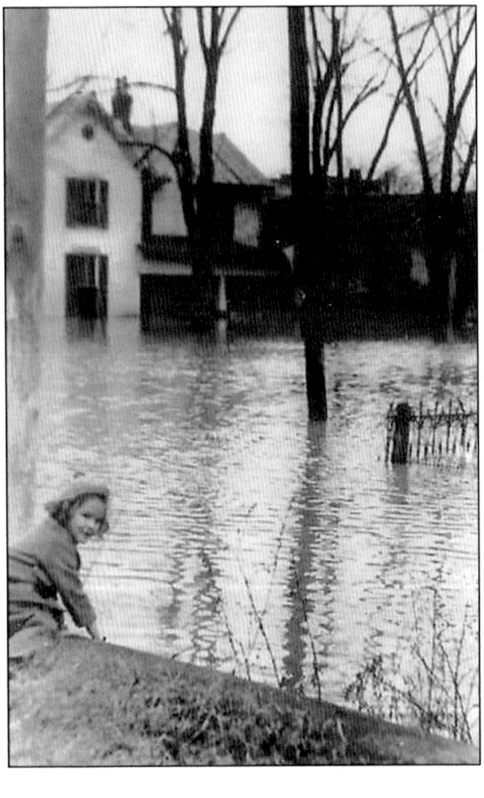

Not everyone thought the floods were bad. A young Laura Lee Smith Butler uses a stick to play in the receding floodwater in Burkesville. Smith is the daughter of Randolph Smith, longtime owner of Smith Pharmacy. (Courtesy of Randolph Smith.)

Two

Working near the Cumberland

The timber industry was always king along the Cumberland River. Thousands of acres of virgin timber lined the riverbanks and filled the valleys with dense forests. Farming along the fertile river bottoms grew at a rapid pace also. Early settlers introduced tobacco, corn, and hemp. Soon these were major crops in the area. But the success in farming was nothing compared to the timber industry.

It was a common sight to see huge log booms floating down the river to a mill. Once processed at the mill, the timber was sent down river to Nashville, Tennessee. Ten million feet of lumber shipped along the Cumberland River in 1895 alone. Demand for carpenters, loggers, and mill workers along the river increased as the timber came to market and settlers worked to build communities, homes, and roads.

As trade along the river and roads improved, revenue for farmers increased as they shipped their goods to larger markets farther away. Development and increased income sparked a demand for more merchandise and more services by community citizens.

The increase in river commerce created demand for banks, restaurants, hotels, and mercantile stores. Community expansion led to an increase in jobs. Populations were augmented as workers from outlying areas moved to town. With this evolution, towns could afford a doctor and build a school. A congregation could build its church and pay a permanent preacher.

It was a natural progression for law enforcement and a jail to follow. This in turn brought lawyers and a court system with a circuit judge who rode from town to town arbitrating cases.

As job opportunities escalated and tax bases increased, towns on the river flourished. For more than 100 years, many towns along the Cumberland River thrived.

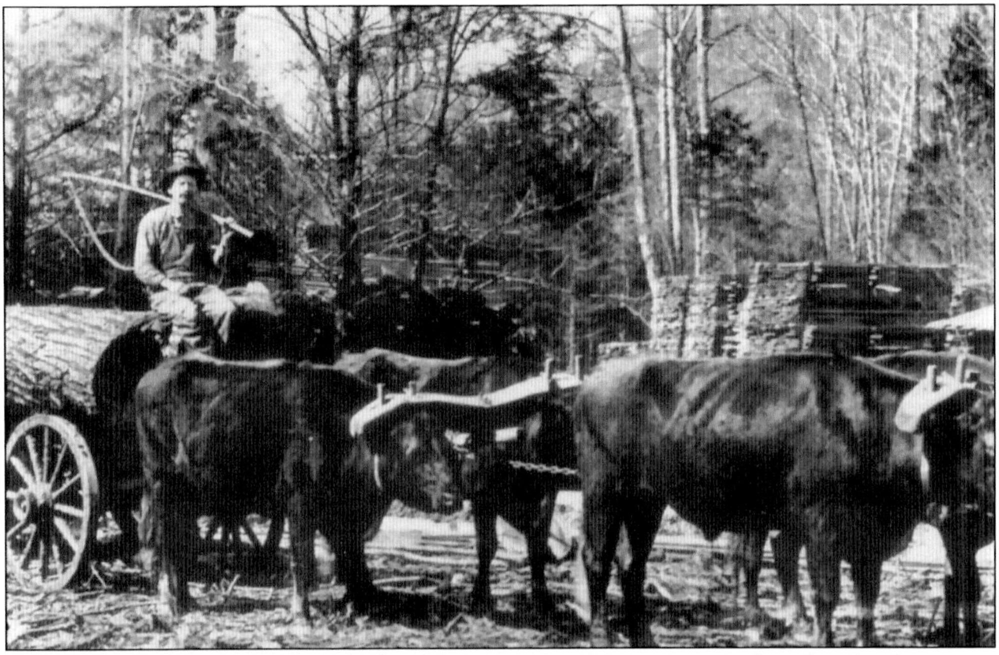

The forests that lined the Cumberland River were rich in virgin timber. Lumber became a prosperous business in the area. Seen here is a man driving a team of oxen. Strong animals were needed to pull the heavy logs to local logging companies. The three most popular hardwood trees were white oak, yellow poplar, and red oak. (Courtesy of the PCHS.)

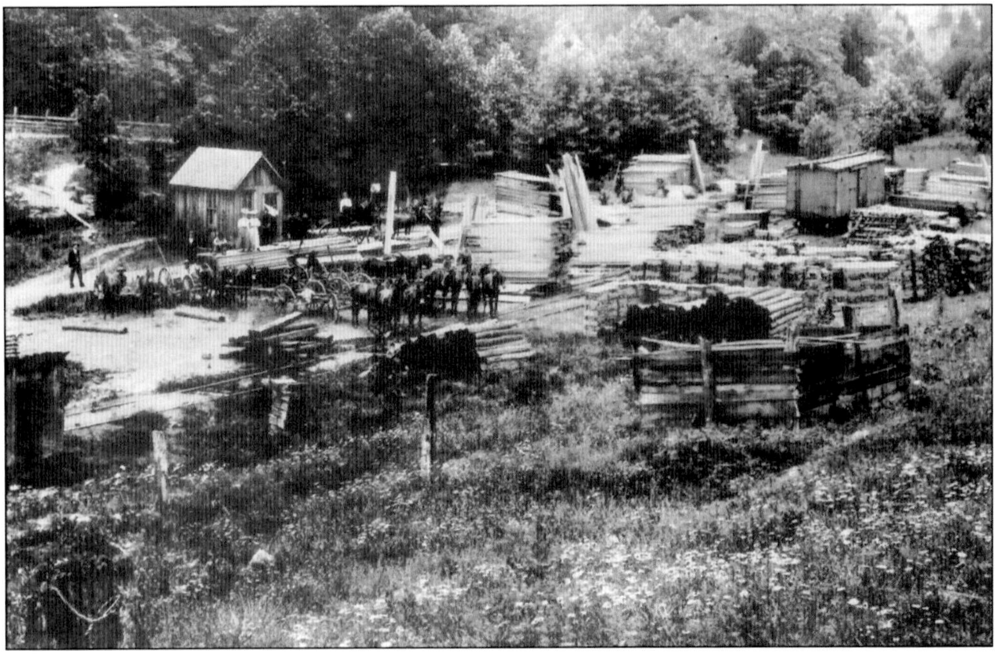

This photograph is of a thriving lumber company near Jamestown, Kentucky, in 1908. Craftsmen needing wood in the 1800s were wheelwrights, who made wagons, sleighs, and carriages; harness makers, who made saddle seats and yokes; carpenters; cabinetmakers; gunsmiths; musical instrument makers; and coopers, who made wooden barrels. (Courtesy of Carole Tupman.)

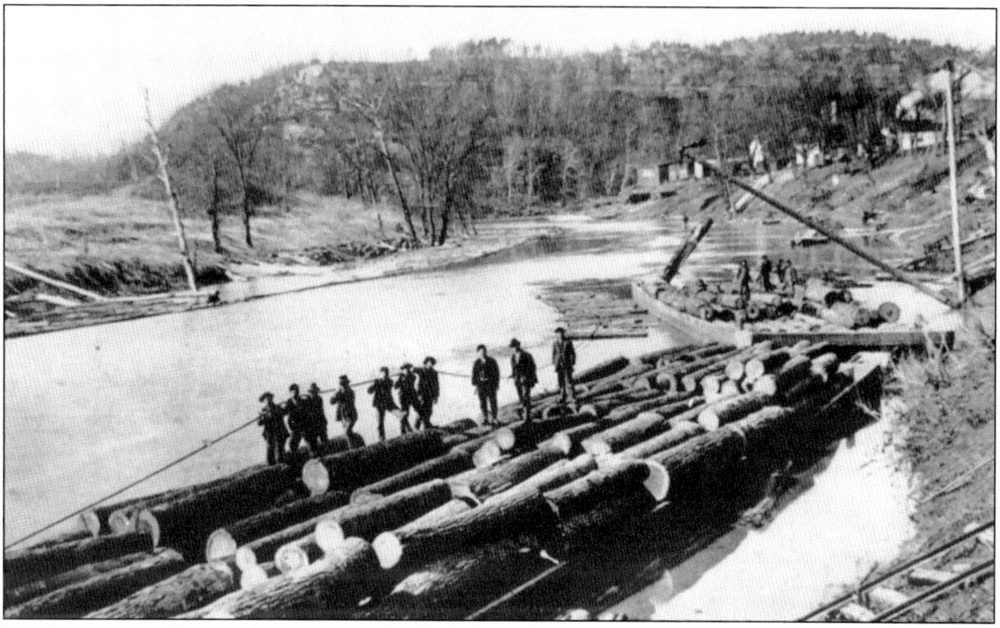

Lumbermen cut logs in the winter and rolled them to the riverbanks. Spring tides rose and floated the logs to towns along the river. The Kentucky Lumber Company in Burnside operated a boom that picked the logs out of the water. During certain periods, the logs were tied together and then brought down by men called "rafters," who rode on these rafts and guided them by the use of long poles. (Courtesy of the authors' collection.)

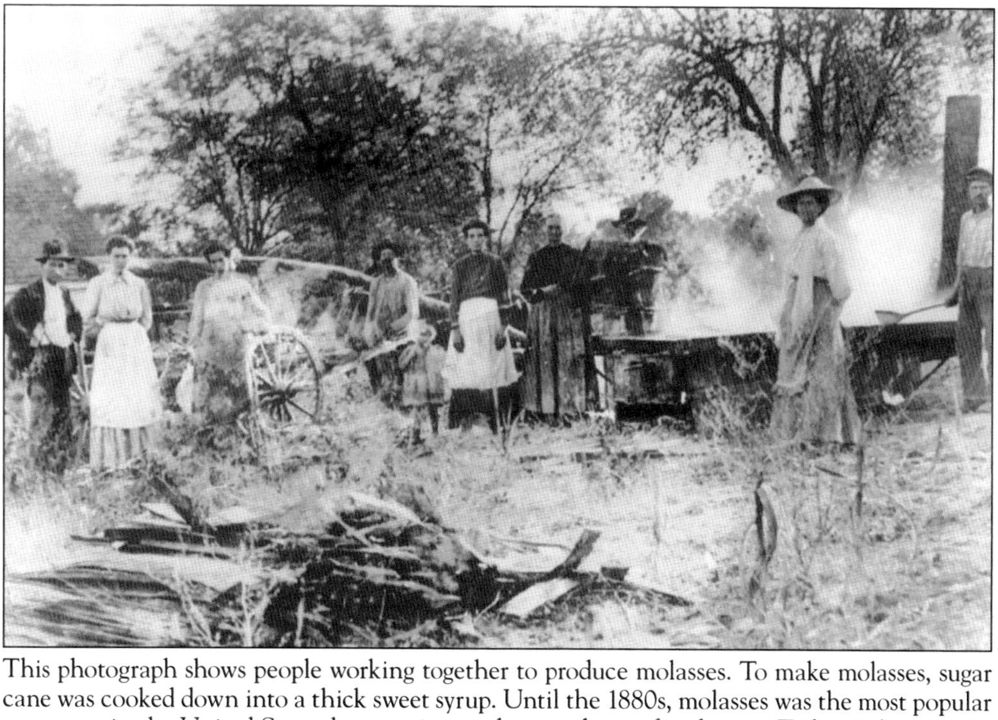

This photograph shows people working together to produce molasses. To make molasses, sugar cane was cooked down into a thick sweet syrup. Until the 1880s, molasses was the most popular sweetener in the United States because it was cheaper than refined sugar. Today molasses costs twice as much as refined sugar. (Courtesy of Rogers Photography.)

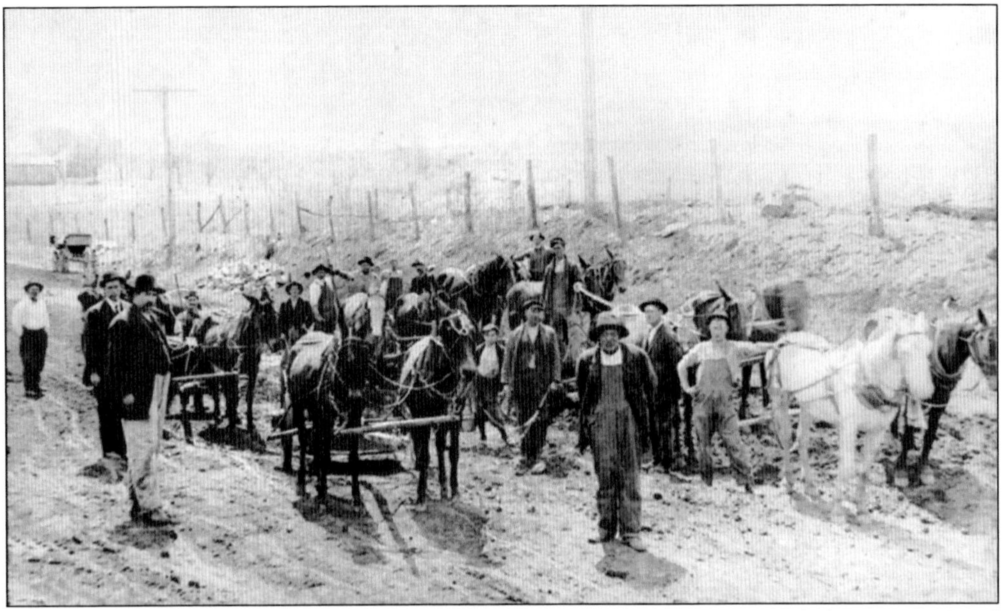

This photograph shows men building a road from Burnside to Somerset in Pulaski County. Road builders of the late 1800s depended solely on stone, gravel, and sand for construction. Early roads such as this were few and far between along the Cumberland River. Most roads were simply dirt paths, which often made for treacherous travel. (Courtesy of Rogers Photography.)

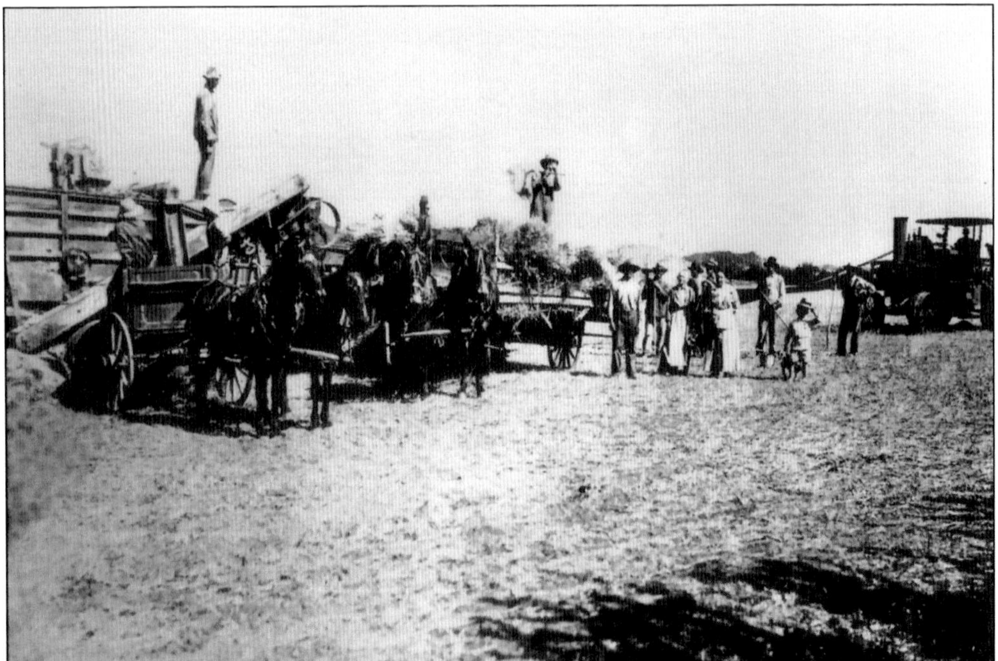

Farming was vital to the people living along the Cumberland River. Here workers are shown threshing the fall harvest. Tobacco, wheat, corn, and oats were common crops in south-central Kentucky. (Courtesy of Carole Tupman.)

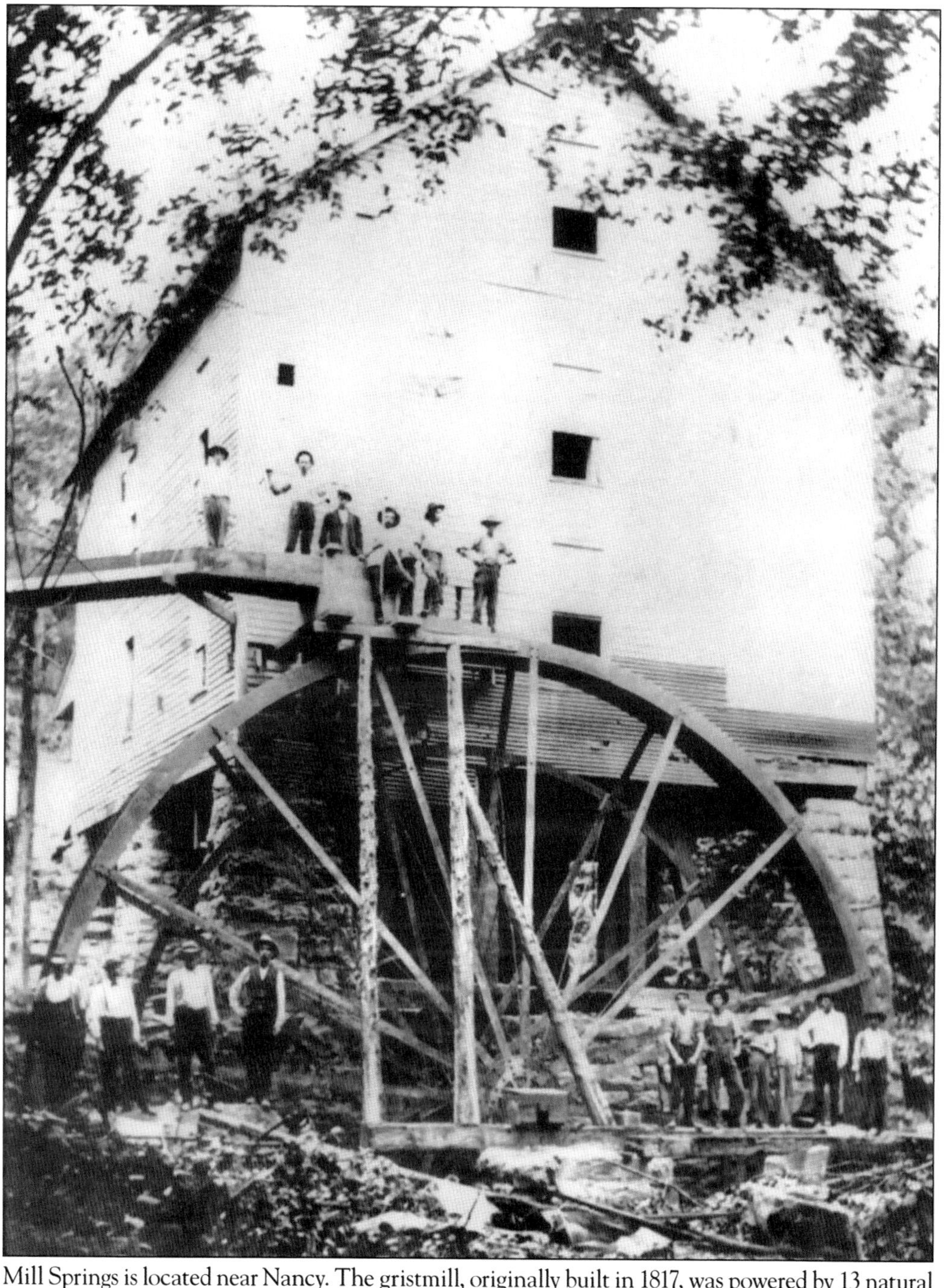

Mill Springs is located near Nancy. The gristmill, originally built in 1817, was powered by 13 natural springs. In 1877, the 34-by-40-foot, three-story mill was erected. This photograph was taken in the 1920s before the 28-foot cedar wheel was replaced by a steel waterwheel. Mill Springs is also known for the famous Civil War battle of Mill Springs, which occurred on January 19, 1862. Confederate army general Felix K. Zollicoffer mistakenly approached Union soldiers and was killed. A bloody battle ensued. The defeat was important because it broke the main Confederate line of defense in Kentucky. (Courtesy of Rogers Photography.)

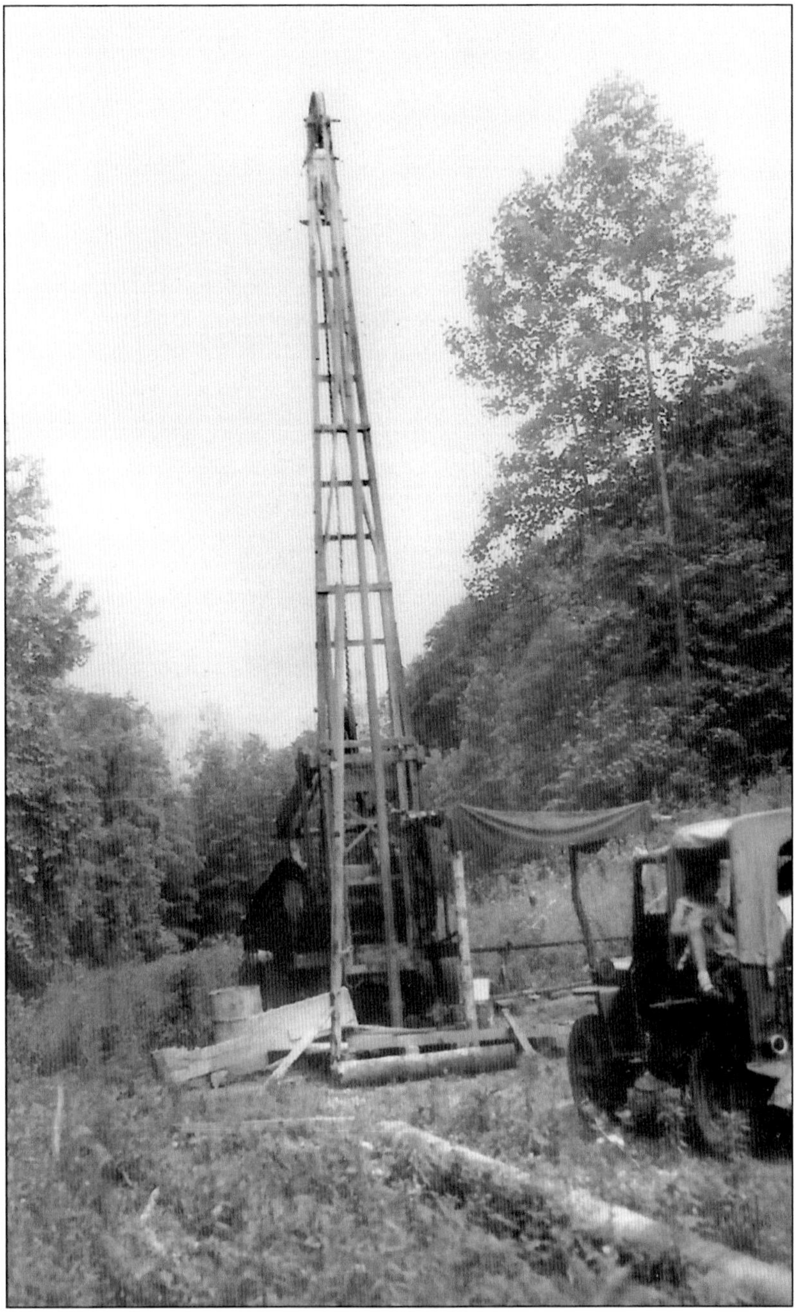

Believe it or not, the first oil gusher in the United States was in Burkesville, Kentucky, in 1829. While searching for salt, an early settler struck oil, and it shot up 50 feet in the air. For three weeks, oil flowed into the Cumberland River. The oil, over 50,000 barrels, caught fire, and the river burned for more than 200 miles. Around 1850, the oil was sold in pint-sized bottles for medicinal purposes at 50¢ a bottle. The label stated that the oil would "cure colic, rheumatism, chronic diseases, burns, scalds, fresh cuts, old sores, and sprains." Today the approximate location of the gusher is marked by a state historical marker on Highway 61 North in Burkesville. (Courtesy of Randolph Smith.)

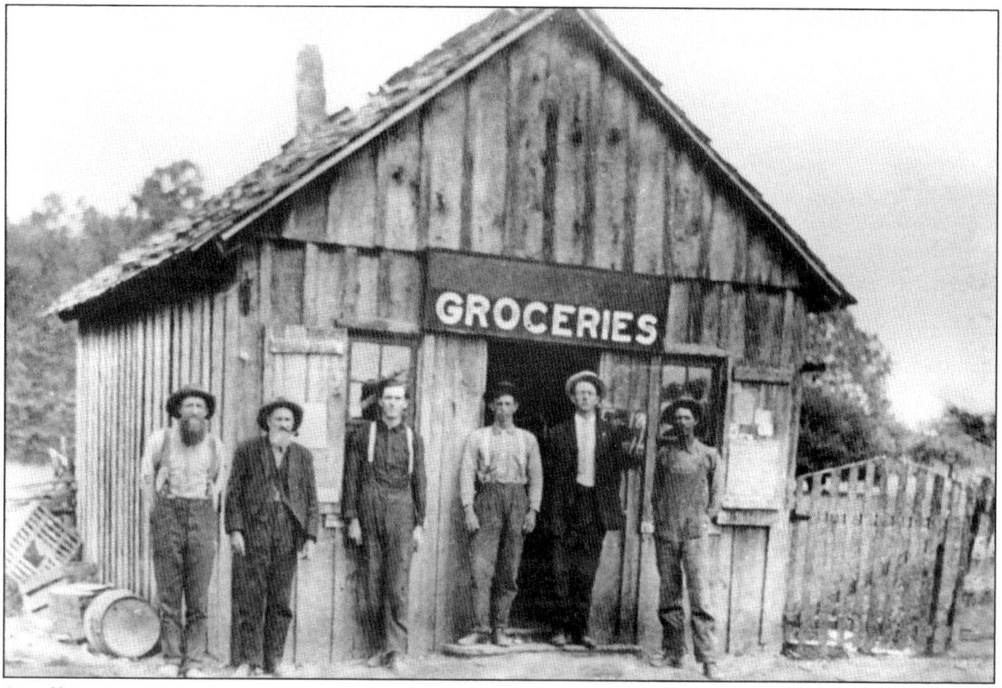

Small stores generally functioned as a general store, post office, and a place to socialize. In rural areas, mail was not delivered to an individual's home. One had to travel to the post office to retrieve mail. This photograph was taken in Pulaski County in 1906 and includes, from left to right, Frank Sowders, Mo Crow, Ben Crow, George Aker, Dan Sowders, and Willie Herrin. (Courtesy of Rogers Photography.)

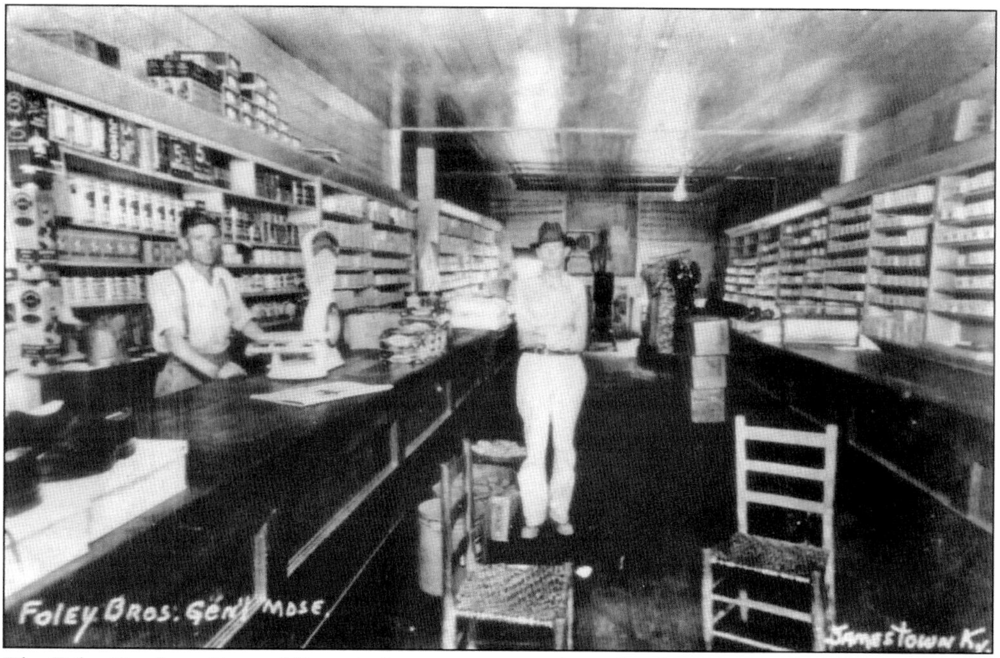

The Foley Brothers General Store in Jamestown served as a focal point in town. This photograph was taken in 1939. (Courtesy of Carole Tupman.)

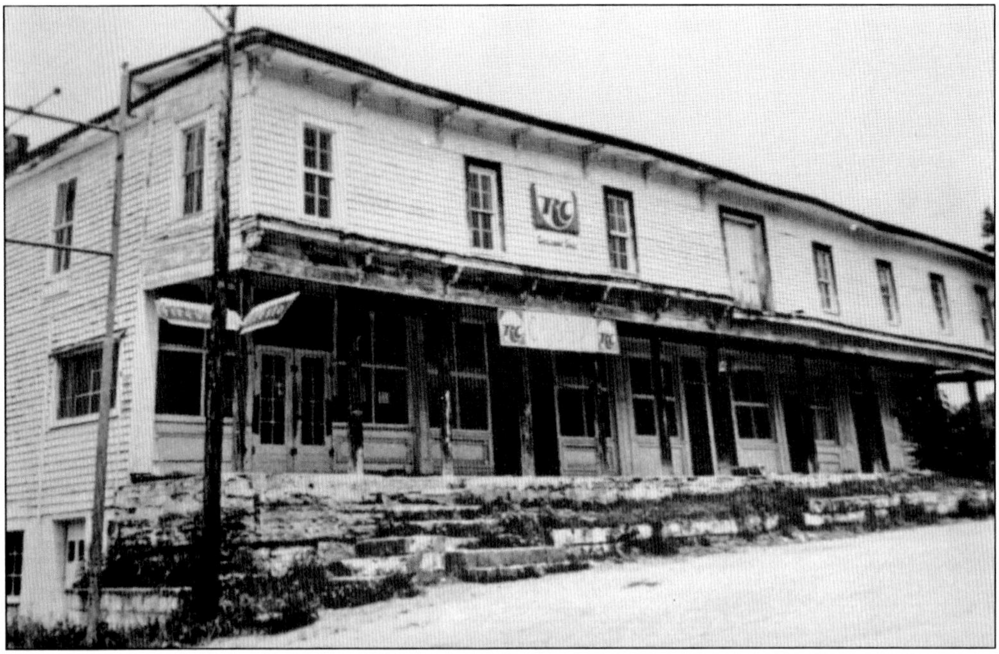

J. D. Irvin's store in Creelsboro opened in 1885 and served as a drugstore, a general store, a furniture store, a funeral home, and a post office. Irvin prided himself in offering the latest merchandise from Nashville. Early mannequins were a novelty in his store that drew spectators on a regular basis, and ready-made dresses brought in customers from miles around. (Courtesy of Debbie Lake.)

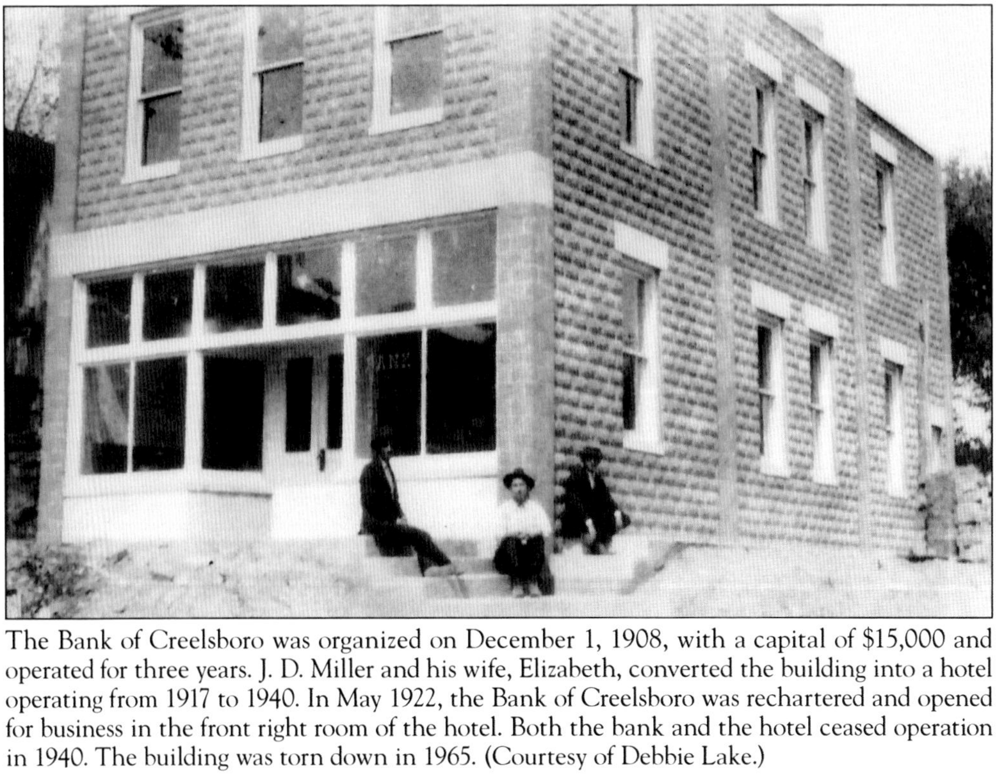

The Bank of Creelsboro was organized on December 1, 1908, with a capital of $15,000 and operated for three years. J. D. Miller and his wife, Elizabeth, converted the building into a hotel operating from 1917 to 1940. In May 1922, the Bank of Creelsboro was rechartered and opened for business in the front right room of the hotel. Both the bank and the hotel ceased operation in 1940. The building was torn down in 1965. (Courtesy of Debbie Lake.)

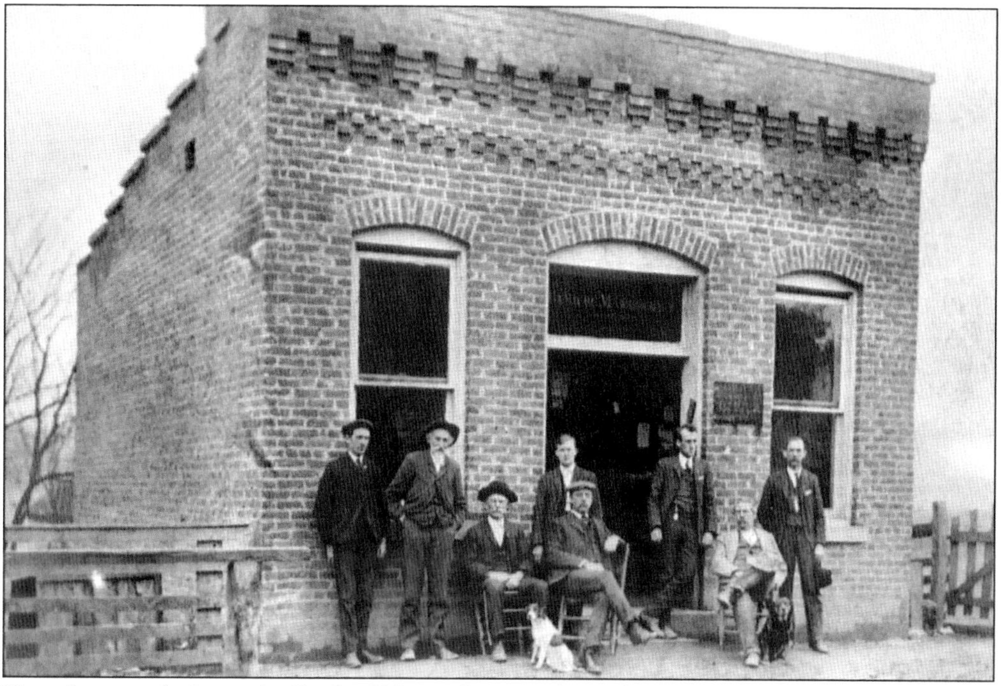

This photograph shows the Bank of Marrowbone in the mid-1800s. The bank was turned into a restaurant called the Vault. It earned this name because the original bank vault was so big and heavy that it could not be removed from the property. (Courtesy of the authors' collection.)

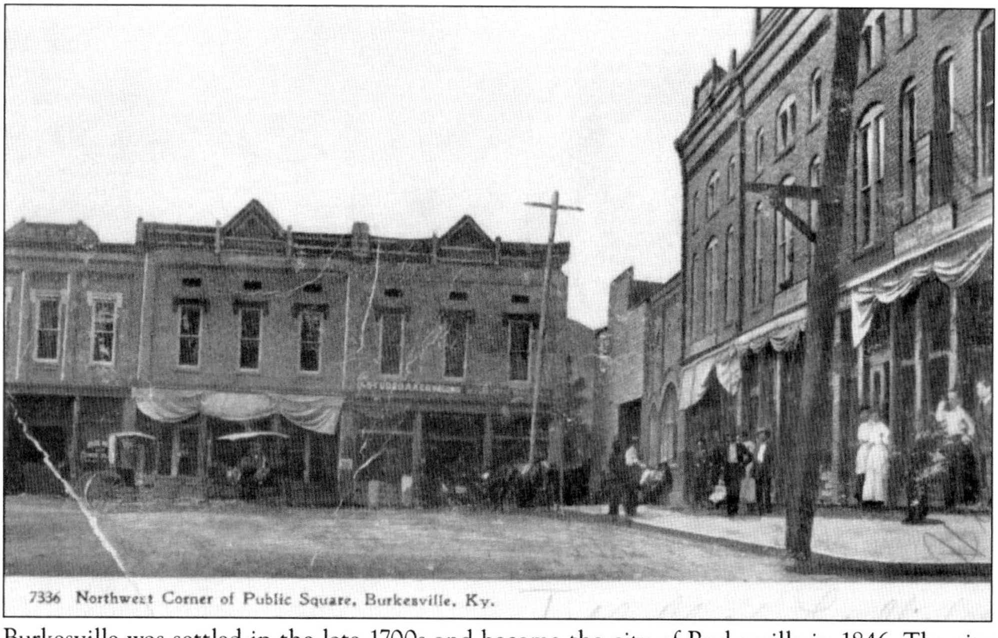

Burkesville was settled in the late 1700s and became the city of Burkesville in 1846. The city thrived thanks to steamboat trade along the Cumberland River and was the center of commerce for Cumberland County. Interestingly enough, Joel Owsley Cheek was born in Burkesville in 1852. Cheek created Maxwell House coffee in 1892. This postcard is postmarked August 28, 1908. (Courtesy of the authors' collection.)

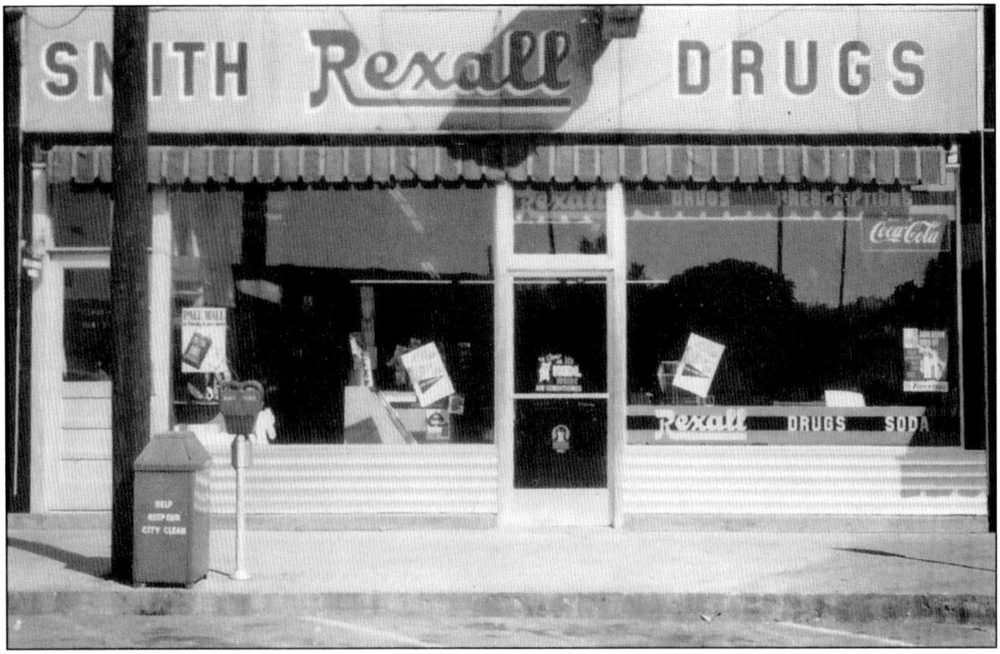

Smith Drugs is one of the oldest pharmacies in the state of Kentucky. Located in Burkesville, the store was opened in 1814 by three brothers: John, Philip, and Ruben Alexander. Since opening, the store has remained in a continuous line of ownership by the Alexander family and later by the Smith family. (Courtesy of Randolph Smith.)

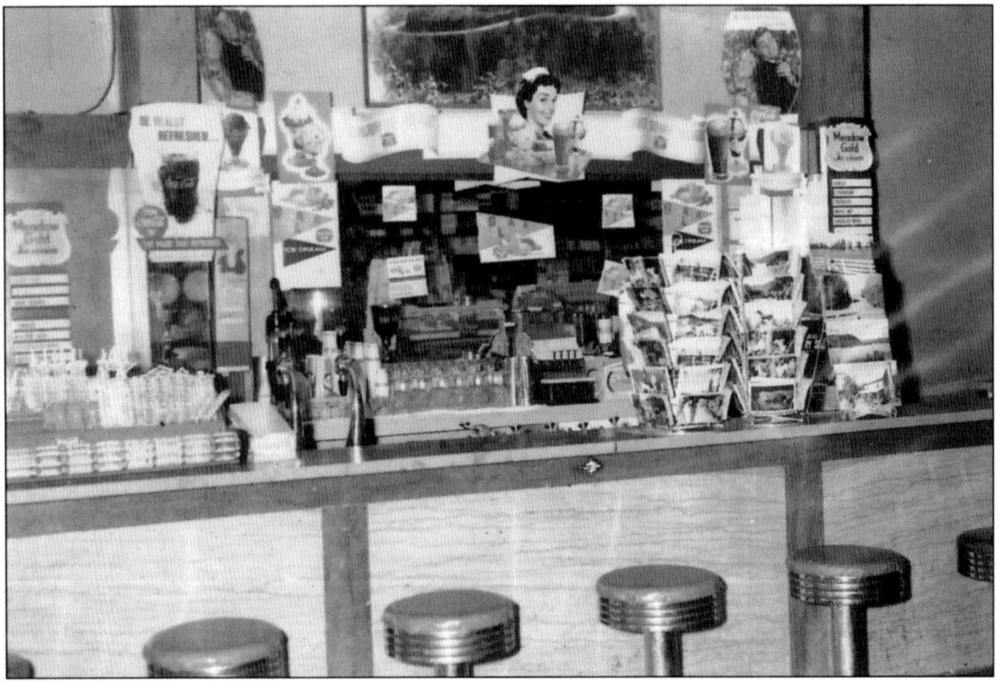

This photograph shows the soda fountain at Smith Drugs. Soda fountains became immensely popular in America during the last quarter of the 19th century. W. F. Alexander brought the soda fountain to Cumberland County in 1877. (Courtesy of Randolph Smith.)

Three

Transportation on the Cumberland

Rough terrain and very few roads along the Cumberland River left the population of the scattered towns and communities nearly inaccessible until 1833, when the first packet boat, the *Jefferson*, chugged upriver toward the head of navigation at Burnside (then called Point Isabel). The *Rose of Sharon* was the first steamboat to travel up the Cumberland from Nashville, Tennessee, to Burnside in January 1846.

Boats of trade, including packets, barges, rafts, ferries, and steamboats, were invaluable to the region. Some communities and towns would have perished without this opportunity for trade.

The sound of the steamboat whistle brought people running to the landing. It was exciting to see what was being off-loaded and who might be stepping from the boat. The boats provided a dependable opportunity for settlers to travel as well as import and export goods. By 1840, the steamboat was queen on the Cumberland, and she held her throne until motor trucks and automobiles forged their way into the area.

The *City of Burnside*, the *Rowena*, and her sister boat, the *Celina*, were common fixtures along the Cumberland. In 1895, the following was shipped downriver to Nashville on steamboats: 10 million feet of lumber, nearly 7 million pounds of barley, 100,000 pounds of cured meat, 3,500 head of livestock, 30,000 hogs, 150,000 chickens, 60,000 gallons of molasses, 100,000 cases of eggs, and 200,000 wooden cross ties.

The early 1900s brought the coming of the horseless carriage and better roads. In time, this put an end to river navigation. But historians agree steamboats were responsible for the growth of trade along the Cumberland River.

The stage was a dependable mode of transportation for early settlers. In 1884, J. W. Hall and Son opened the first stagecoach business in the area. Charles Burton bought the stage in 1896 for $900. The company prospered, and Burton added a second coach in 1897 and a third in 1898. The Burton stagecoach operated daily between Burnside and Monticello until its final run in November 1915.

The most dependable modes of transportation were the train and the automobile. Trains arrived in the area in the late 1800s, and automobiles made their way into the area in the early 1900s. With improved railway systems and the creation of the interstate system, the world of transportation narrowed to these two entities as the most sustainable modes of transportation around the Cumberland River.

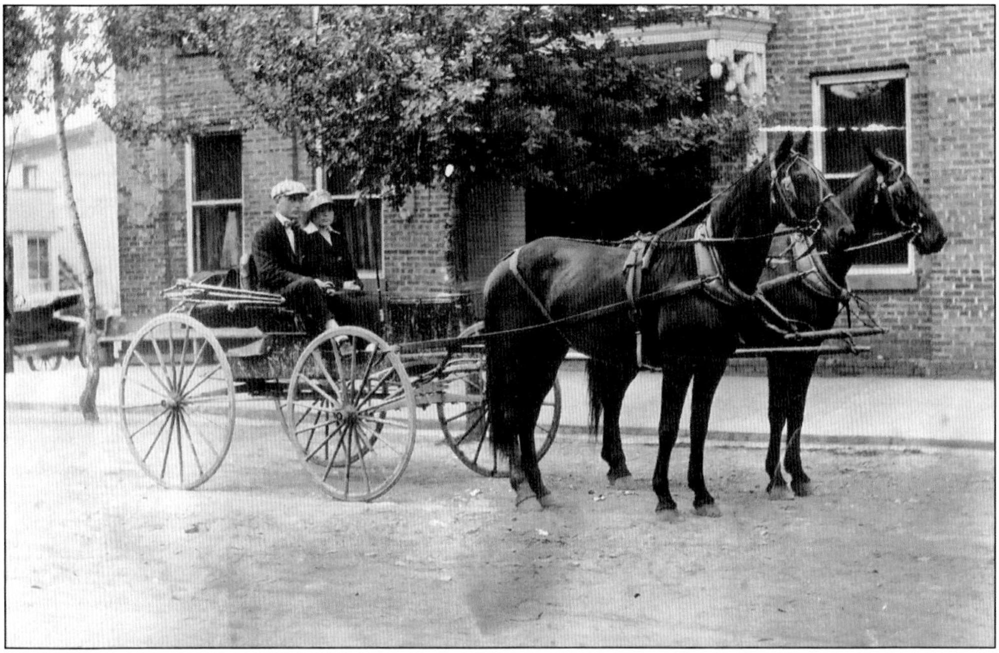

From 1865 to 1915, a horse and buggy was the primary mode of short-distance personal transportation. Buggies cost an average of $25 to $50 and could easily be hitched and driven by men, women, or children. This photograph was taken in downtown Burkesville in 1903. (Courtesy of Randolph Smith.)

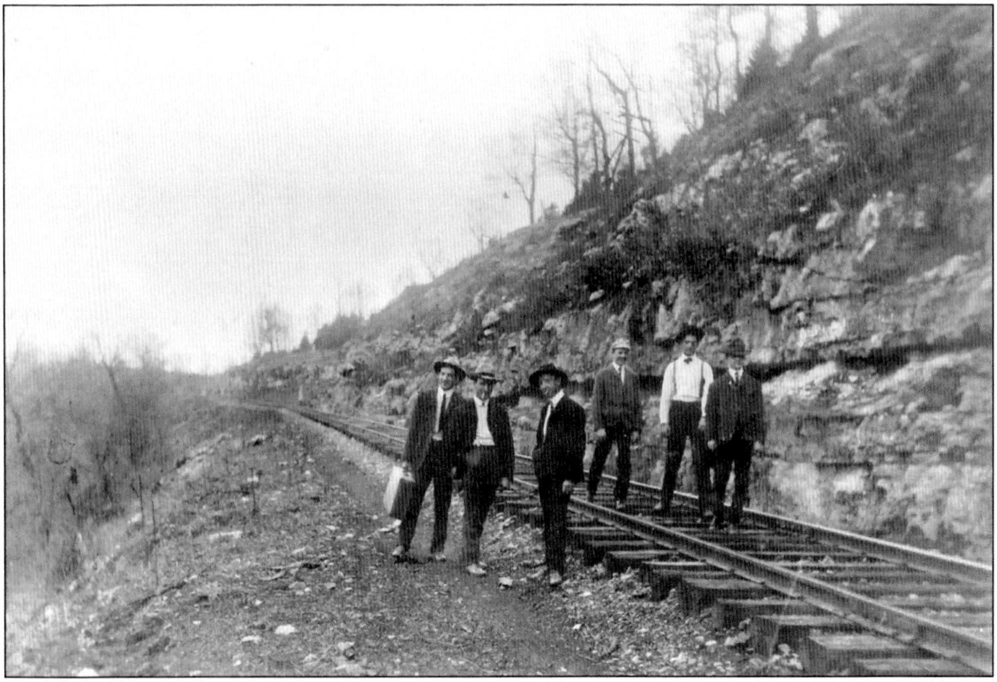

People of all ages and all ranks of society used the rail system in south-central Kentucky. In this photograph, William Noah Babbs (third from the left) and his friends walked along the tracks to Burnside, where they boarded a train toward Cincinnati, Ohio. (Courtesy of the PCHS.)

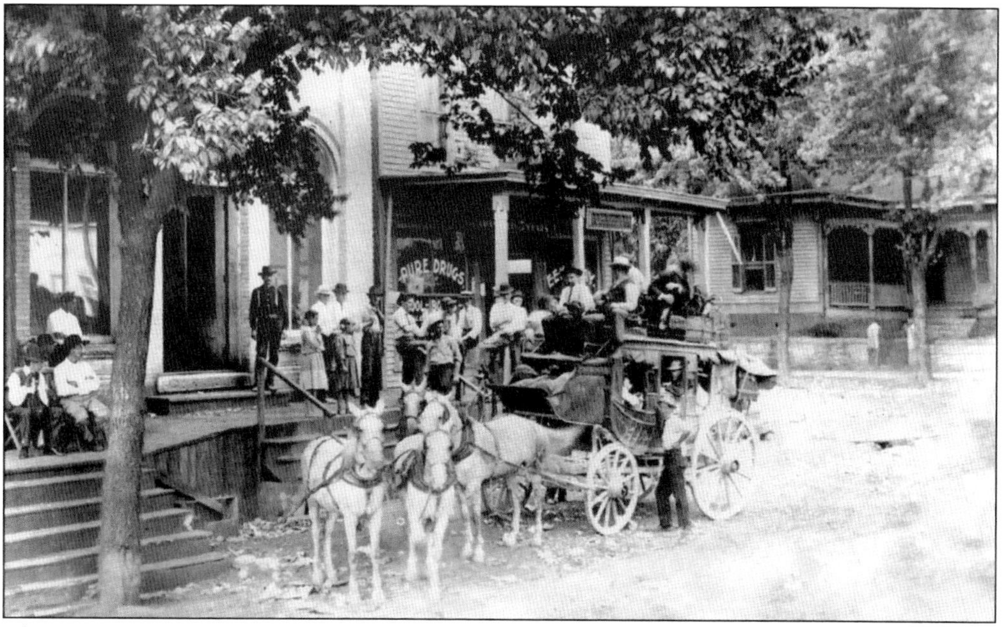

The Burton Stage from Monticello to Burnside was the last stagecoach to operate in the eastern half of the United States. A one-way ticket cost $1.50, and the 20-mile journey took 4 to 5 hours. The stage operated until 1915. Charles Burton lovingly kept the stage until his death in 1973. Due to a family squabble, the stage was auctioned off in 1978 to Kenneth Ballou of Burkesville for $38,750. (Courtesy of the authors' collection.)

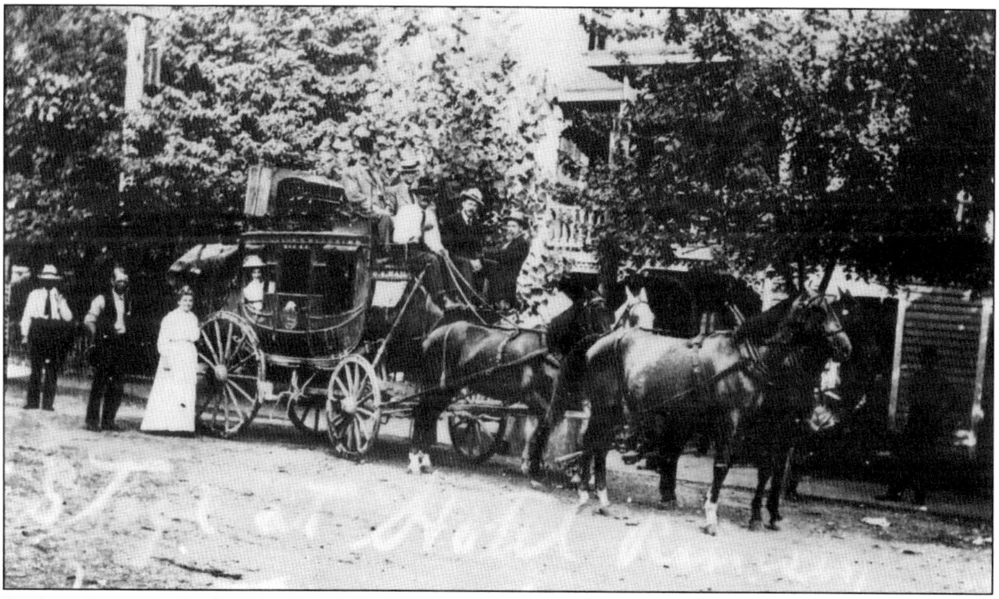

In this photograph, the Burton Stage waits in front of the Hotel Ramsey in Monticello. The stage left Monticello at 6:00 a.m. and arrived in Burnside at 11:00 a.m. In the afternoon, the stage left Burnside at 1:30 p.m. and arrived in Monticello at 7:00 p.m. There were many stops along Monticello Pike. But the most important stop was at the halfway point near Frazer. There tired horses were exchanged for fresh ones. The journey was too long for one set of horses. (Courtesy of the PCHS.)

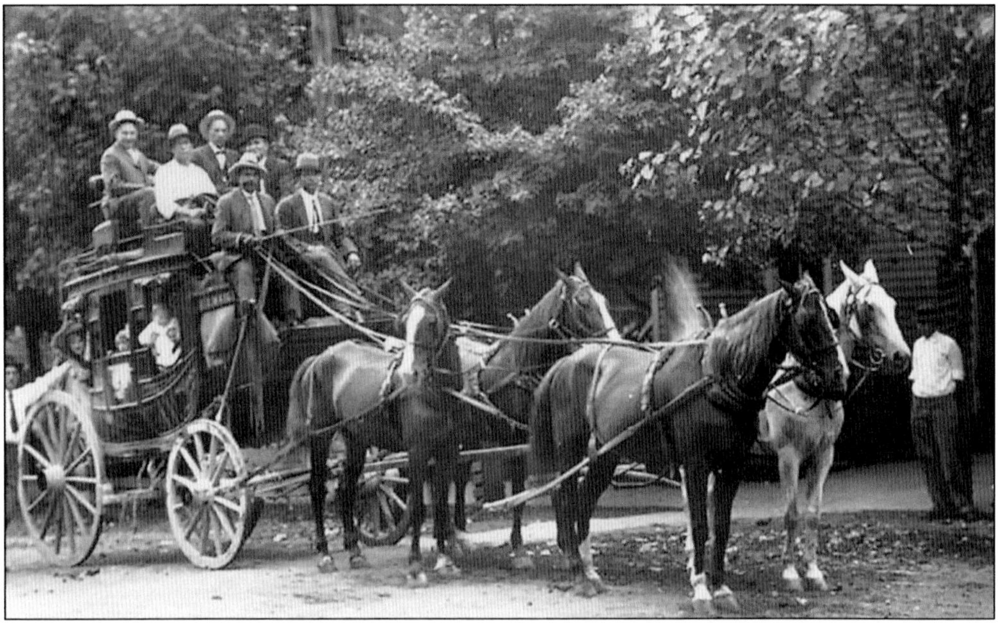

After paying the $1.50 fare, passengers and the mail were loaded onto the stagecoach. A total of 15 passengers could ride the stage—nine passengers could ride inside and five on top, plus the driver. Baggage was carried on the rear of the coach and covered by a huge oiled leather flap. There was no glass in the windows. During inclement weather, oiled leather flaps were rolled down and fastened at the bottom of the window. (Courtesy of John T. Carter.)

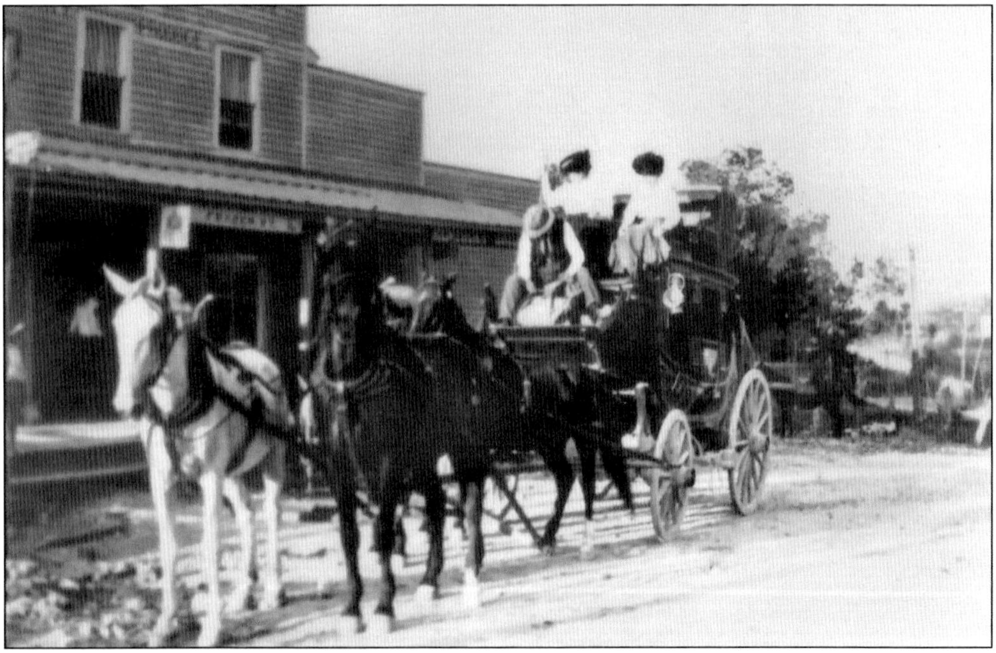

The Burton Stage transported passengers between Burnside and Monticello daily. Here the stage is shown in 1910 in front of the Shadoan Store and Post Office. The stagecoach stopped at small post offices along the way, which enabled dependable transportation of the mail from community to community. (Courtesy of the PCHS.)

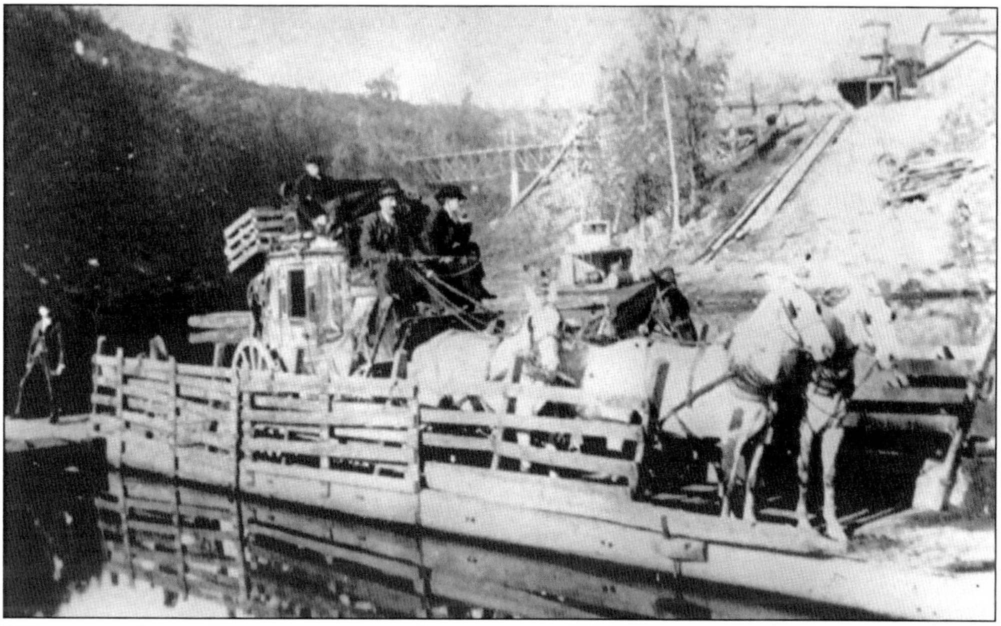

When a road met the river, a means of crossing was of the greatest importance. The Burton Stage crossing the Cumberland River by ferry was a common sight in the bottoms of Burnside until the Highway 90 Bridge to Bronston was completed. In this photograph, the bridge is nearly complete. Many ferries operated along the Cumberland River. The exact number of ferries would be impossible to determine. (Courtesy of Carol Ann Lewis Lovell.)

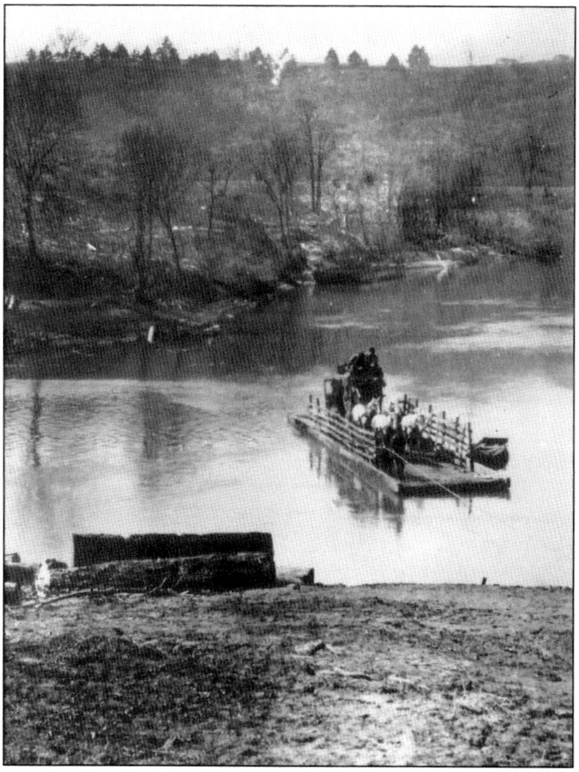

In the early days of river travel, there were no motors on the ferry. The ferry was either propelled with oars or ropes were fastened on the bank of each side of the river and the ferry was pulled across. This photograph shows the Burton Stage crossing the Cumberland River on a ferry near Waitsboro. (Courtesy of the PCHS.)

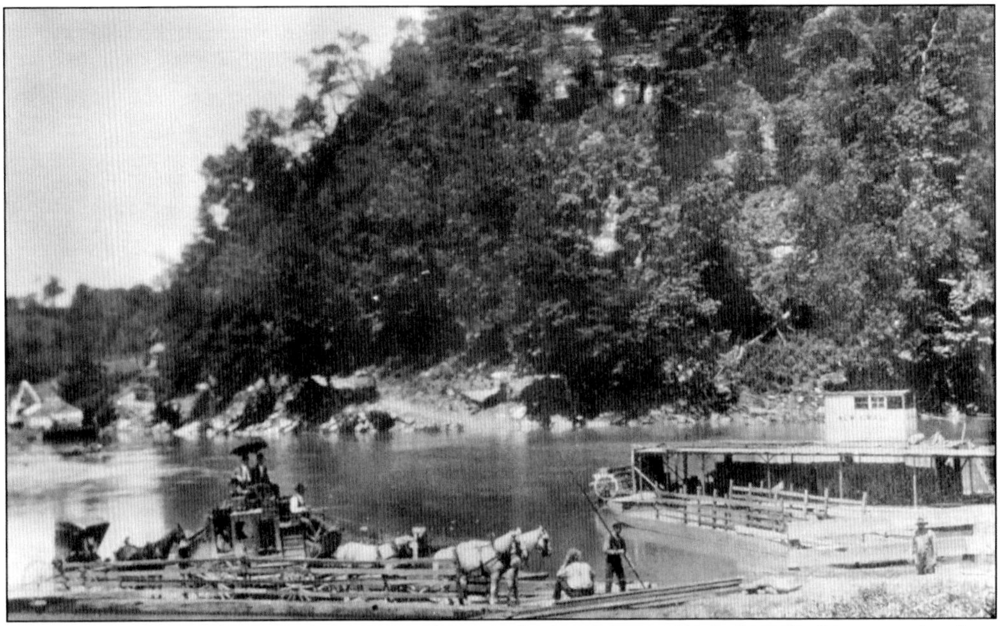

Ferries were essential to people crossing the Cumberland River. Each ferry had its own landing on the shore. To operate a ferry, it was required that a franchise be bought, boats be built to specifications, and an operator's license be purchased. Wagon boats were 52 feet long and 8 feet wide with railings and banisters high enough to insure safety. A horse boat was 25 feet long and 7 feet wide with a safe railing and banister. (Courtesy of the PCHS.)

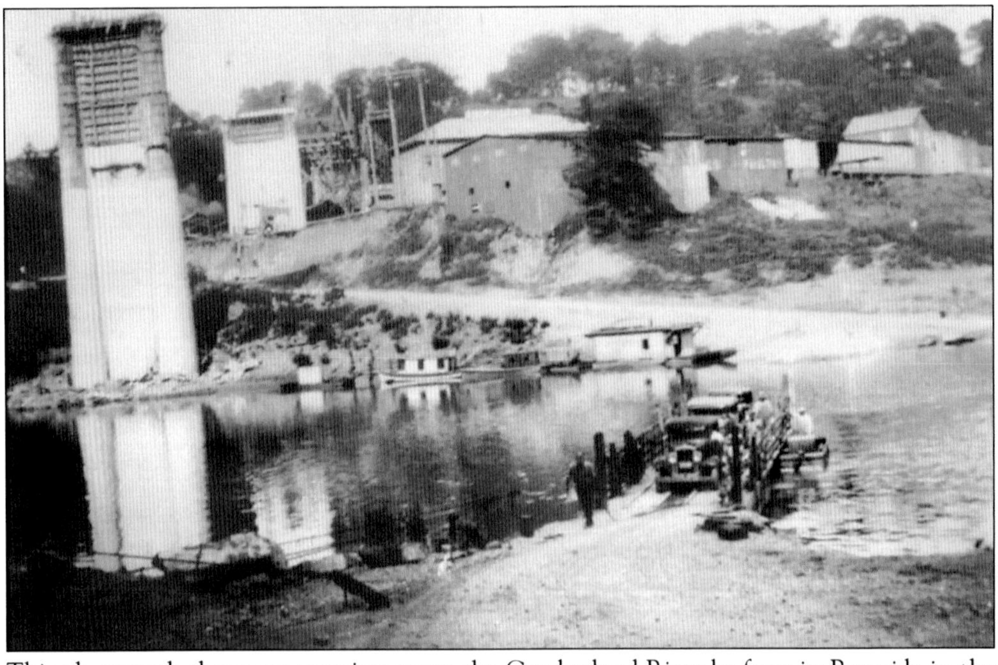

This photograph shows cars coming across the Cumberland River by ferry in Burnside in the summer of 1930. Construction of the "General Burnside Bridge" was in its early stages. Ferries were a key part of river traffic. They worked hand in hand with steamboats and the stage to complete the "river highway." (Courtesy of John T. Carter.)

The Rowena Ferry opened for business in 1848. In the early 1900s, fees were as follows: six-horse wagon with driver, 65¢; four-horse wagon with driver, 45¢; two horses, light wheel wagon with driver, 25¢; two-wheel carriage with driver, 25¢; horse and rider, 10¢; cattle per head, 5¢; hog per head, 5¢; stud horse, 25¢; sheep or goats each, 1¢. Prices were determined by the Fiscal Court, and all laws were strictly enforced. (Courtesy of Debbie Lake.)

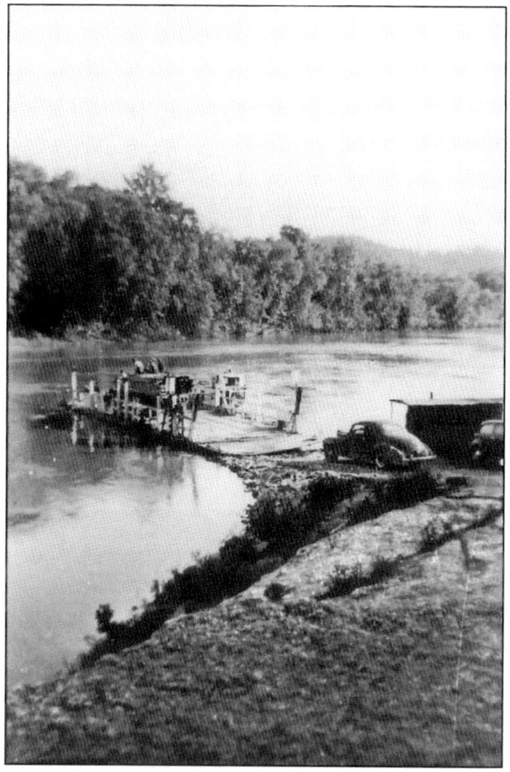

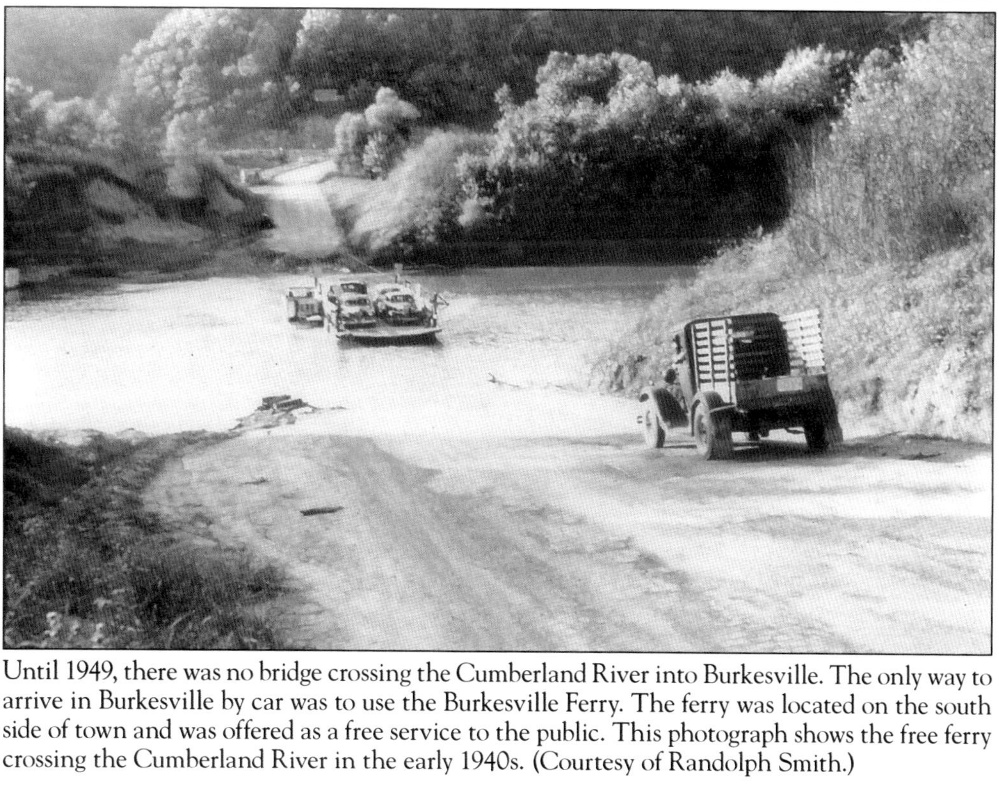

Until 1949, there was no bridge crossing the Cumberland River into Burkesville. The only way to arrive in Burkesville by car was to use the Burkesville Ferry. The ferry was located on the south side of town and was offered as a free service to the public. This photograph shows the free ferry crossing the Cumberland River in the early 1940s. (Courtesy of Randolph Smith.)

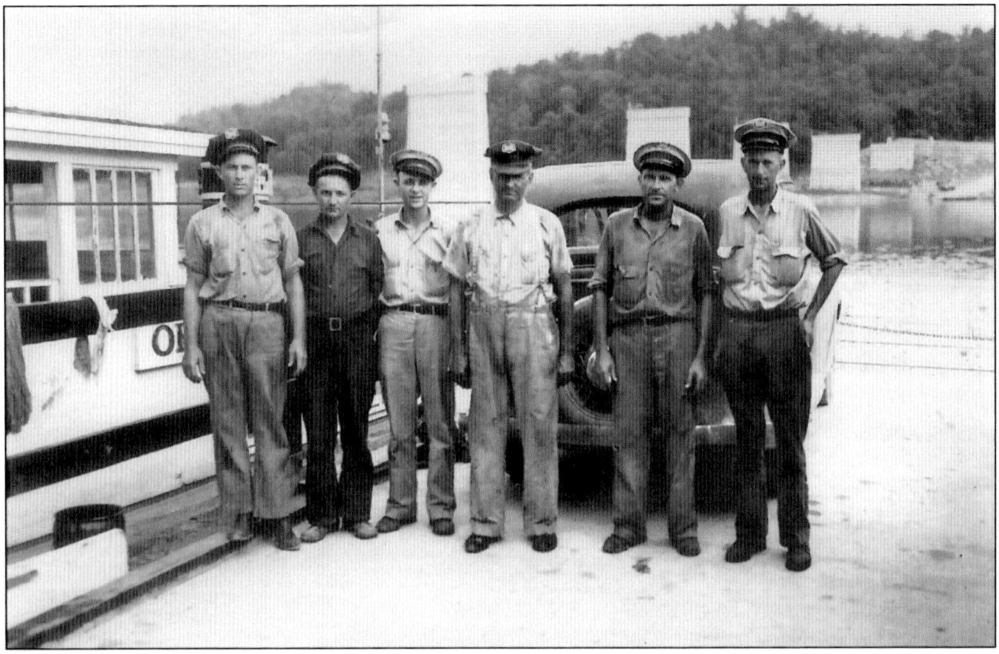

This photograph shows the crew of the Rowena Ferry in the late 1940s. When Highway 35 was built in the early 1930s from Jamestown to Albany, the ferry became state-operated and for the first time was propelled by a tugboat attached to the side. The ferry operated 24 hours a day free of charge. (Courtesy of Debbie Lake.)

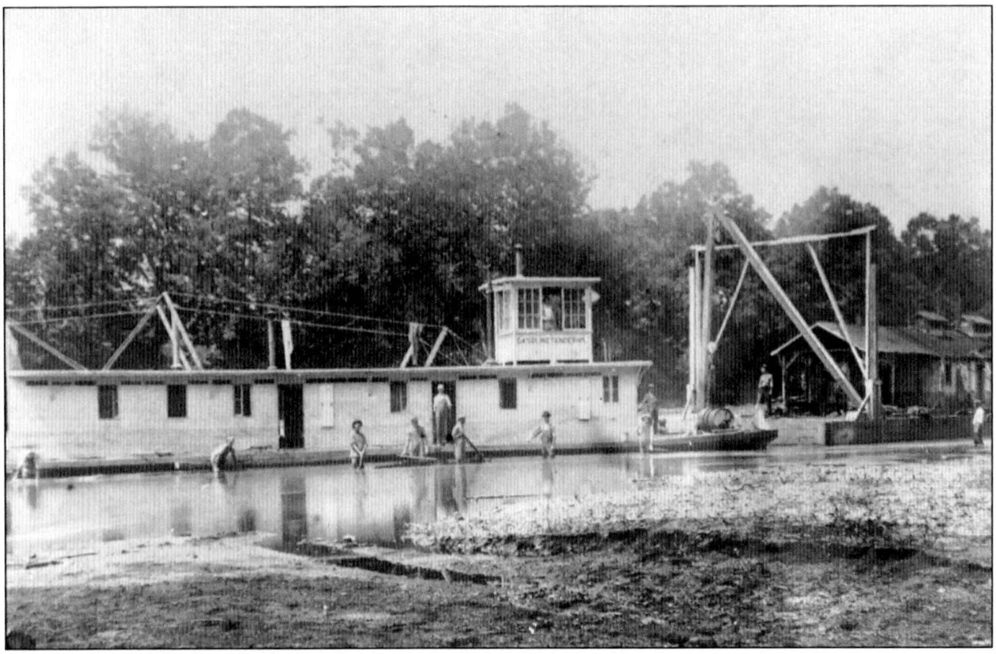

The *Oil King* delivered gasoline up and down the Cumberland River. An oil refinery operated in Creelsboro from 1922 to 1930. Oil was pumped from local wells, refined, and moved by tanker boat. It was reported that 100 wells in the area pumped oil for about eight years. (Courtesy of Carole Tupman.)

This photograph shows a ferry crossing the Cumberland River and transporting Don O'Brien's shiny 1951 Mercury. Ferries transported livestock, people, wagons, and automobiles across the Cumberland River. During the Civil War, they were also used to transport soldiers and supplies across the Cumberland. (Courtesy of Don O'Brien.)

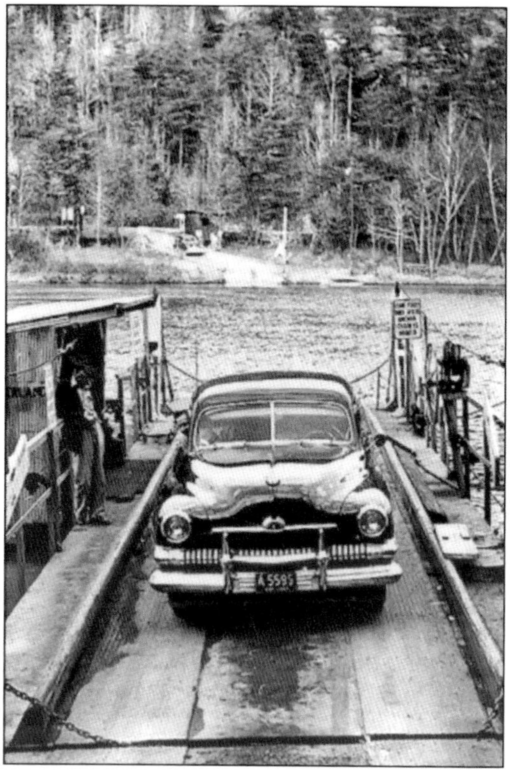

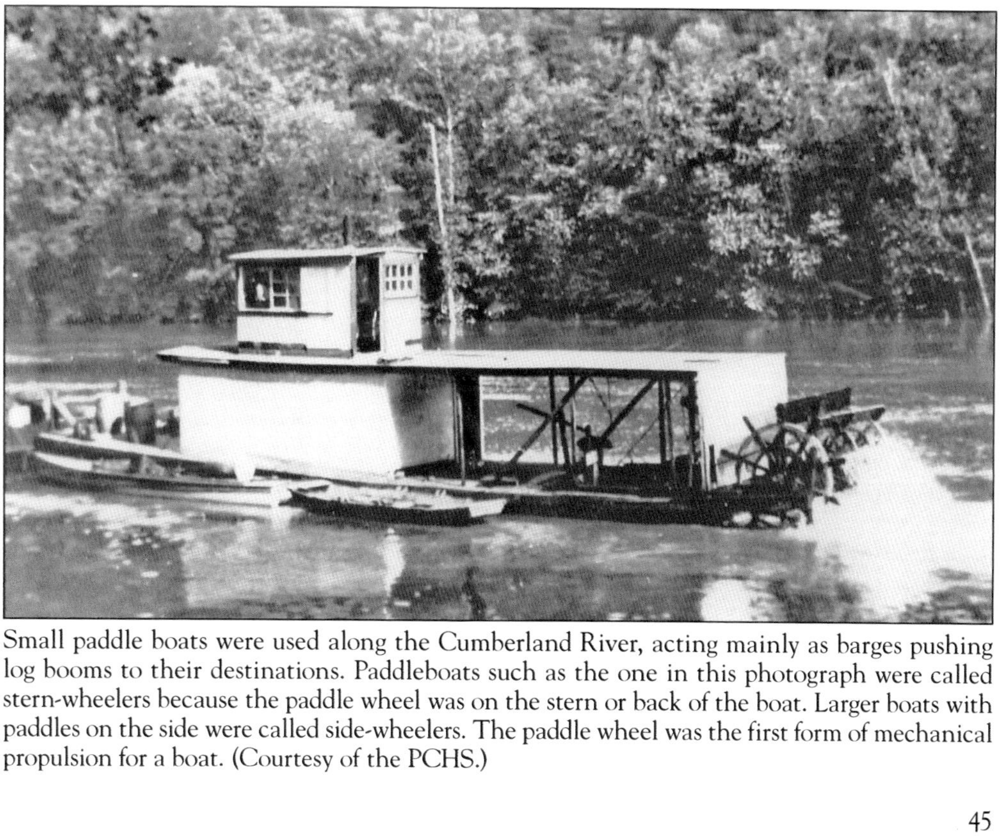

Small paddle boats were used along the Cumberland River, acting mainly as barges pushing log booms to their destinations. Paddleboats such as the one in this photograph were called stern-wheelers because the paddle wheel was on the stern or back of the boat. Larger boats with paddles on the side were called side-wheelers. The paddle wheel was the first form of mechanical propulsion for a boat. (Courtesy of the PCHS.)

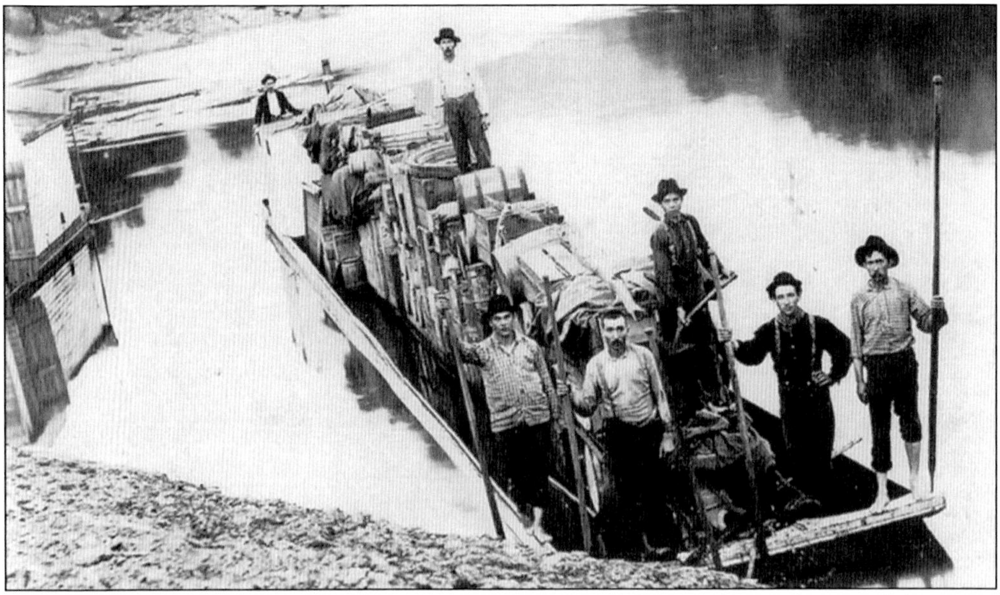

Ferry transportation was needed to cross the South Fork and the Cumberland River while steam-powered paddleboats took passengers and freight to landings along the river. Two major river transportation operations along the Cumberland were the Burnside Burkesville Transportation Company (B&B) and the Cumberland Transportation Company. After two decades of competition, Cumberland Transportation purchased B&B's operation in 1917. (Courtesy of the "Mayor" of Marrowbone.)

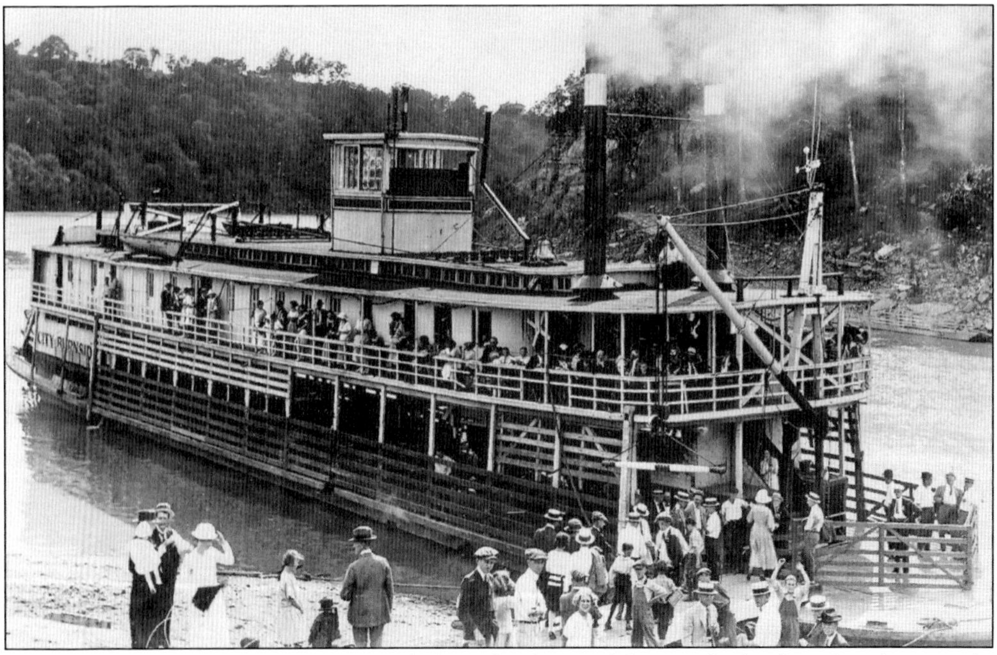

Many steamboats were built and repaired along the shores of the Cumberland. In this photograph, the *City of Burnside* is shown. She was named after the town where she was built. Most of the larger towns along the Cumberland had a steamboat named in their honor, such as the *Rowena*, the *Creelsboro*, the *Burkesville*, and the *Albany*. (Courtesy of the PCHS.)

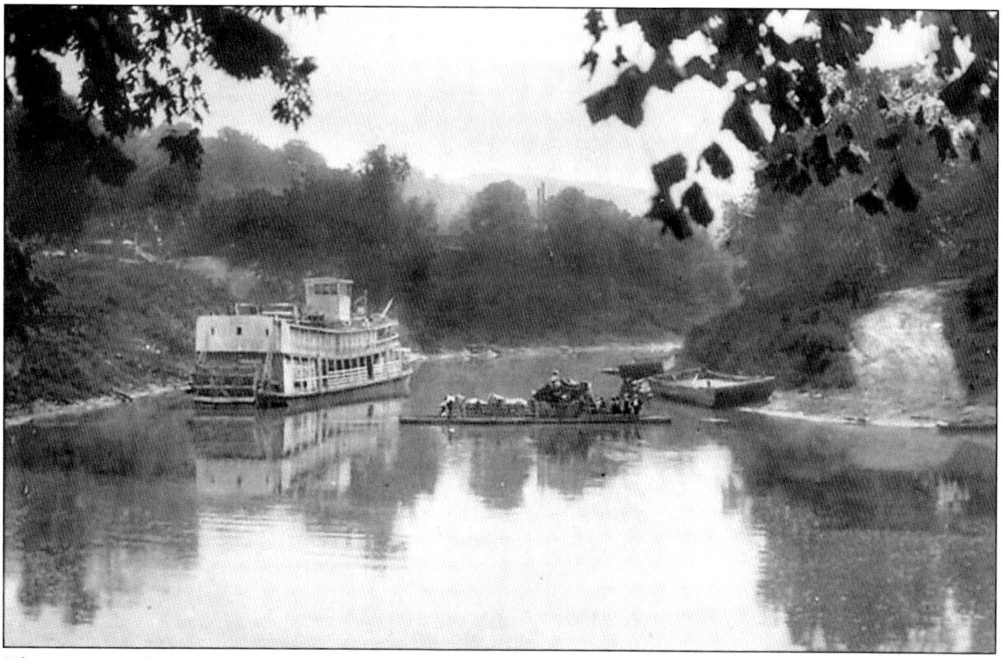

The river could be very dangerous. The pilot had to operate the boat and act as navigator as well. They had to know every inch of the river to avoid snags, shallow spots, and other obstacles. Mark Twain said, "A steamboat pilot was the only unfettered and entirely independent human being that lived in the earth." (Courtesy of the PCHS.)

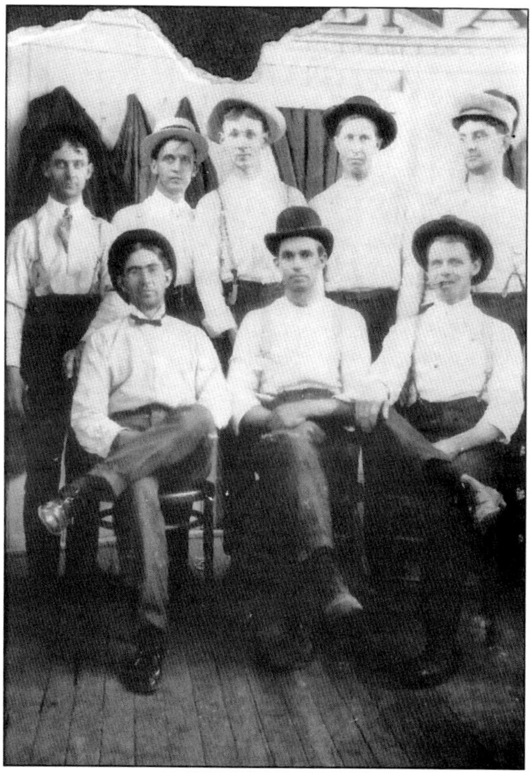

This rare photograph shows the crew of the *Rowena*. From left to right are (first row) Abner Jones, first clerk; Clate Heath, captain; and Logan Horn, first mate; (second row) Lewis Campbell, pilot; Frank Faulkinburg, second pilot; Lanus McMurfry, second clerk; Roy Baker, third clerk, and Gordon Thurston, second mate. (Courtesy of Debbie Lake.)

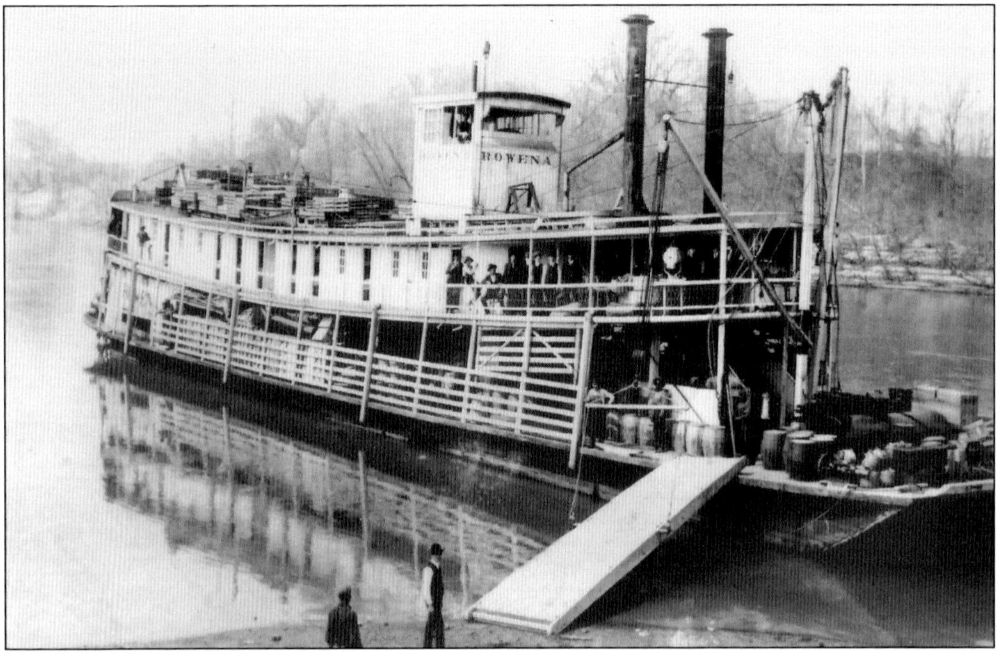

The *Rowena* was owned by the B&B and carried cargo to and from Nashville, Tennessee. It was rare for a steamboat to last more than five years due to boiler-room explosions, stateroom fires, or running against snags in the water, which ripped open the hull. The *Rowena* was rare; she was 22 years old when she sank in 1934. (Courtesy of Debbie Lake.)

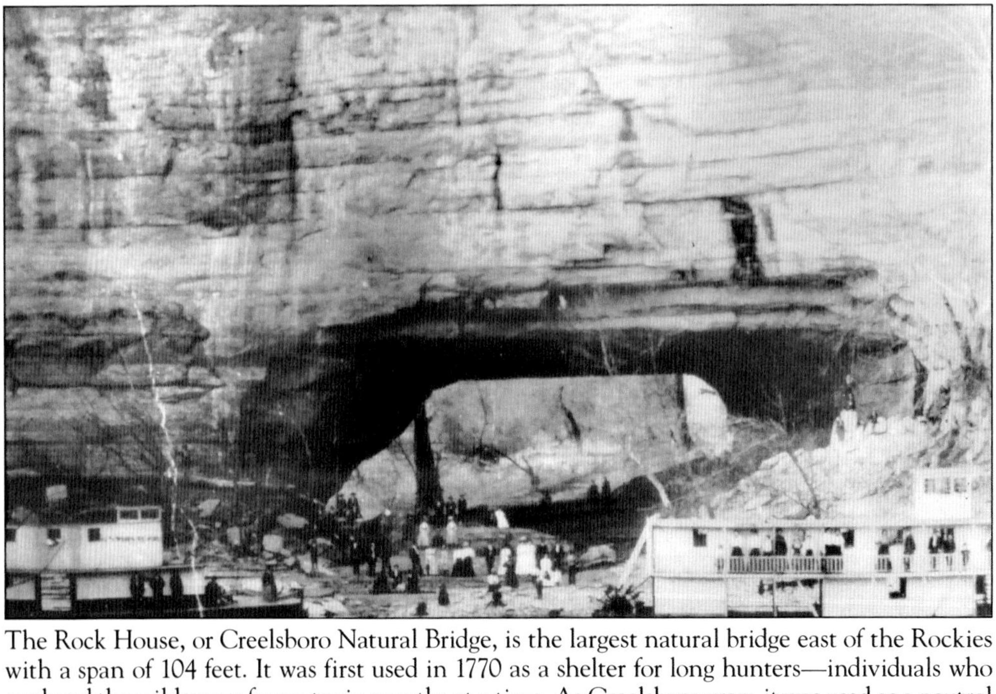

The Rock House, or Creelsboro Natural Bridge, is the largest natural bridge east of the Rockies with a span of 104 feet. It was first used in 1770 as a shelter for long hunters—individuals who explored the wilderness for up to six months at a time. As Creelsboro grew, it was used as a neutral spot for Creelsboro town meetings. The natural bridge was a popular stopping place for river traffic. The Rock House is currently located on private property. (Courtesy of Carole Tupman.)

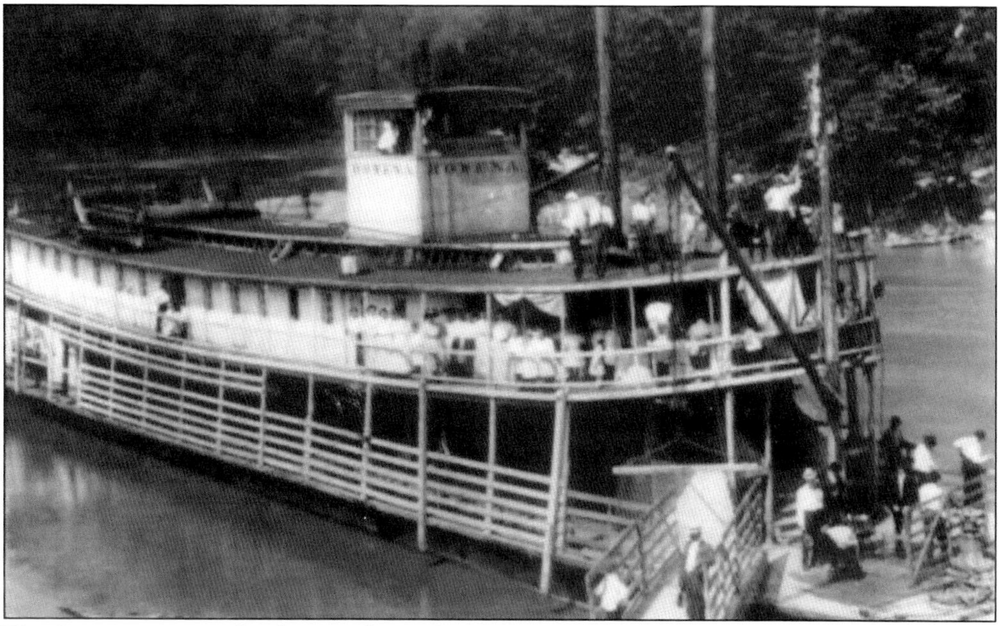

The *Rowena* was 168 feet long and 29.7 feet wide. Two stern boilers supplied the power to the 12-foot paddle wheel. The hull was flat, and the boat had a carrying capacity of 250 tons. The boat offered delicious meals served in a large dining room. Twenty staterooms and 56 berths were available for 60 passengers. The 275-horsepower steam engines averaged a speed of 10 miles an hour. (Courtesy of the PCHS.)

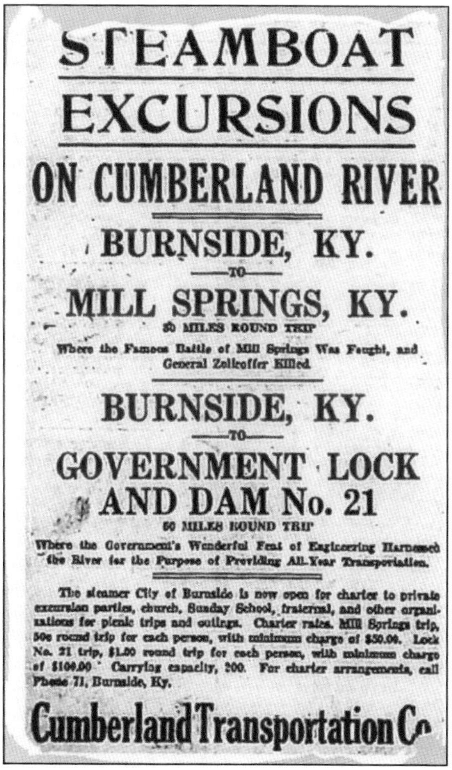

STEAMBOAT EXCURSIONS

ON CUMBERLAND RIVER

BURNSIDE, KY.

—TO—

MILL SPRINGS, KY.

30 MILES ROUND TRIP

Where the Famous Battle of Mill Springs Was Fought, and General Zollicoffer Killed.

BURNSIDE, KY.

—TO—

GOVERNMENT LOCK AND DAM No. 21

60 MILES ROUND TRIP

Where the Government's Wonderful Feat of Engineering Harnessed the River for the Purpose of Providing All-Year Transportation.

The steamer City of Burnside is now open for charter to private excursion parties, church, Sunday School, fraternal, and other organizations for picnic trips and outings. Charter rates. Mill Springs trip, 50c round trip for each person, with minimum charge of $50.00. Lock No. 21 trip, $1.00 round trip for each person, with minimum charge of $100.00. Carrying capacity, 200. For charter arrangements, call Phone 71, Burnside, Ky.

Cumberland Transportation Co

Steamboats were used for excursions along the Cumberland. This is an advertisement by the Cumberland Transportation Company and reads, "The steamer *City of Burnside* is now open for charter to private excursion parties, church, Sunday School, fraternal and other organizations for picnic trips and outings." Rates were 50¢ per person round-trip from Burnside to Mill Springs or $1 per person round-trip from Burnside to Lock 21. (Courtesy of John T. Carter.)

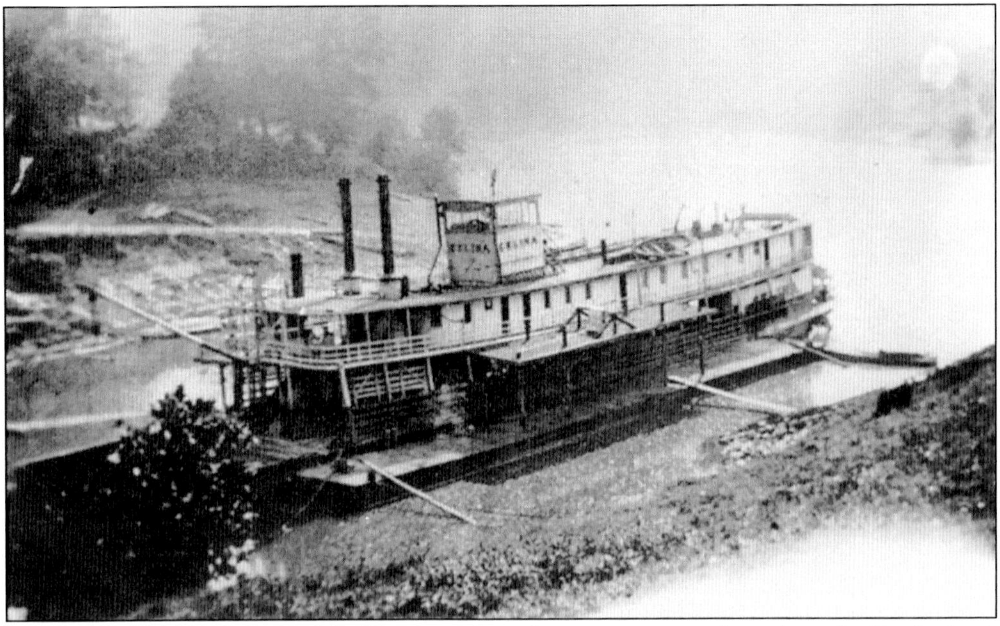

The *Celina* was the sister boat of the *Rowena* and another common steamboat along the Cumberland. In 1925, the *Celina* was pushing a barge up river. Passengers noticed the boat leaning to one side. The crew instantly knew they were in trouble and shouted for everyone to jump to the barge. Just as they did, the *Celina* sank, and only 3 feet of the boat extended above the water. (Courtesy of John T. Carter.)

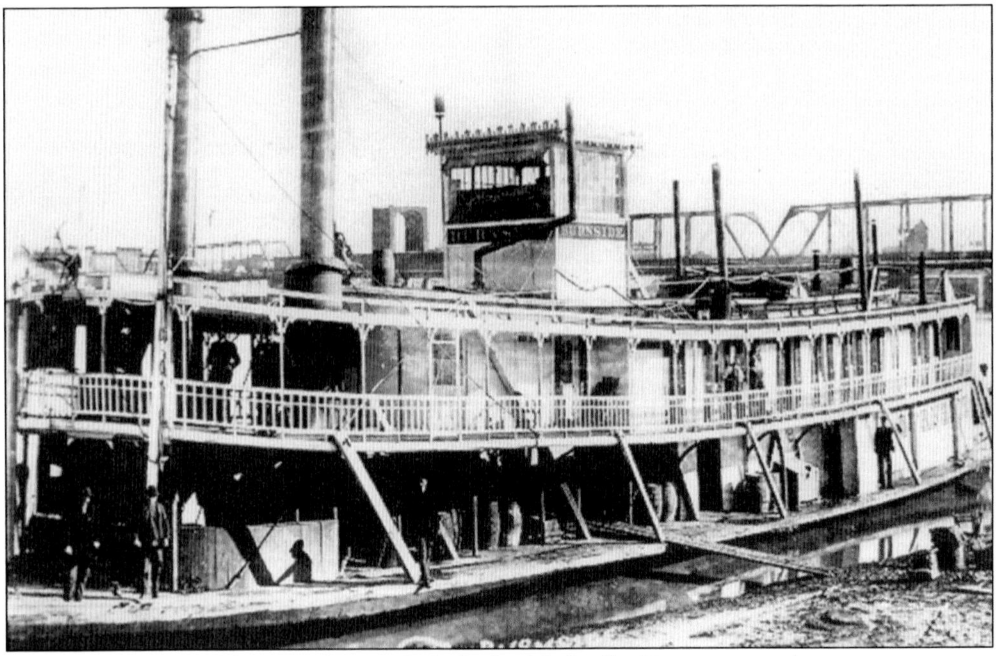

This photograph is of the *City of Burnside* docked in Nashville, Tennessee, ready to transport cargo and passengers up the Cumberland. The steamboat was a regular visitor to the port in Nashville. Nashville was a major city with a population of 17,000 residents in 1860 and an astounding 80,000 residents in 1900. (Courtesy of the PCHS.)

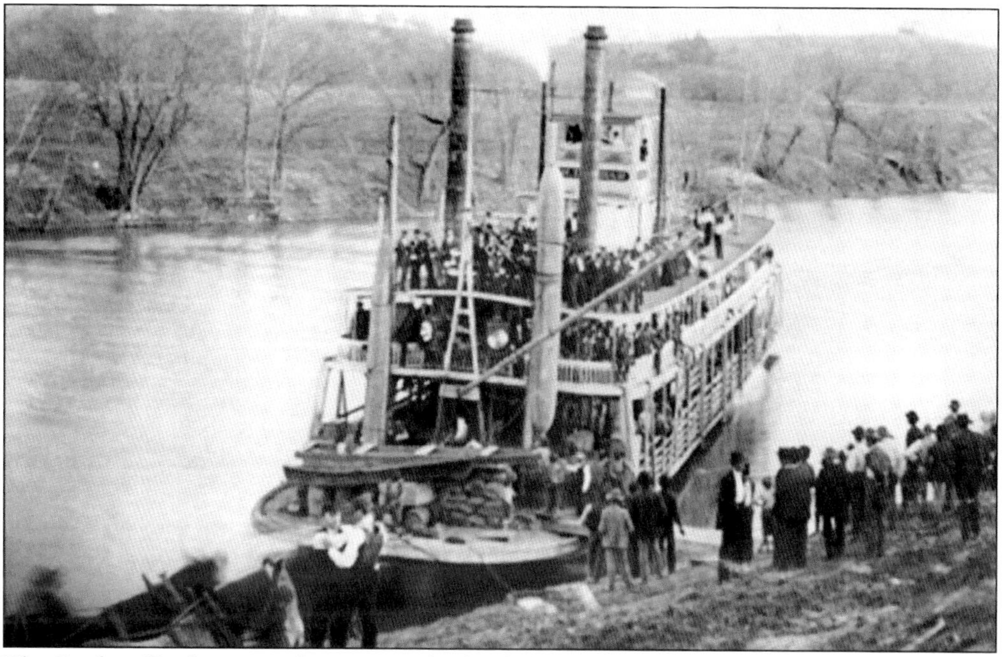

The *Reuban Dunbar* waits for items to be loaded and unloaded at the Burkesville Landing. Capt. Tom Rhyman steered the *Reuban Dunbar* to Nashville and back once a week. Burkesville was one of the biggest landings along the Cumberland River. The last riverboat to dock at the Burkesville Landing was in 1929. (Courtesy of Randolph Smith.)

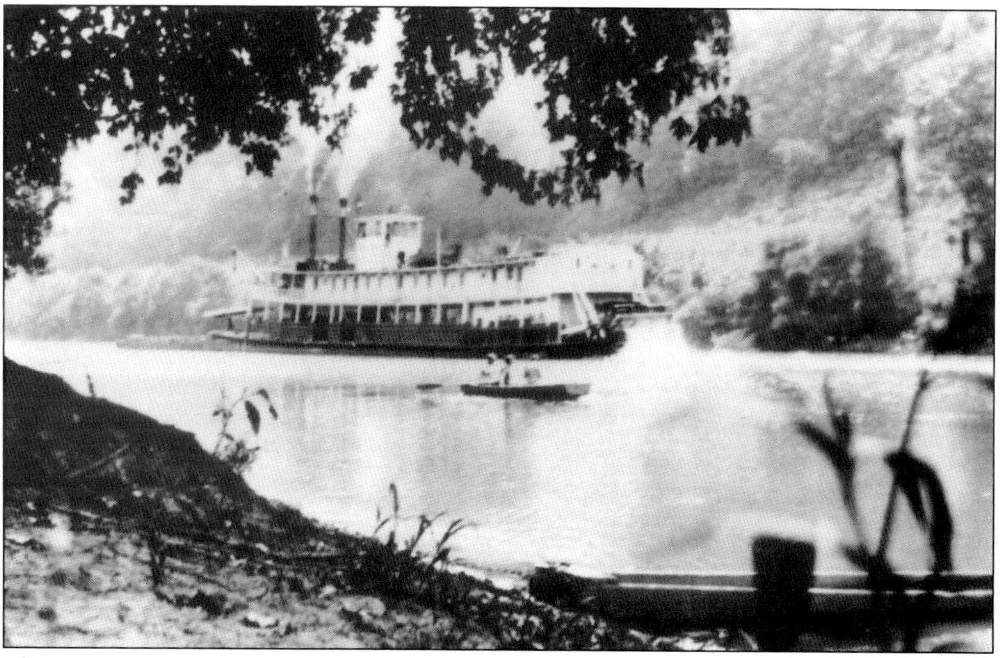

The *Rowena* sank on June 20, 1934, on her way to Paducah, Kentucky. This marked the end of a 100-year era of river transportation. The steamboat's whistle was salvaged and repaired. It currently sits, unused, atop the Fruit of the Loom manufacturing facility in Jamestown, Kentucky. (Courtesy of the PCHS.)

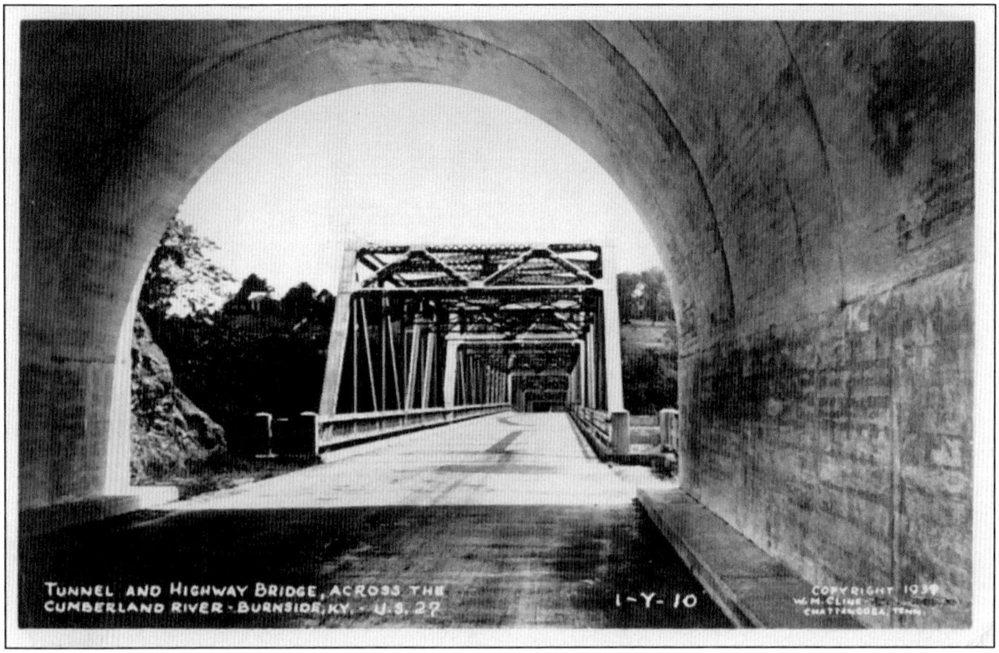

The General Burnside toll bridge was completed in 1931. The toll was a hefty 45¢. Due to the Great Depression, the state reduced the toll to 30¢ and finally to 15¢. Pedestrians could cross for a nickel. By 1945, the construction bonds were paid off seven years ahead of schedule. (Courtesy of the authors' collection.)

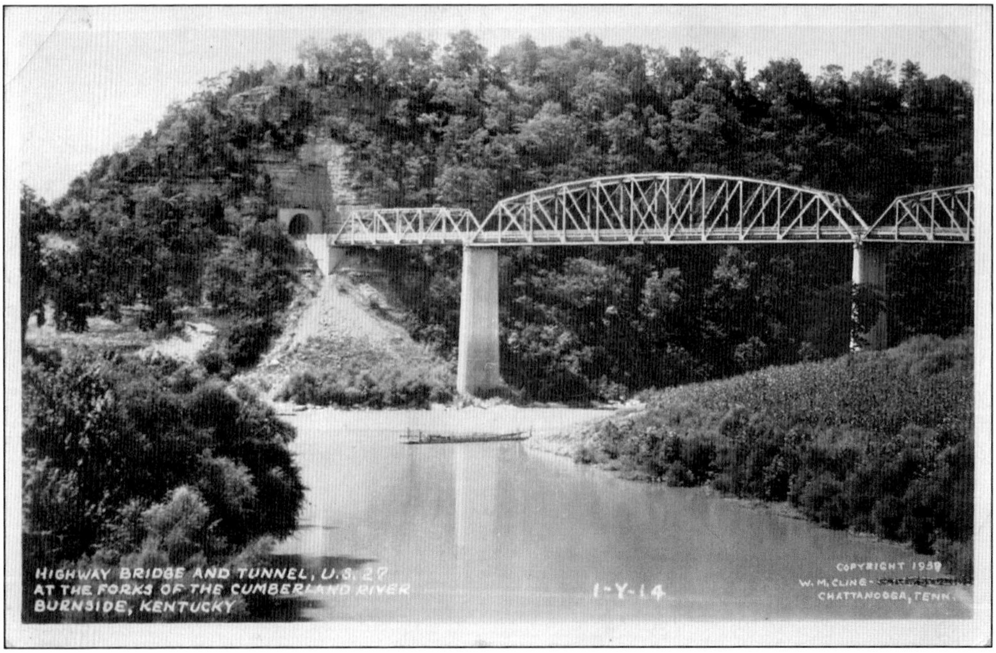

This photograph shows the span of the General Burnside Bridge. The bridge was 1,393 feet long and 90 feet tall. Flood gauges were painted onto the side of the concrete pillars, which could be read during high water. Construction on the bridge started in the summer of 1930, and the bridge was completed a year later. (Courtesy of the authors' collection.)

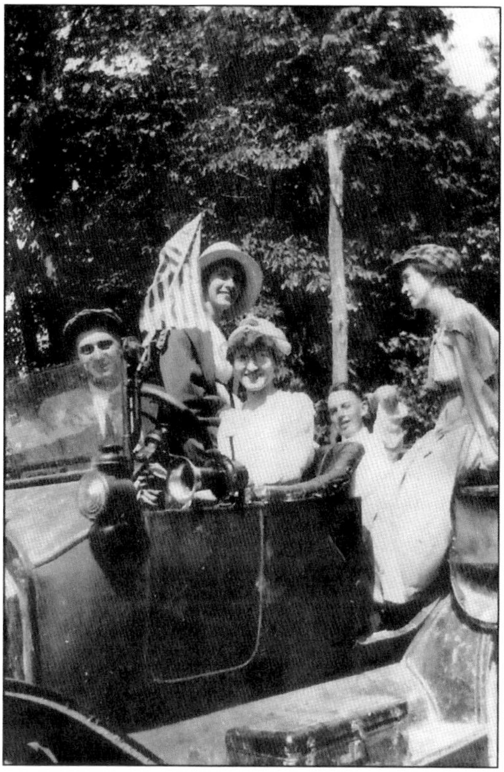

In 1945, after World War II ended, employment and prosperity came back to the area. In spite of gasoline and tire rationing and a halt in the manufacture of new cars, Americans took to the road as never before. (Courtesy of Randolph Smith.)

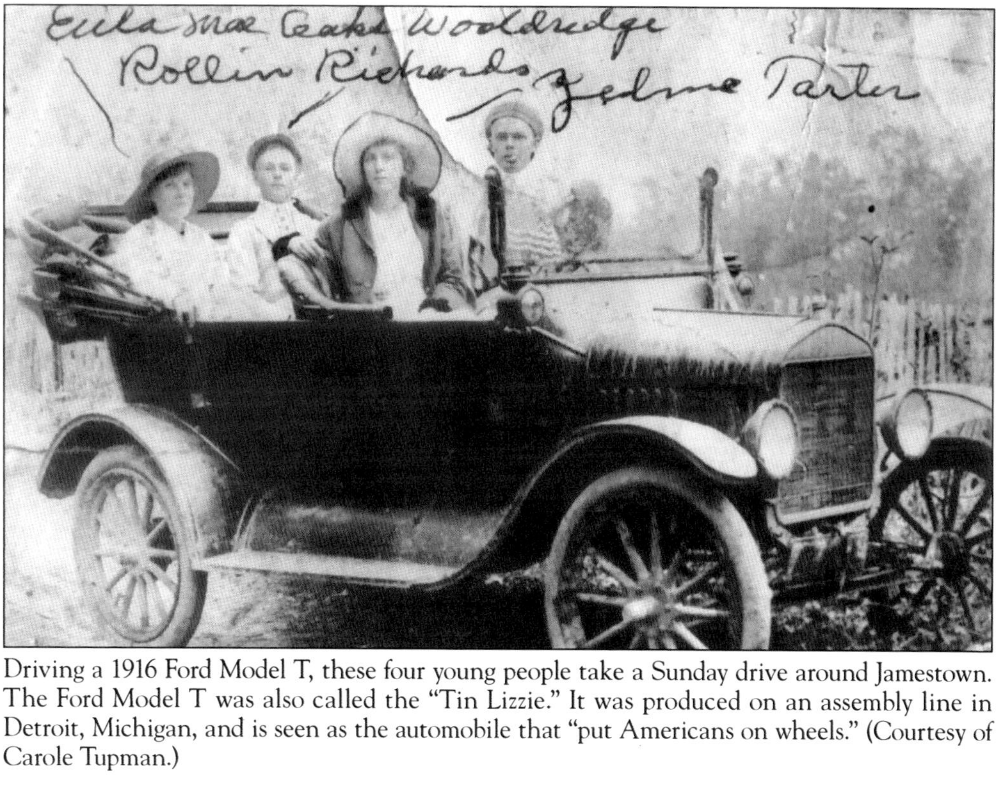

Driving a 1916 Ford Model T, these four young people take a Sunday drive around Jamestown. The Ford Model T was also called the "Tin Lizzie." It was produced on an assembly line in Detroit, Michigan, and is seen as the automobile that "put Americans on wheels." (Courtesy of Carole Tupman.)

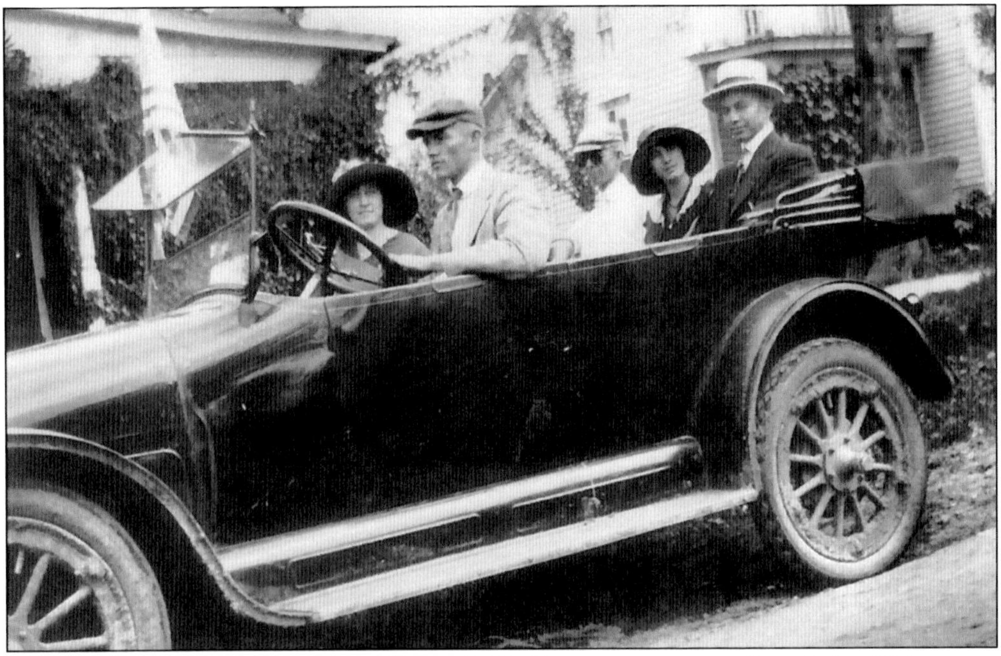

Ford produced the Model T from 1908 to 1927. The car was originally sold for $850, but as production became more efficient, the price for the car decreased. In the 1920s, a new Model T could be purchased for $300. These Burkesville natives enjoy a day in their 1927 Model T. (Courtesy of Randolph Smith.)

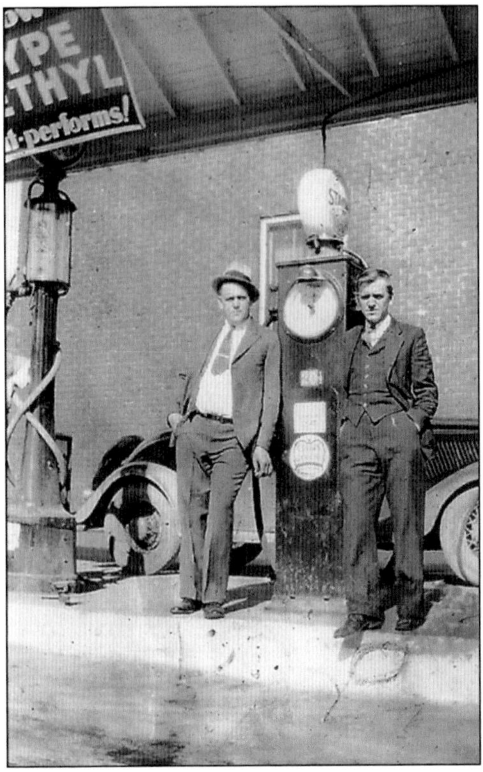

The Model Ts relied on gravity for ethyl to flow from the fuel tank to the carburetor and could not climb a steep hill if its fuel was low. The immediate solution was often to drive up steep hills in reverse. In this photograph, Philip (left) and Charles Cox stand at the ethyl station in Burnside. (Courtesy of Ron Holcomb.)

Prior to the completion of the Wolf Creek Dam, there was still a choice when it came to crossing the Cumberland River. In spite of new bridges, numerous car owners preferred the old way and chose to cross the river by ferry. This photograph was taken in 1942 on the Burnside-to-Bronston ferry. There are several ferries still in operation downriver from Wolf Creek Dam. (Courtesy of John T. Carter.)

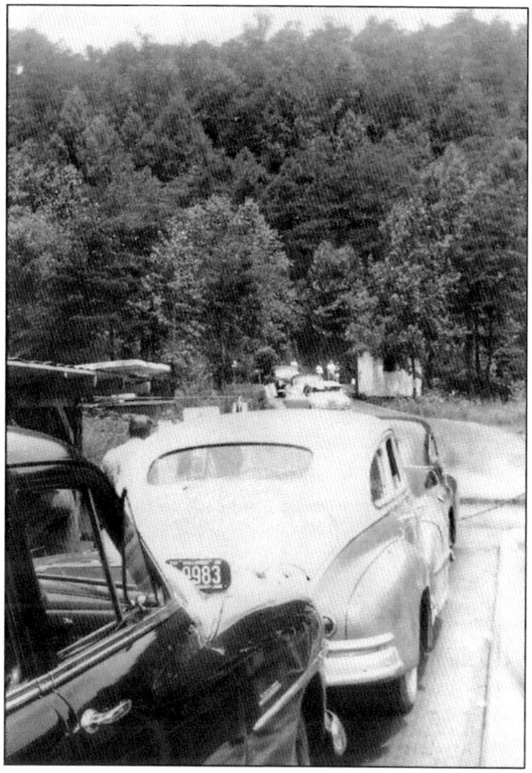

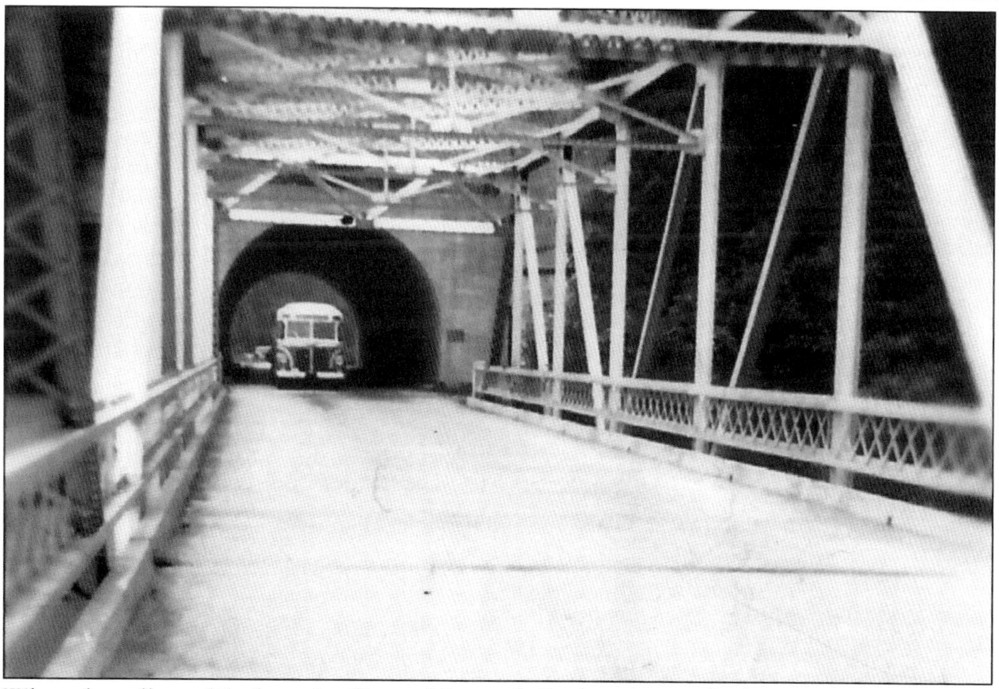

When the toll was lifted on the General Burnside Bridge, three vehicles crossed the bridge to symbolize the evolution of travel. The stagecoach crossed first, followed by the Tin Lizzie, and finally this Greyhound bus. (Courtesy of Tom Moody.)

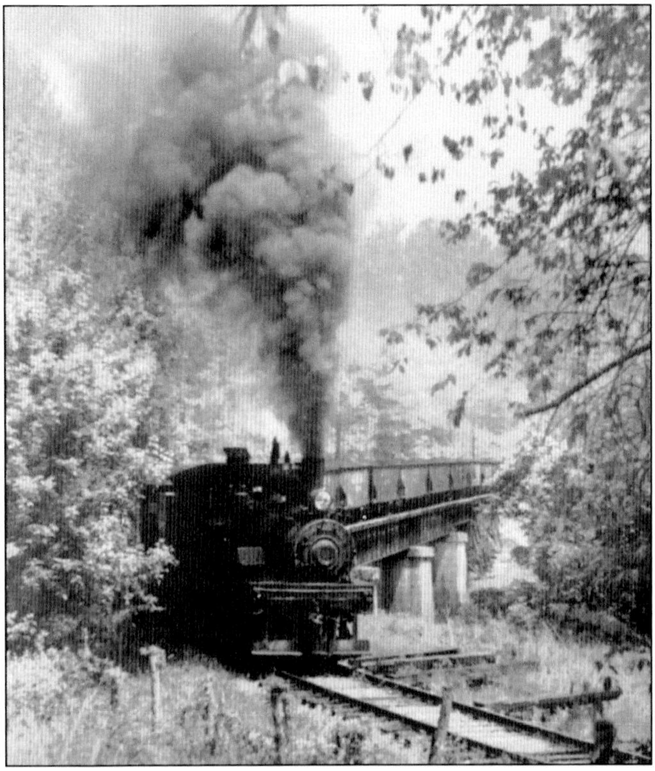

Freight trains first arrived in Burnside at the request of Gen. Ambrose Burnside. The Civil War general suggested that President Lincoln have a railroad built in order to ship war supplies into the South. A survey was conducted in 1863. The Cincinnati Southern Railway, later known as the Southern Railway, was completed in 1880. The first freight train arrived in Burnside in February 1880, and the first passenger train was welcomed by town residents in March 1880. (Courtesy of the authors' collection.)

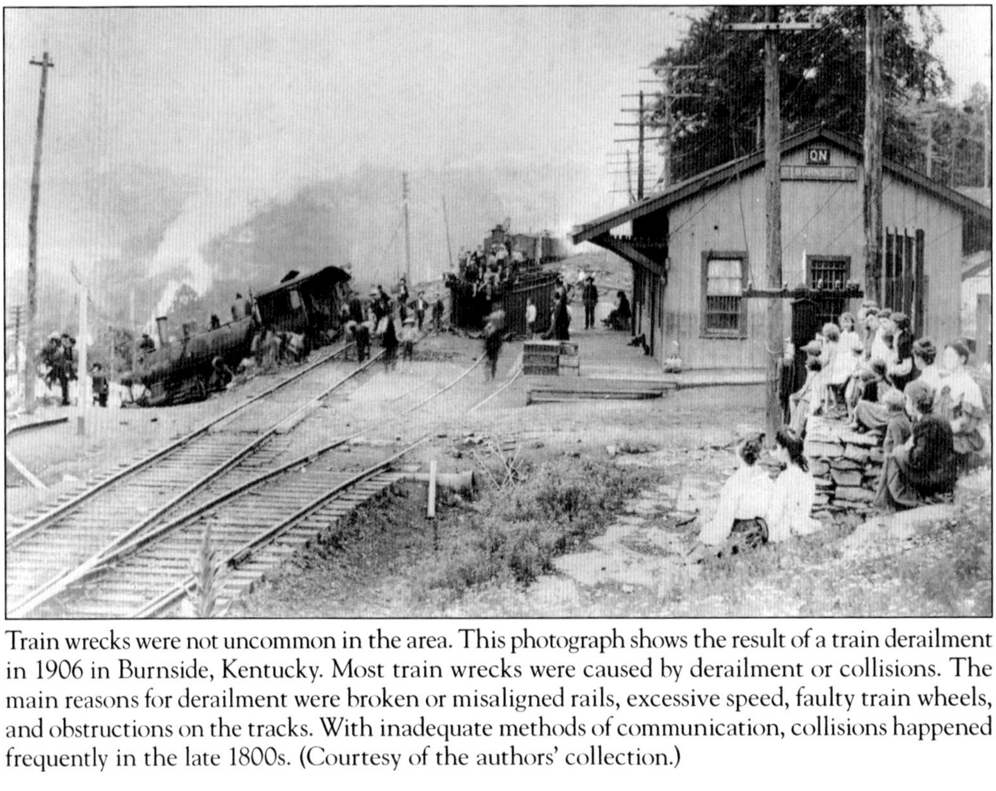

Train wrecks were not uncommon in the area. This photograph shows the result of a train derailment in 1906 in Burnside, Kentucky. Most train wrecks were caused by derailment or collisions. The main reasons for derailment were broken or misaligned rails, excessive speed, faulty train wheels, and obstructions on the tracks. With inadequate methods of communication, collisions happened frequently in the late 1800s. (Courtesy of the authors' collection.)

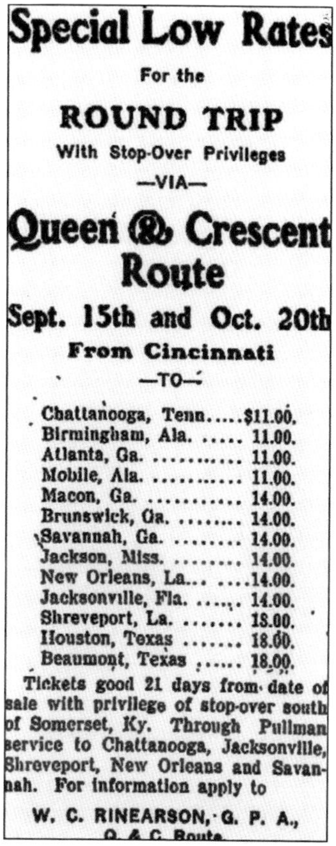

Special Low Rates

For the

ROUND TRIP

With Stop-Over Privileges

—VIA—

Queen & Crescent Route

Sept. 15th and Oct. 20th

From Cincinnati

—TO—

Chattanooga, Tenn.	$11.00.
Birmingham, Ala.	11.00.
Atlanta, Ga.	11.00.
Mobile, Ala.	11.00.
Macon, Ga.	14.00.
Brunswick, Ga.	14.00.
Savannah, Ga.	14.00.
Jackson, Miss.	14.00.
New Orleans, La.	14.00.
Jacksonville, Fla.	14.00.
Shreveport, La.	18.00.
Houston, Texas	18.00.
Beaumont, Texas	18.00.

Tickets good 21 days from date of sale with privilege of stop-over south of Somerset, Ky. Through Pullman service to Chattanooga, Jacksonville, Shreveport, New Orleans and Savannah. For information apply to

W. C. RINEARSON, G. P. A., Q. & C. Route.

This newspaper advertisement from 1903 offers a list of prices to ride the rail from Cincinnati, Ohio, (the Queen City) to New Orleans, Louisiana (the Crescent City). Burnside was a popular town for trains to stop for the night on the trip between the two large cities. (Courtesy of John T. Carter.)

Passengers found traveling more convenient on the railroad. Quick one-day trips to Lexington or Cincinnati were not uncommon for residents along the Cumberland. Coney Island, Chester Park, and the zoo were favorite attractions in Cincinnati, Ohio. One could purchase a round-trip ticket from Burnside to Cincinnati and back to Burnside for $1.50. (Courtesy of the authors' collection.)

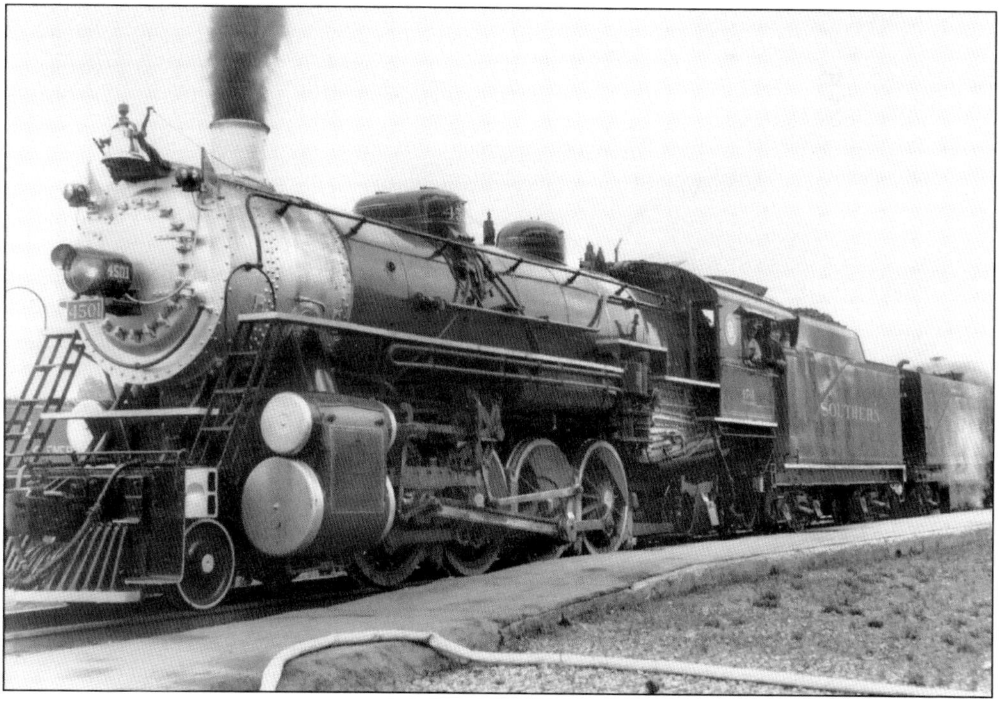

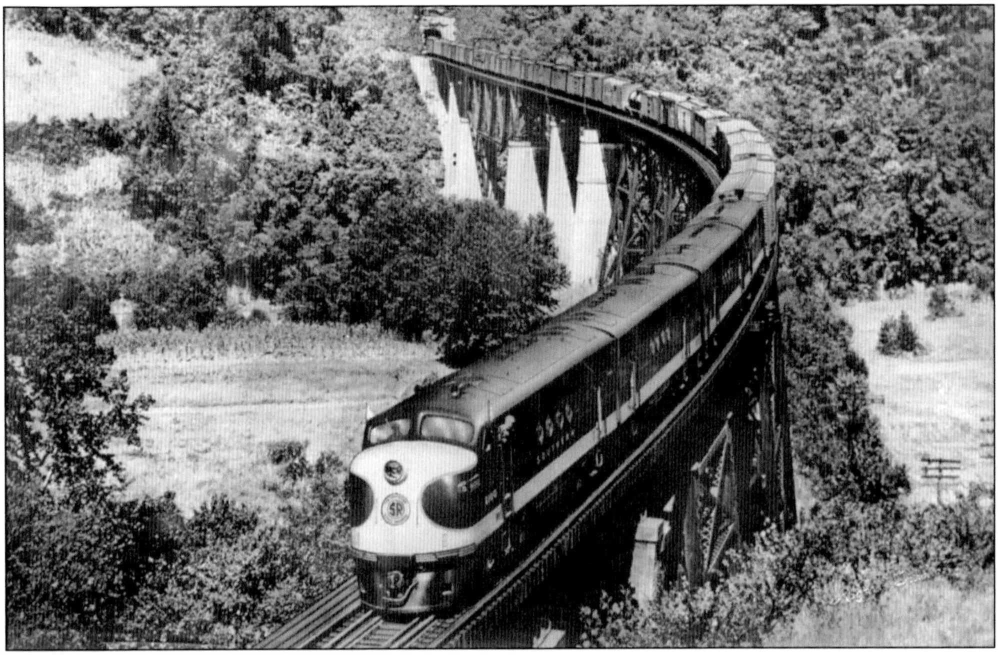

This photograph shows the world's first diesel-electric freight locomotive crossing Burnside's Cumberland River Bridge in May 1941. Credited with being the "greatest single locomotive of the 20th century," the locomotive was a highly successful workhorse. It is on display at the National Museum of Transportation in St. Louis, Missouri. (Courtesy of the authors' collection.)

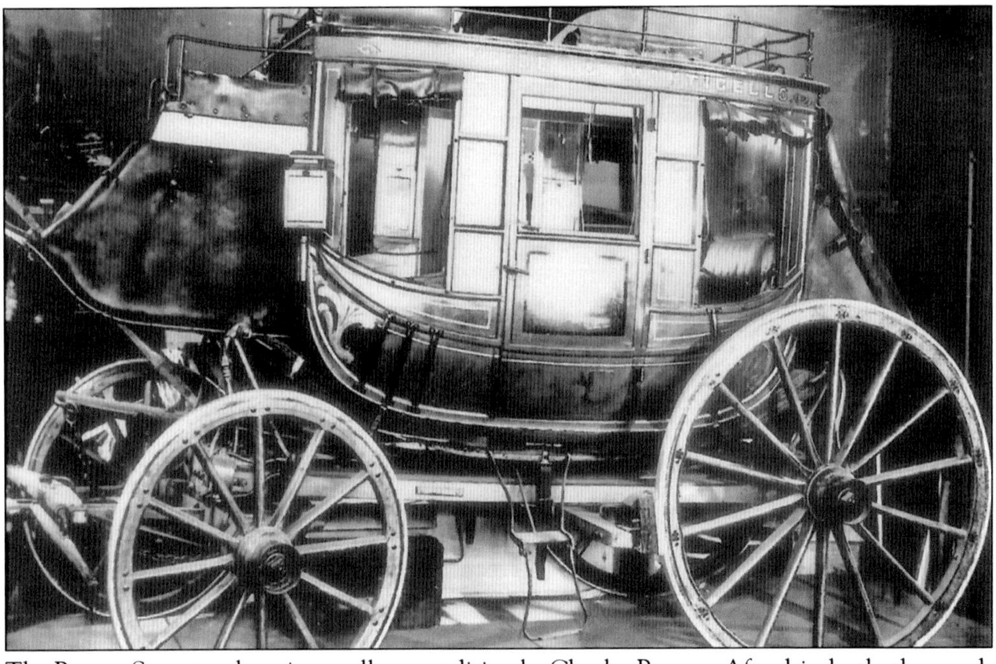

The Burton Stage was kept in excellent condition by Charles Burton. After his death, the coach was auctioned off on July 29, 1978, for $38,750. Wells Fargo of California purchased the coach on December 20, 1978, for $85,000. It currently resides in the Wells Fargo building and museum in Los Angeles, California. (Courtesy of the PCHS.)

Four

Booming Burnside

The story of Burnside begins with a tragic tale of a young girl named Isabel who suffered from a broken heart. One night, in a moment of distress, she threw herself from a cliff into the Cumberland River. The cliff was situated high above a protruding piece of land at the juncture of the Cumberland and the South Fork Rivers. The piece of land was then called Point Isabel.

During the Civil War, Union army general Ambrose Burnside commandeered the town as a staging area for his invasion of Tennessee and the town was called Camp Burnside. Twenty-five years after the Civil War ended, the town was incorporated in 1890 as Burnside with a population of 500.

The thriving town was divided into "Upper" and "Lower" Burnside. "Upper" Burnside was built high above "Lower" Burnside and was home to the more affluent business owners and well-paid employees.

"Lower" Burnside was in the valley alongside the Cumberland. It was the heart of the town and teamed with commerce. Initially, the town had lumber mills, a spoke and stave company, a general store, a hotel, a schoolhouse, a livery, and a blacksmith shop. The town supported one drugstore and two doctors.

Burnside was perfectly located for trade because it was the head of navigation along the Cumberland River and was the largest railroad shipping hub between Cincinnati, Ohio, and Chattanooga, Tennessee.

As trade heightened, jobs became more numerous, and the town grew to several thousand residents by 1897.

Unfortunately, spring rains generally brought flooding. People expected the floods. When water rose, neighbor helped neighbor move furniture and belongings to higher ground. As water receded, everyone cleaned up and moved back in to their homes and businesses. Flooding was frequent, and residents were accustomed to this way of life.

Despite the flooding, the timber, the river, and the railroad made Burnside flourish.

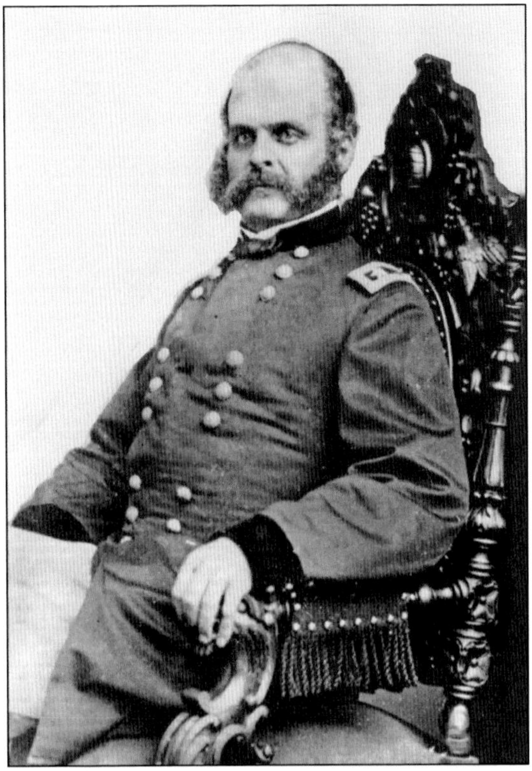

Union army general Ambrose Everett Burnside (May 23, 1824–September 13, 1881) set up camp in Point Isabel, later named Burnside in his honor. Burnside went on to become the governor of Rhode Island. He is well known for his facial hair, known as sideburns. (Courtesy of Rogers Photography.)

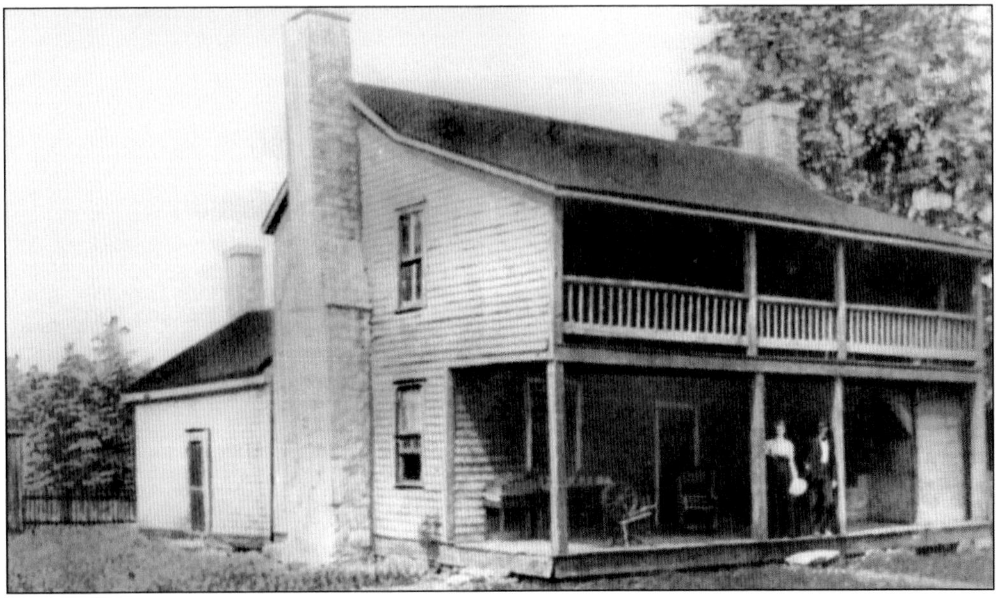

The first settlers in the area were John Beaty and his wife, Polly, who married in 1796. They built a house on the west side of the Cumberland River overlooking Point Isabel. In the early 1800s, the Reverend James Ballou purchased much of the land in the valley of Point Isabel. He, his wife, Susanah, and their 15 children lived in a home in the center of the valley. The Ballou home was used as the headquarters of General Burnside during the Civil War. (Courtesy of Rogers Photography.)

The Drug Store was the first store of its kind in Burnside. Dr. Littleton Cook, one of the few licensed physicians in the county, opened the store in 1884. Nicholas Stigall clerked in the store for $6.25 a month plus board. Stigall earned his medical degree from the University of Louisville and returned to Burnside in 1901. Dr. Stigall spent the next 47 years as the best loved and busiest physician in town. (Courtesy of the PCHS.)

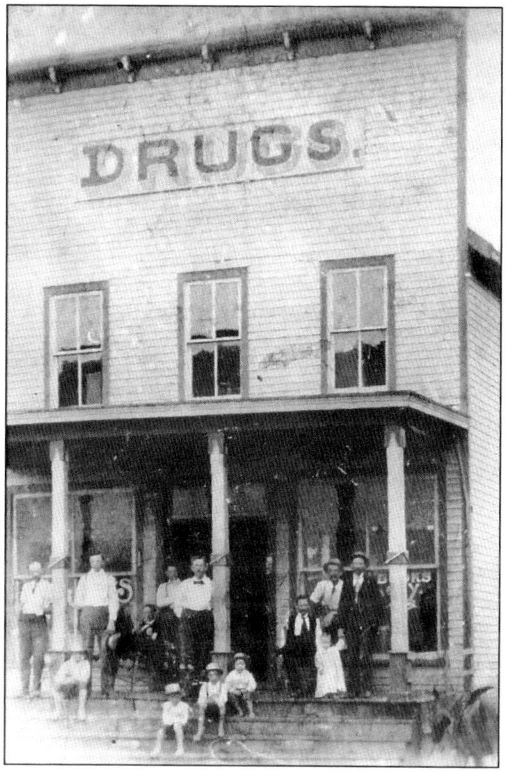

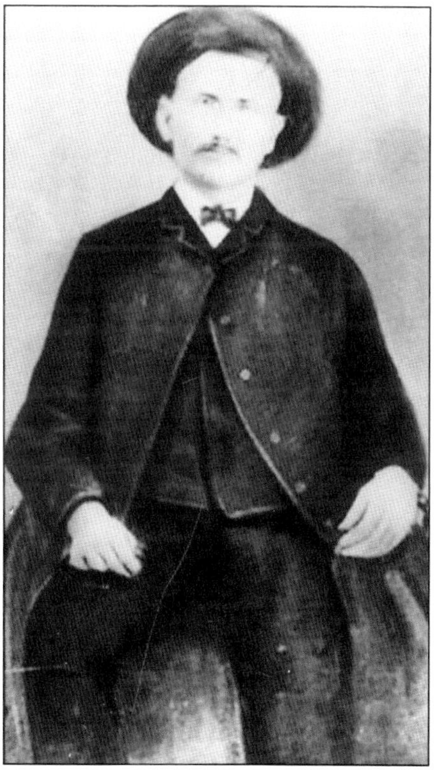

John Morgan Fitzgerald (pictured at left) was killed in the streets of Burnside on August 13, 1913, at the age of 51. An intoxicated Josh Tarter shot the city marshal, John Coomer, in the neck and fled. Tarter jumped onto the Cumberland River Ferry and forced ferryman Ben Brown to take him across the river. A posse was quickly organized to capture Josh Tarter. The posse saw Tarter on the ferry and ordered him to return to Burnside. Tarter refused to return and opened fire on the posse. John Morgan Fitzgerald was shot and died instantly. Six weeks later, Marshal John Coomer died from his gunshot wound. Tarter only served five years for the murders. (Courtesy of Judith Waddell.)

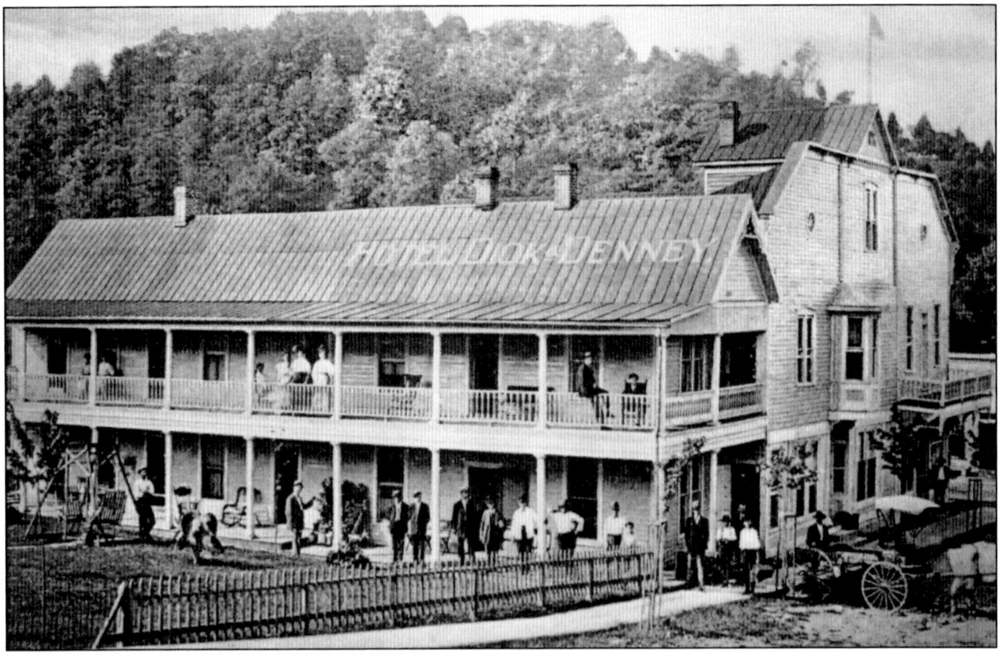

G. S. Dick and Joseph R. Denney from Mill Springs opened a livery, store, and hotel in 1900. The Hotel Dick and Denney was a popular hotel in Burnside and attracted traveling businessmen until it was destroyed by fire only a few years after opening. Fire was a common cause of destruction to homes and businesses in the area. (Courtesy of Dudley Bryant.)

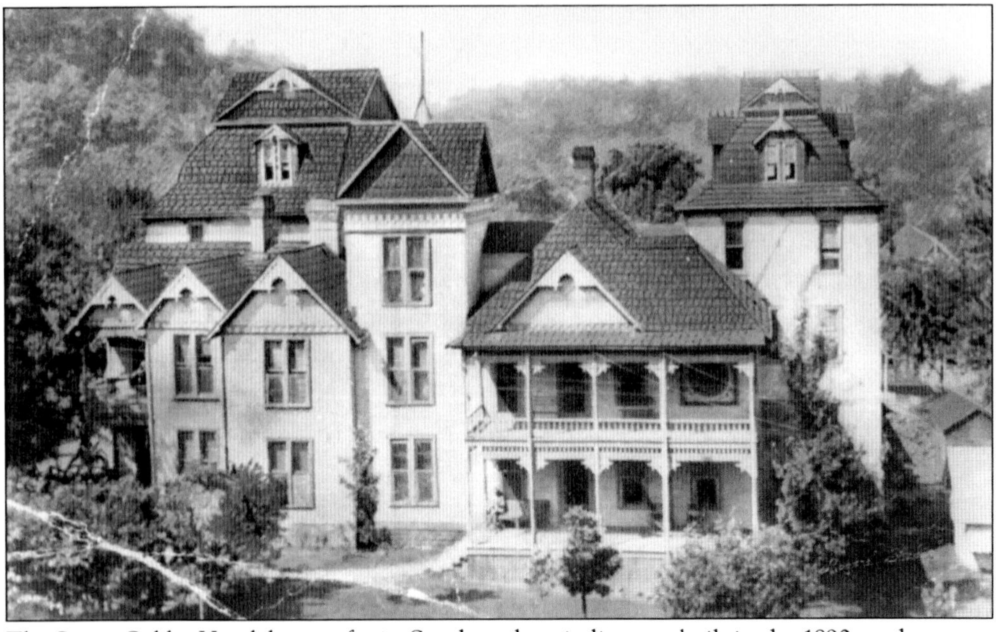

The Seven Gables Hotel, known for its Southern hospitality, was built in the 1890s and was one of the most popular hotels in the region. It was not uncommon to arrive in Burnside by train, spend the night at the Seven Gables, and board a steamboat heading west the next day. It was customary for guests to add their business cards to the collection of cards lining the walls in the lobby. (Courtesy of the authors' collection.)

The Seven Gables Hotel also had a well-known restaurant. On February 2, 1913, the Seven Gables dinner menu included roast possum and sweet potatoes, stewed chicken, roast pork and roast mutton, stewed prunes, stewed peaches, mashed potatoes, corn, string beans, macaroni, baked beans, celery, sweet pickles, slaw, cherry pie, peach pie, white bread, biscuits, and corn bread. The food was served "family style" and passed around the table in large bowls. (Courtesy of the PCHS.)

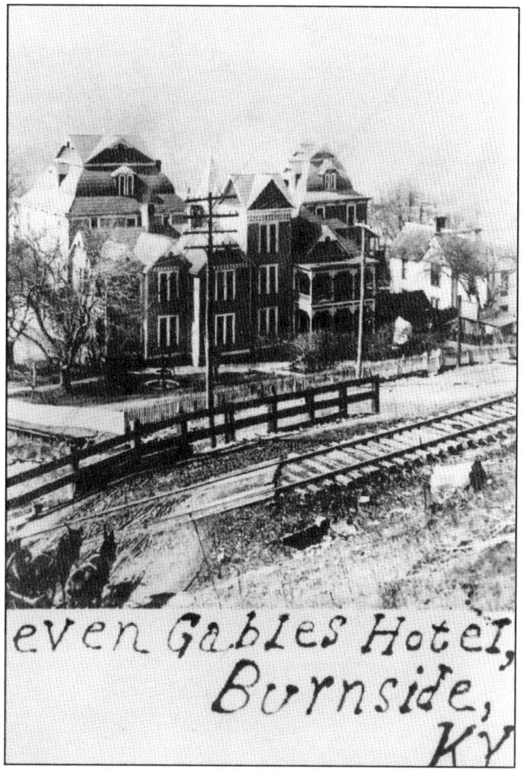

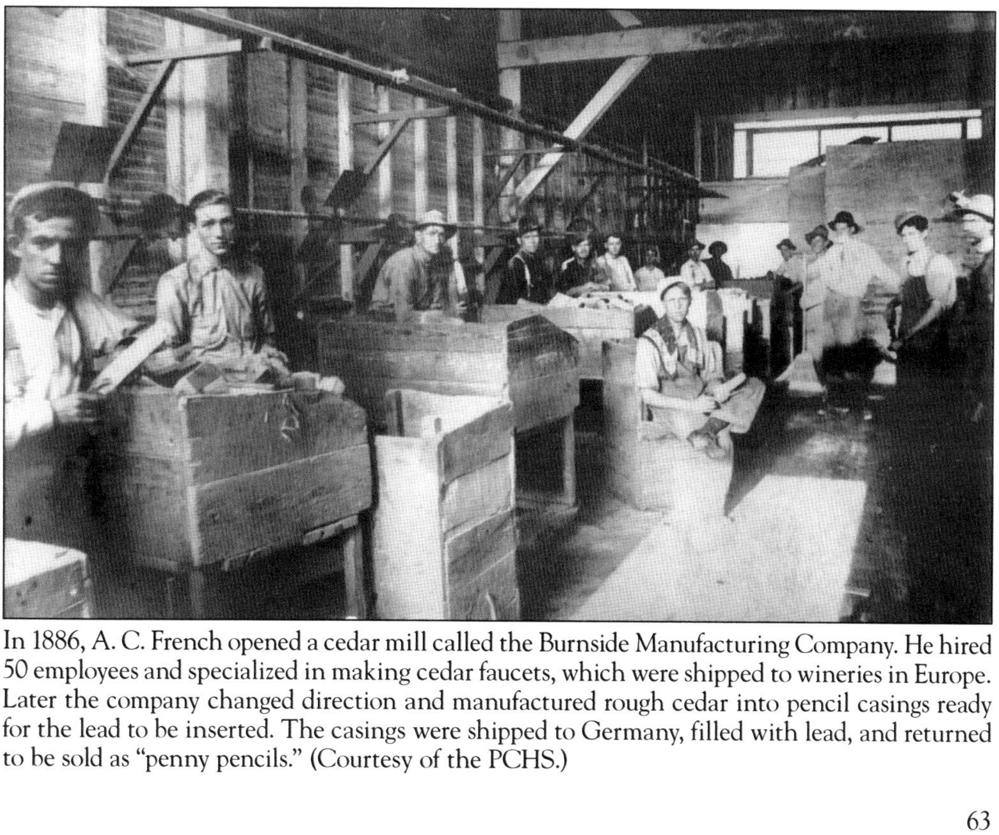

In 1886, A. C. French opened a cedar mill called the Burnside Manufacturing Company. He hired 50 employees and specialized in making cedar faucets, which were shipped to wineries in Europe. Later the company changed direction and manufactured rough cedar into pencil casings ready for the lead to be inserted. The casings were shipped to Germany, filled with lead, and returned to be sold as "penny pencils." (Courtesy of the PCHS.)

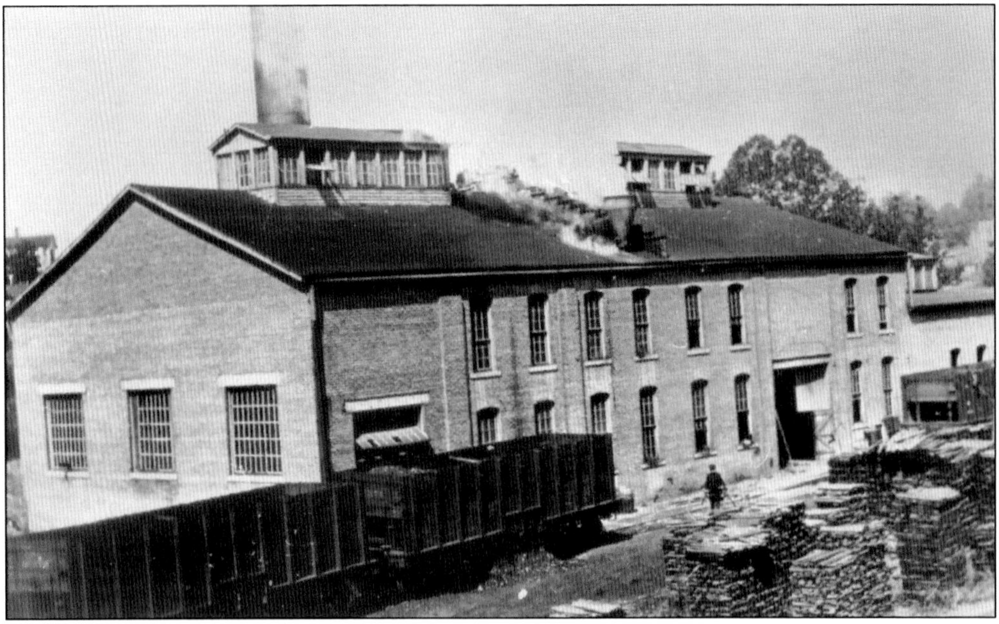

The Burnside Veneer Company received large quantities of logs by barge, river, and rail. It was one of the largest manufacturers of rotary-cut veneer in the country. The veneer company's whistle could be heard for miles around and almost acted as a town clock, blowing early in the morning when work began, again at noon, and in the afternoon when work ended. The whistle blew short blasts when there was a fire in town. (Courtesy of the PCHS.)

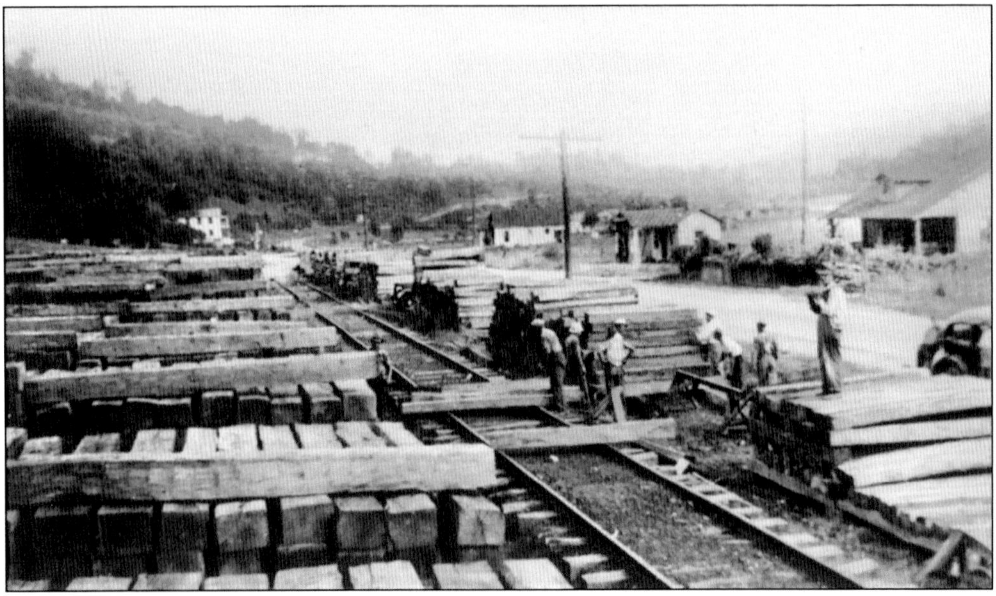

The Grissom-Rakestraw Lumber Company shipped vast amounts of lumber mainly to furniture manufacturers. The lumber was dried near the railroad and often had to be tied down when floodwater rose so it would not float away. As wood dries, it shrinks in size and weighs less, which reduces shipping costs. Dried wood also has improved usability, enhanced heat insulation, reduced susceptibility to insect damage, and increased strength. Wood that has not been dried is called "green wood." (Courtesy of Rogers Photography.)

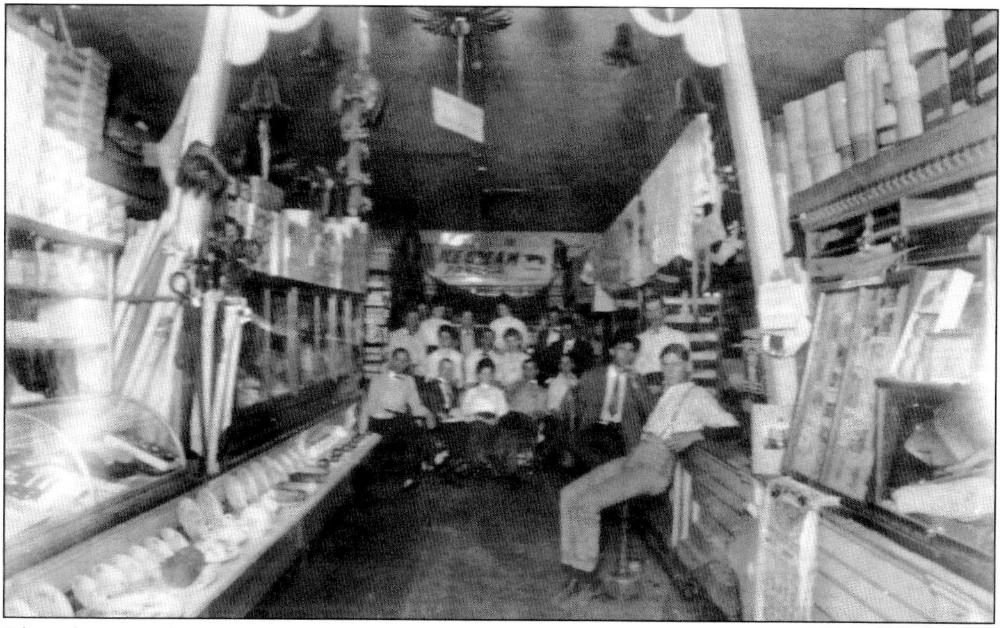

This photograph was taken inside the George P. Taylor produce store in the late 1800s. The store sold a variety of feed, hides, dried herbs, and more. It was successful and continued to grow through the years. Christine Helton Miller remembered the store selling "everything you could ever want or need." In this photograph, the employees pose with an advertisement for ice cream hanging behind them. (Courtesy of Carol Ann Lewis Lovell.)

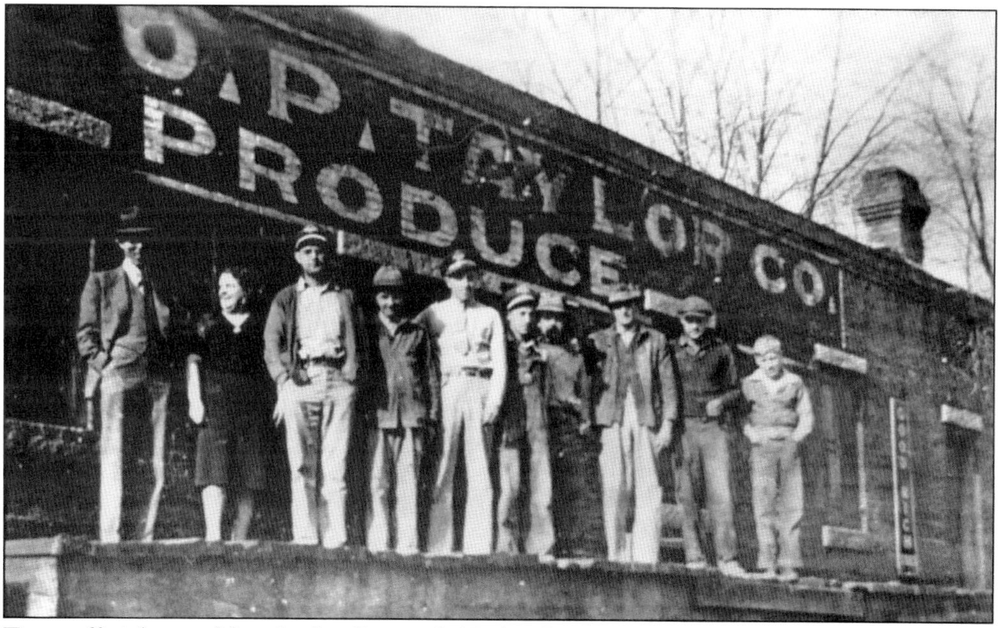

Town officials stand beside the George P. Taylor Company store in this photograph. Taylor shipped eggs and freshly killed chickens. The cleaned chickens were placed on ice and shipped to Chattanooga, Tennessee; Cincinnati, Ohio; and even to New York. For a constant supply of ice, Taylor built an ice manufacturing plant. Howard Hunter could be seen daily driving his horse-drawn wagon, yelling "ice for sale." (Courtesy of Tom Moody.)

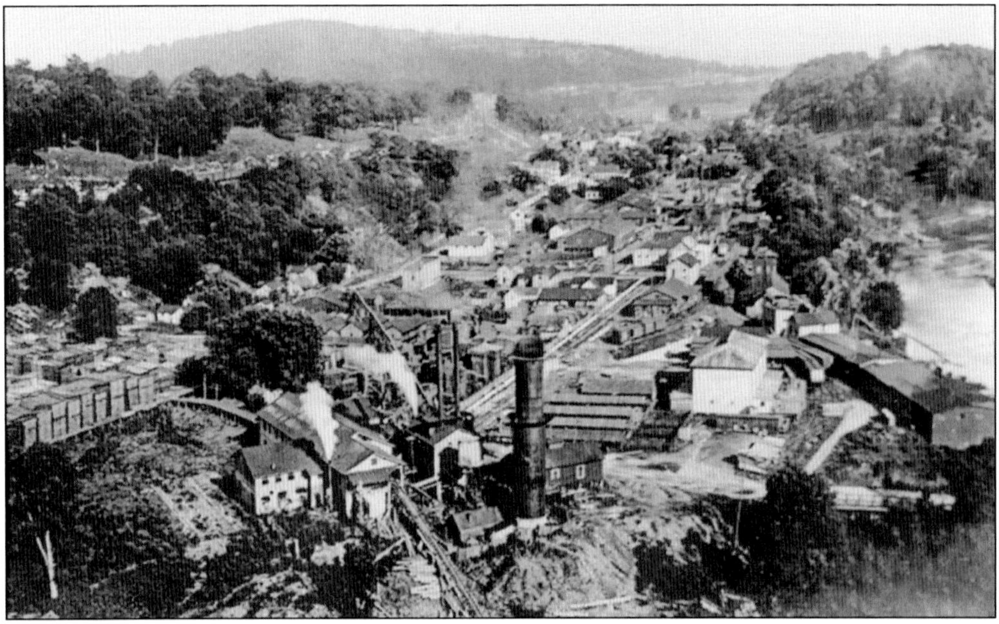

Burnside was booming in the early 1920s, as this photograph shows. The Burnside Veneer Company, originally Chicago Veneer, is seen beside the large smokestack. Elias Thomas Simpson, father of Harriette Simpson Arnow, worked there "feeding the hog," which meant he loaded a large fuel chute leading to the boiler room. Simpson worked 10 hours a day, 6 days a week, and earned $1 a day. (Courtesy of Rogers Photography.)

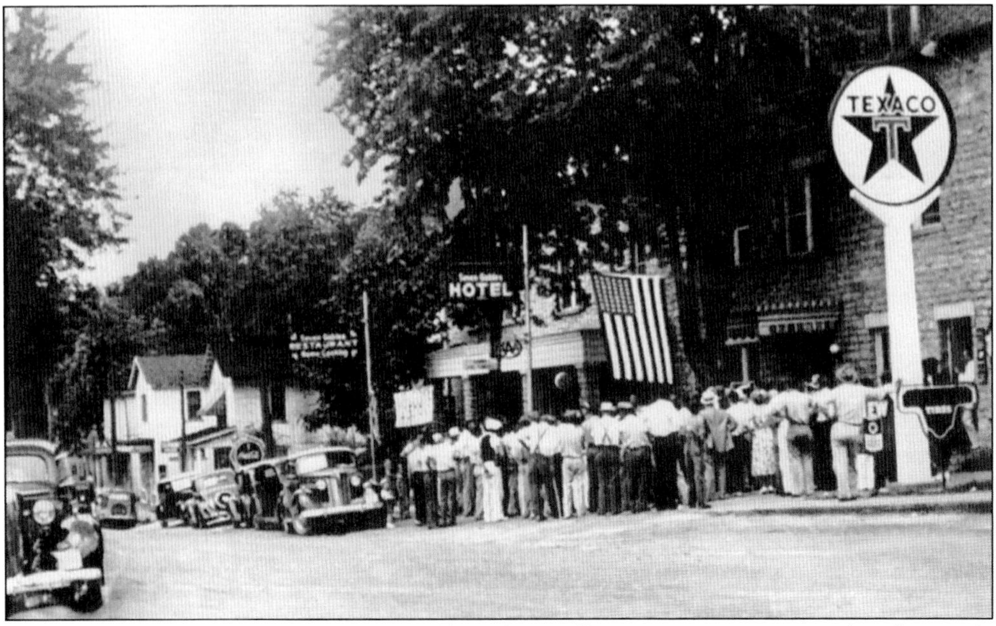

Town residents stand outside the Seven Gables to hear Albert Benjamin "Happy" Chandler speak. Happy was elected the 44th governor of Kentucky in 1935. At the time, he was only 37 years old and was known as the "Boy Governor." Happy was a state senator from 1939 to 1945. In 1955, Happy returned to the governor's mansion as the 49th governor of Kentucky. He died in 1991 at the age of 92. (Courtesy of the authors' collection.)

In 1945, the toll was lifted from the General Burnside Bridge, and the "Free Bridge" celebration ensued. Townspeople parked alongside the road in order to take part in the festivities. In this photograph, James Hail locks his car door while his children impatiently wait on the curb. The tunnel leading to Burnside was 183 feet long. (Courtesy of the PCHS.)

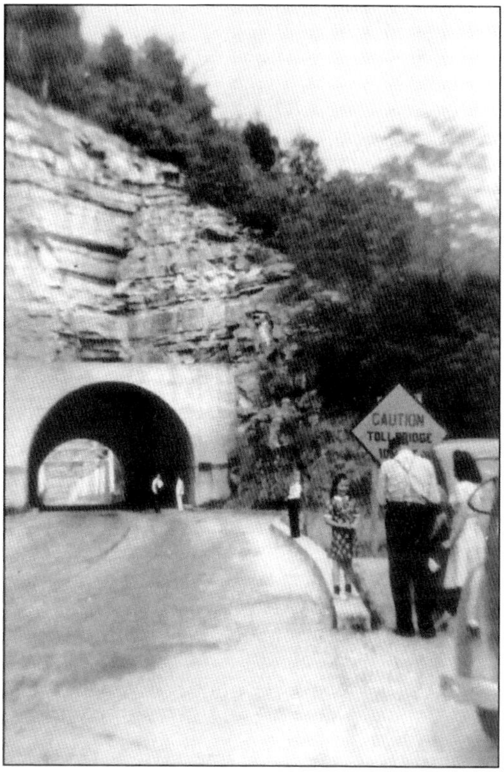

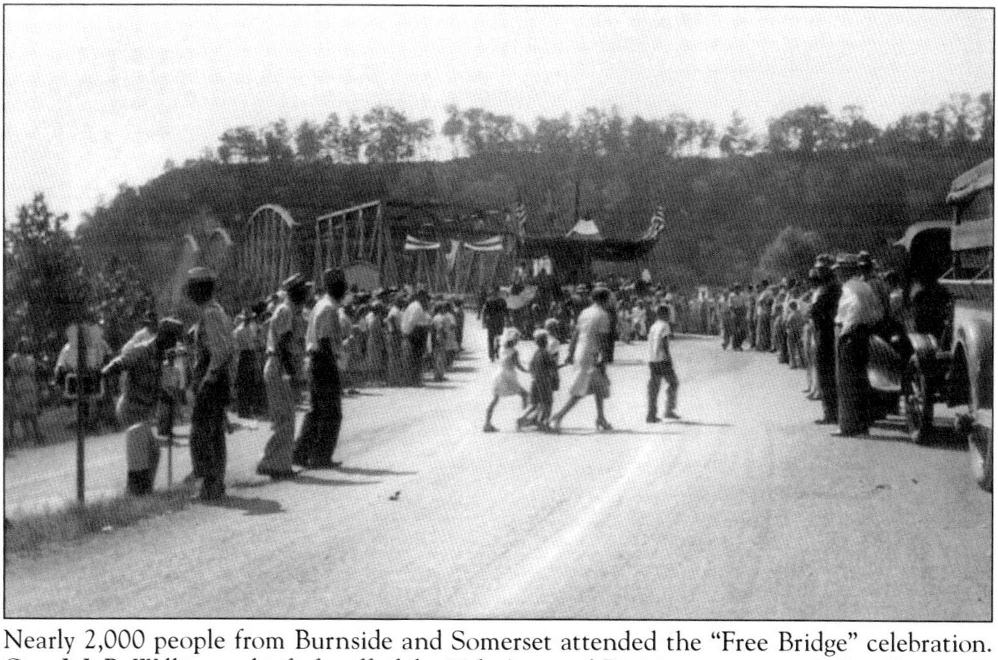

Nearly 2,000 people from Burnside and Somerset attended the "Free Bridge" celebration. Gen. J. J. B. Williams, chief of staff of the 11th Armored Division, represented Gov. Simeon S. Willis and gave a brief address. Dignitaries from the General Assembly and four county judges were in attendance. At 4:15 p.m. on August 25, 1945, a ribbon was cut to symbolize the elimination of the toll. (Courtesy of Tom Moody.)

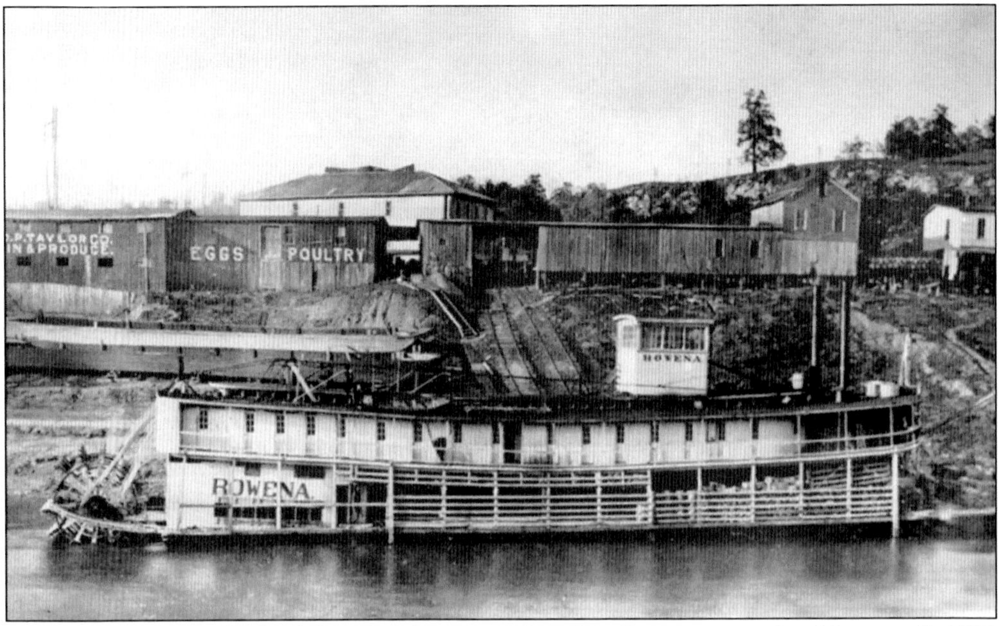

The *Rowena* waits to be loaded with a shipment of poultry. In an invoice dated January 5, 1897, the George P. Taylor Company sold George Cowan 30 pieces of poultry. His order included 13 turkeys for $9.36, 1 tom turkey for 90¢, 3 ducks for 84¢, and 13 geese for $4.24. Cowan paid his bill totaling $15.34 with a check. (Courtesy of Rogers Photography.)

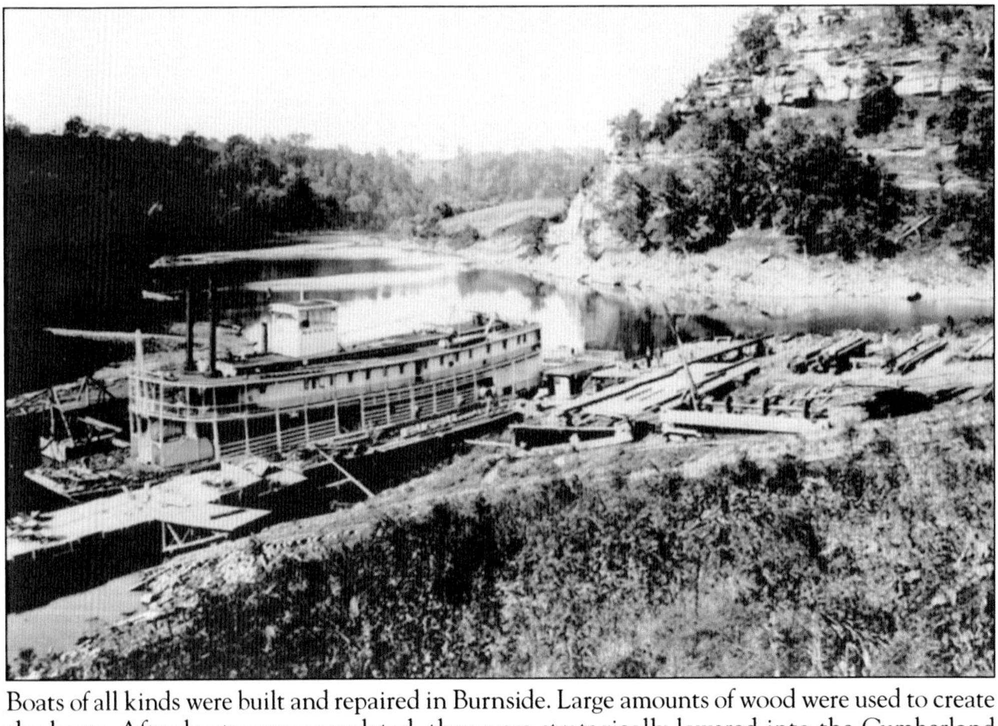

Boats of all kinds were built and repaired in Burnside. Large amounts of wood were used to create the boats. After boats were completed, they were strategically lowered into the Cumberland River. This photograph was taken in the early 1900s and shows the *Rowena* docked in Burnside for repairs. (Courtesy of the authors' collection.)

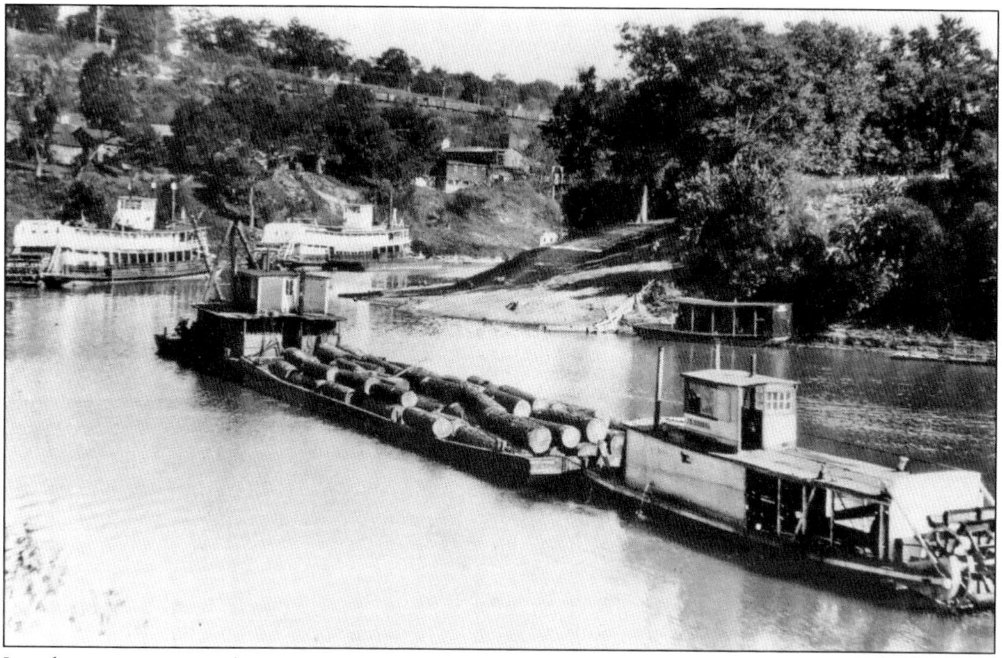

Log booms were vital to Burnside's lumber companies. Logs were cut and allowed to float downstream. The logs were retrieved, loaded onto a barge, and hauled along the river to lumber companies. The road seen in this photograph led to Bronston. It also served as a ferry landing. (Courtesy of the PCHS.)

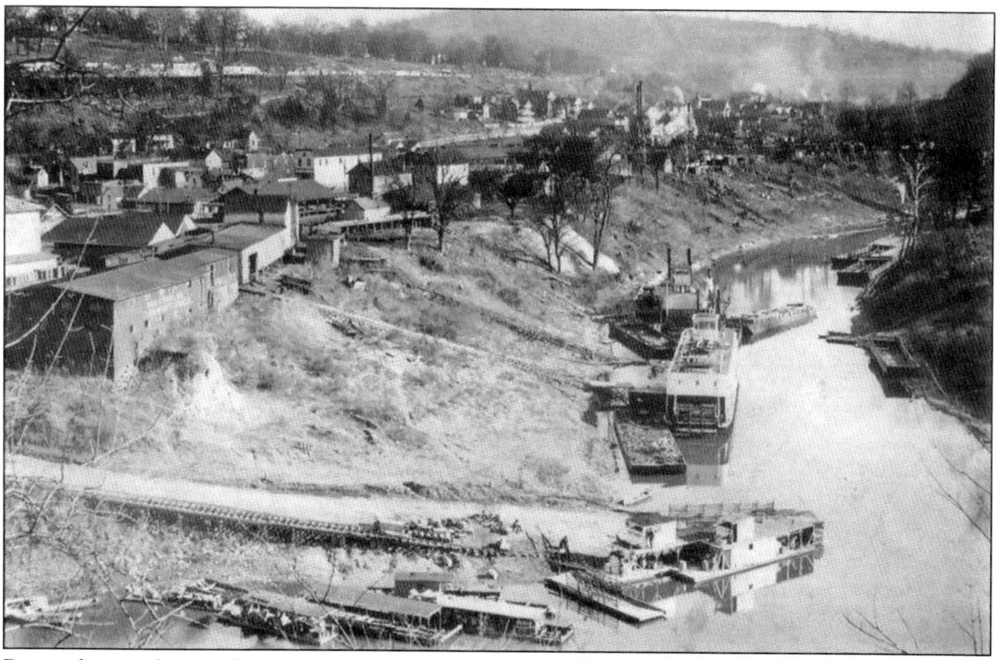

Burnside was the northernmost navigational point on the Cumberland River. It was one of the most popular ports of trade along the river. This photograph shows a typical river traffic scene. Steamers, barges, and ferries are seen in this photograph, which was taken in the early 1900s. (Courtesy of Carol Ann Lewis Lovell.)

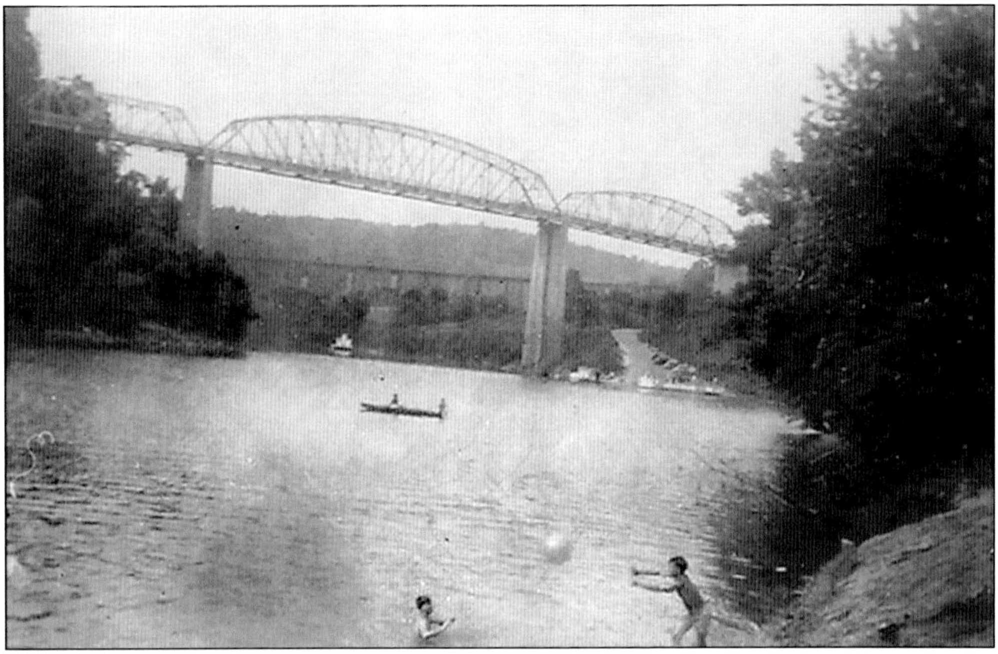

The Burnside Beach was a fun and popular place to go to enjoy the Cumberland River. In this photograph, two boys play ball while two people fish in the middle of the river. The bridge above the boys is the General Burnside Bridge, otherwise known as the U.S. Highway 27 Bridge. In the distance is the railroad bridge that crossed the Cumberland River. (Courtesy of Judith Waddell.)

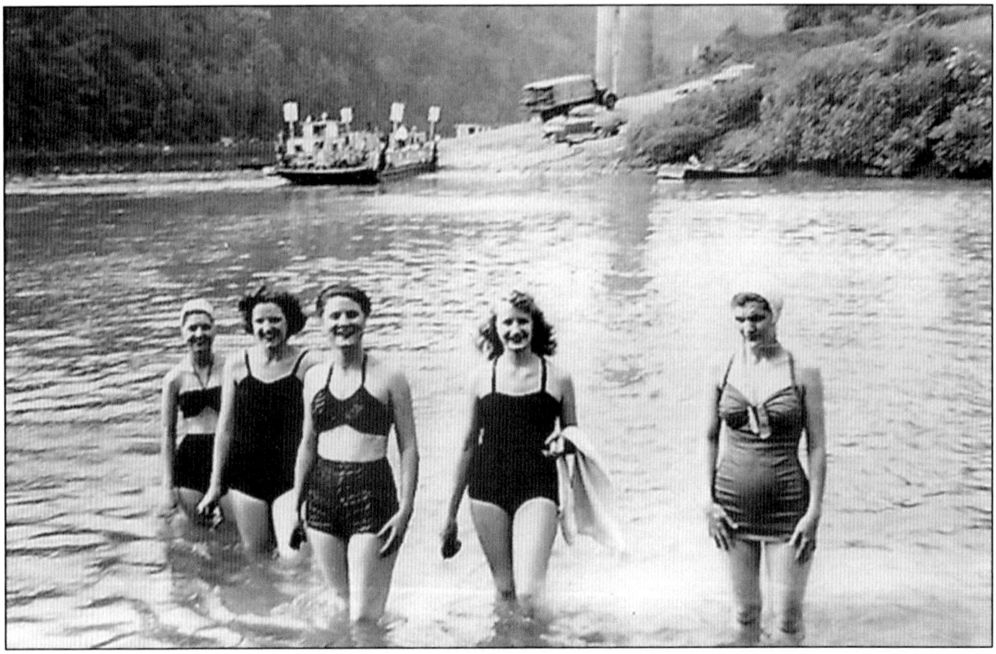

From left to right, Jean Greene, Allese Criswell, Inez Criswell, Annetha Walters, and Louise Greene enjoy an afternoon of swimming and sunbathing in the Cumberland River. Behind the ladies in this photograph, a large truck has just driven off of the ferry and is heading up the hill to Burnside. (Courtesy of Jim Fitzgerald.)

Thomas Moody (right) and his friend Samuel Weaver pose for the camera next to the fire hydrant in front of the Dick and Denney Electric Shop. Burnside residents pumped their water from a reservoir in "Upper" Burnside. The water was forced out through gravity, and the people of "Lower" Burnside had very good water pressure. However, if the water supply was depleted, fire protection was unavailable. (Courtesy of Tom Moody.)

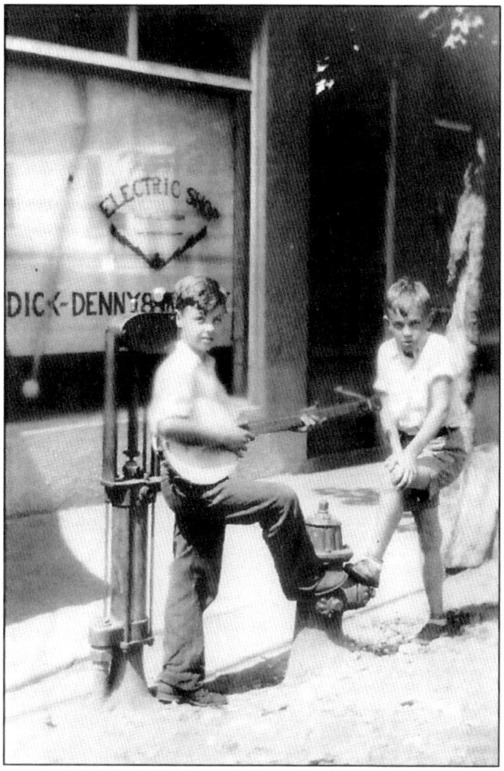

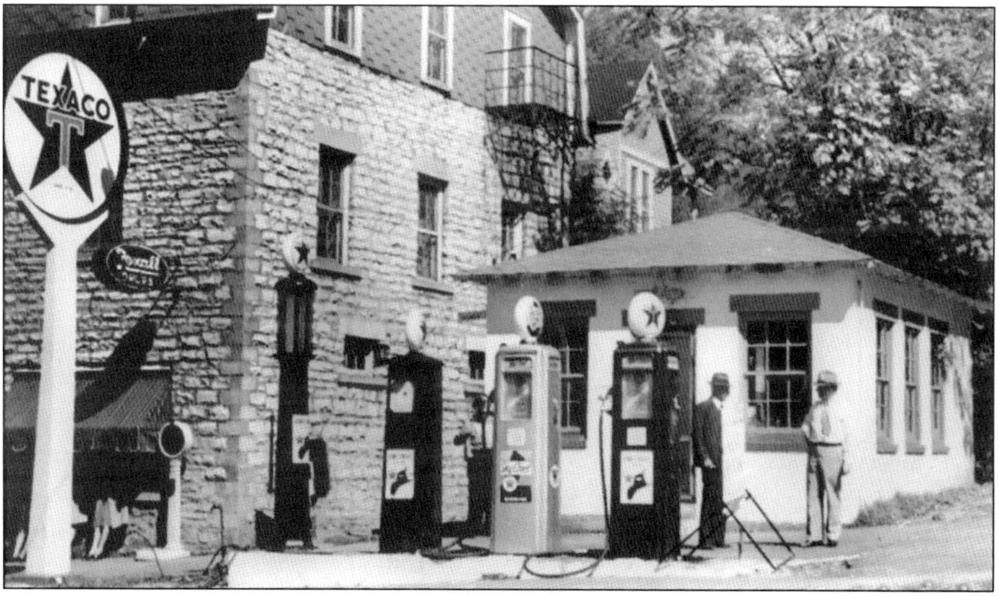

The Texaco gasoline station was next door to the Seven Gables. At one point, Burnside's streets were lined with businesses, retail stores, hotels, and restaurants. Other companies in Burnside included Drake Lumber, Burnside Sand Company, Burnside and Burkesville Transportation Company, Cumberland Grocery Company, Merchants Hardware, Matt Lloyd's Moving Pictures, Oil Well Supply Company, French Coal Company, Coffey Spokes and Staves, and Phillippi Bakery to name a few. (Courtesy of Tom Moody.)

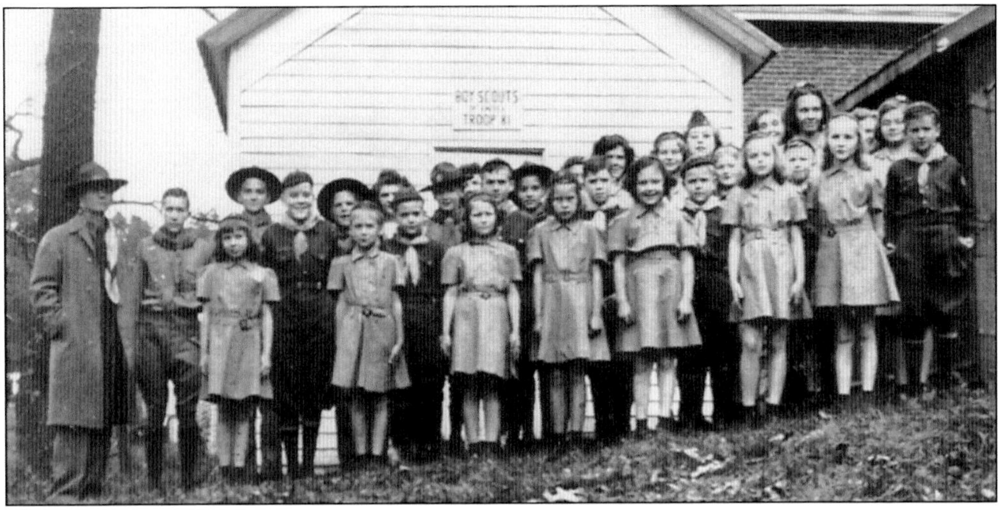

Myra Bass purchased a Scouting guide in London, England, in 1908. Upon her return to Burnside, she gathered 15 boys to form the first Boy Scout troop in the United States—two years before the Boy Scouts of America was formed. They were an independent troop and never officially became part of the national Scout organization. The boys named their group the "Eagle Troop." After five years, the group disbanded because of a newfangled game called basketball. The original 15 members were George Burgess, James Burgess, Roger Cooper, Lloyd Fitzgerald, Tommy Lenahan, Yateman Latimer, Vear Mann, Narvel Marcum, Dee Nunn, Hubert Phillips, Horace Smith, Edgar Garland, Baker Grissom, Crippen Greno, and Owens Wright. This photograph is of the Scouts in Burnside in the early 1950s. (Courtesy of John T. Carter.)

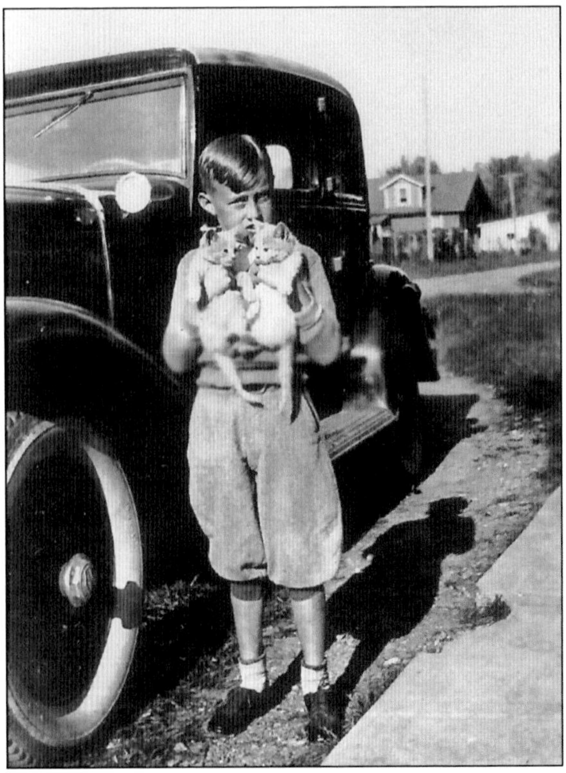

A young Thomas Moody holds his two kittens beside his mother's car. Moody said there were only two cars in Burnside in the late 1920s, and his mother owned one of them. One day as she pulled into the baseball field, she sideswiped the only other car in Burnside. She never drove again. (Courtesy of Tom Moody.)

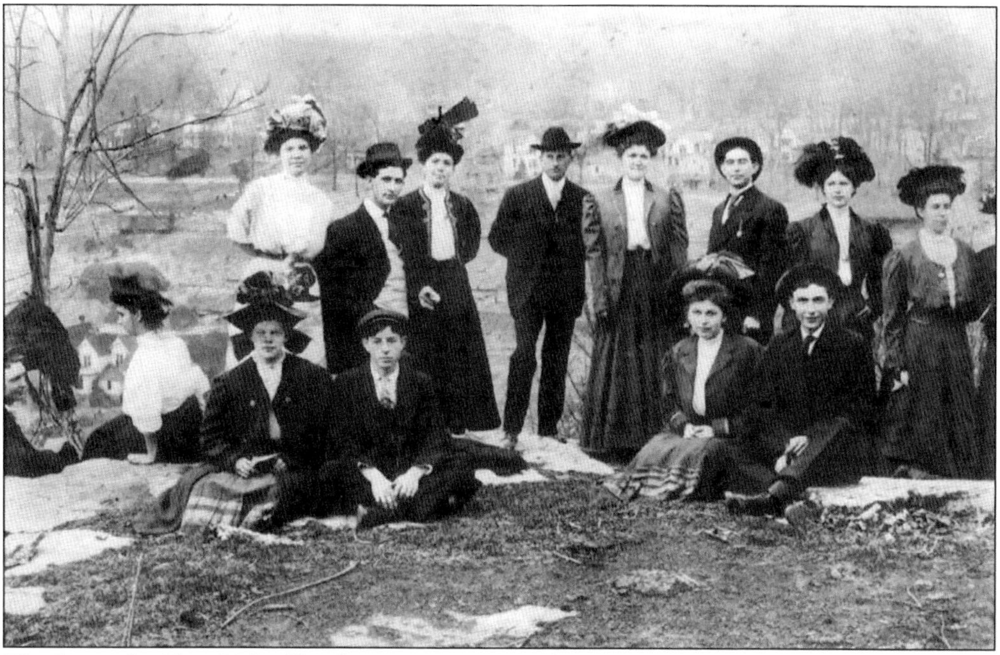

The Burnside Glee Club offered entertainment to the local townspeople with its music. Glee clubs originated in England and were generally made up of all male singers. Over time, glee clubs became a choir of mixed voices specializing in short songs. This photograph was taken atop Bunker Hill, which is now General Burnside Island. (Courtesy of Carol Ann Lewis Lovell.)

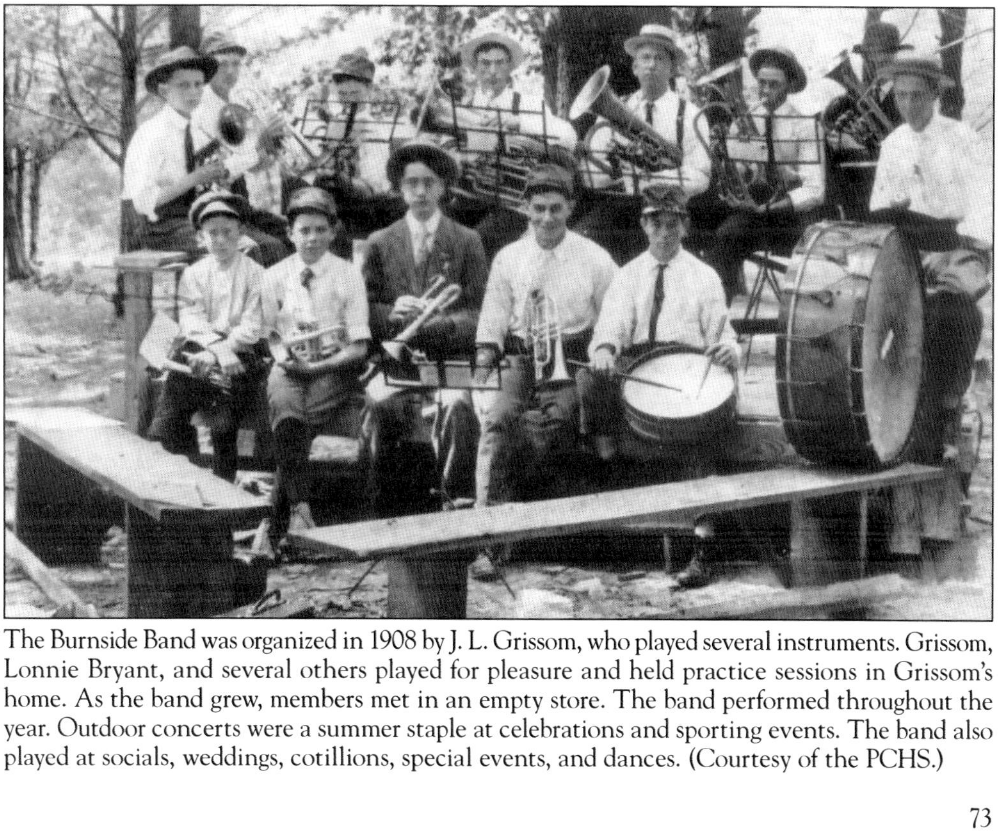

The Burnside Band was organized in 1908 by J. L. Grissom, who played several instruments. Grissom, Lonnie Bryant, and several others played for pleasure and held practice sessions in Grissom's home. As the band grew, members met in an empty store. The band performed throughout the year. Outdoor concerts were a summer staple at celebrations and sporting events. The band also played at socials, weddings, cotillions, special events, and dances. (Courtesy of the PCHS.)

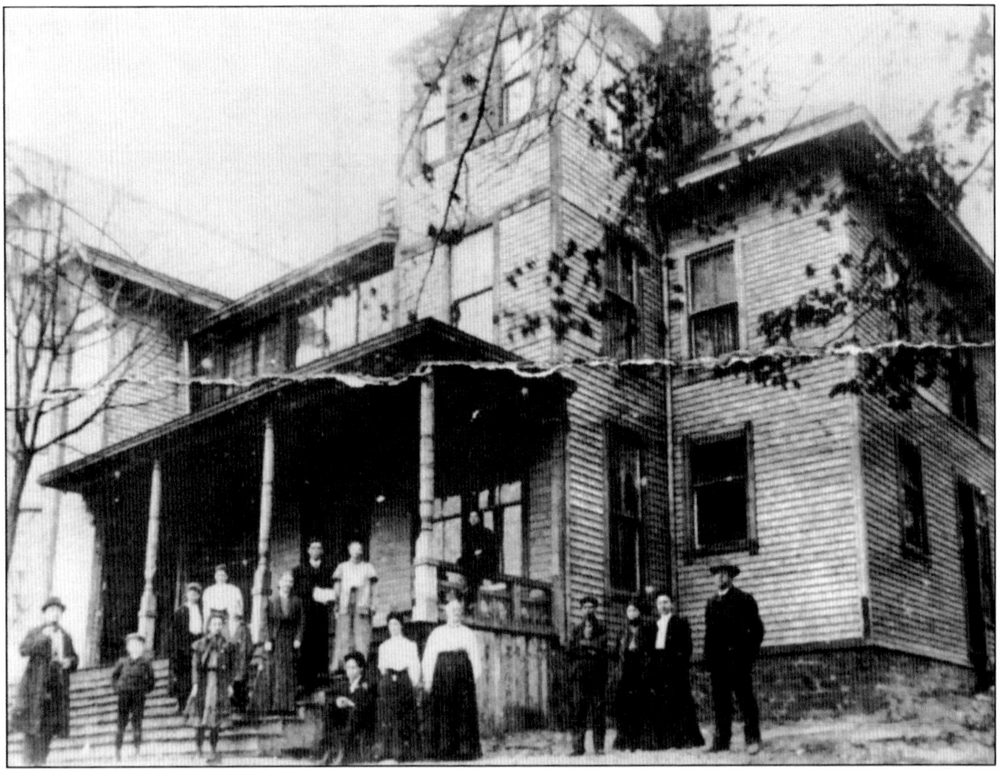

The Burnside Academy was the first Wesleyan preparatory school in Kentucky and opened in 1896. The building was originally erected for $21,000 and meant to serve as a hotel. It was instead donated by Col. C. W. Cole for educational work. The first floor was reserved for school rooms. The second and third floors were occupied by the principal and boarding students. Classes offered included writing, spelling, geography, geology and natural philosophy, physiology and hygiene, history, rhetoric and literature, Latin, Greek, French, German, arithmetic, algebra, plane and solid geometry, and trigonometry. The school was only open for five years before it burned in 1901. This is the only known photograph of the school. (Courtesy of the PCHS.)

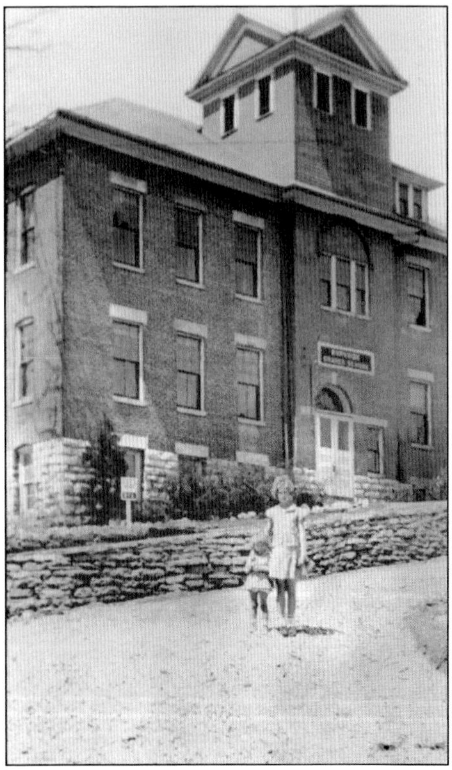

The Burnside Graded School was open to all children from both "Upper" and "Lower" Burnside and operated 10 months out of the year. Children from the two social classes did not mesh well. People living on the hill were called "hillbillies," while people living in the bottoms were called "river rats." (Courtesy of Rogers Photography.)

Edith Moody was a resident of "Lower" Burnside and played basketball for the Burnside High School girls' team in the early 1930s. This picture was taken in 1931. Edith was the big sister of Thomas Moody. Tragically, in 1932, two days before Edith was to depart for the University of Kentucky, she was killed in an automobile accident. (Courtesy of Tom Moody.)

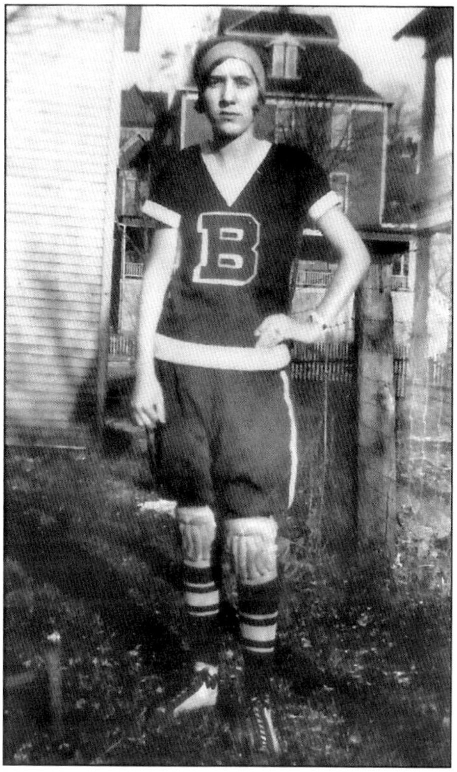

The Burnside High School men's basketball team of 1943 was, from left to right, Conrad Bryant, Billy Bob Coomer, Arvil Barnes, coach Lewis Fisher, Ralph Smith, Gerald Walters, and Louis Fitzgerald. James Naismith, a physical education teacher, invented the basketball in 1891. Initially players dribbled a soccer ball up and down a court of unspecified dimensions. The ball was thrown into a peach basket to earn points. A hammock-style basket was introduced in 1893. In 1903, an open-ended net was created. (Courtesy of John T. Carter and Judith Waddell.)

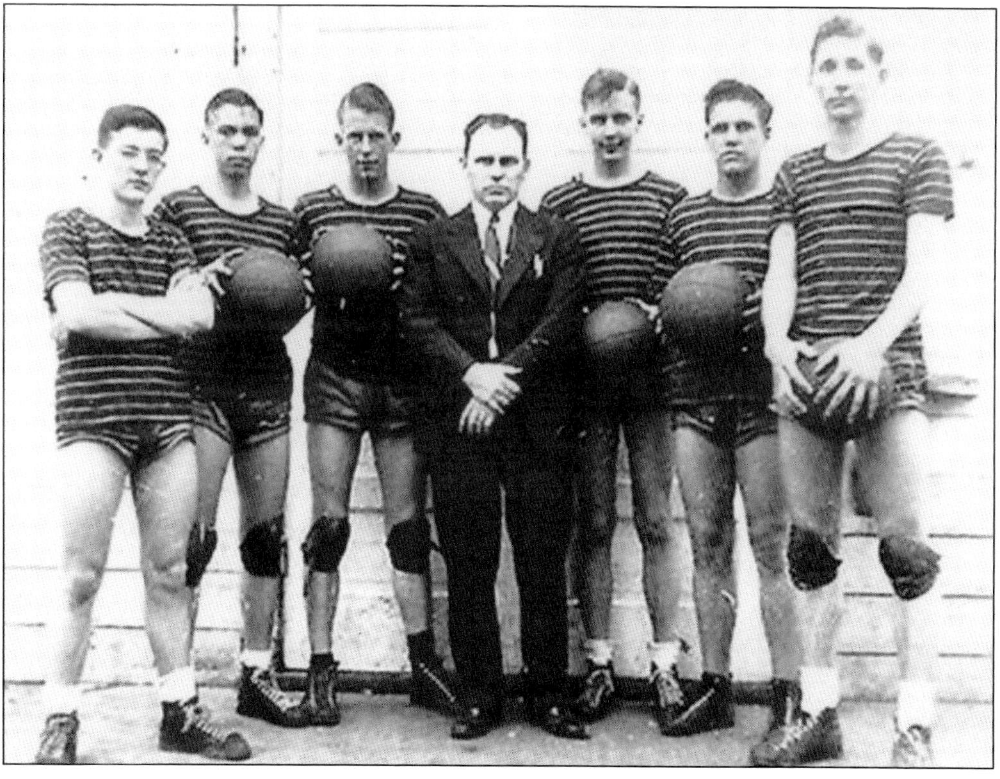

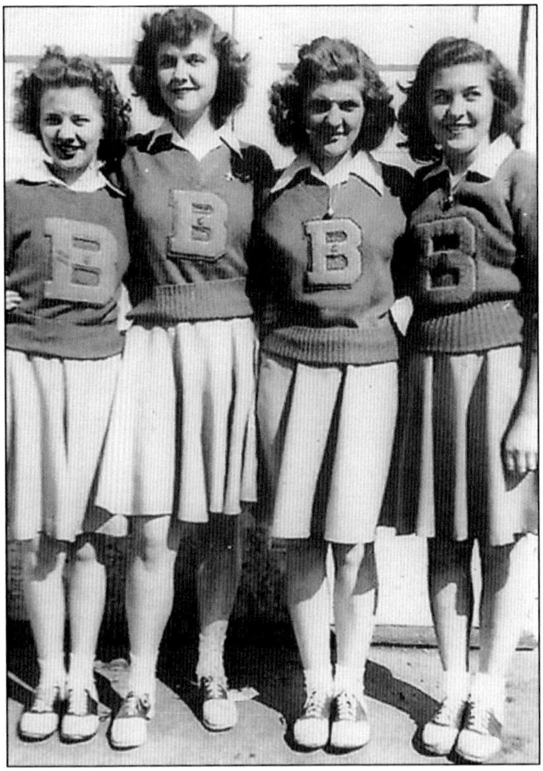

The cheerleaders for Burnside High School in 1945 were (from left to right) Sue Finley, Joanne Smith, Louise Greene, and Dora Fitzgerald. Cheerleaders, once known as "yell leaders," became more popular as more people became fans of basketball and football. In the 1930s, cheerleaders performed pom-pom routines using paper poms. In the early 1940s, cheerleaders added gymnastics to their routines, and soon after, cheerleading became more of a female sport. (Courtesy of John T. Carter and Judith Waddell.)

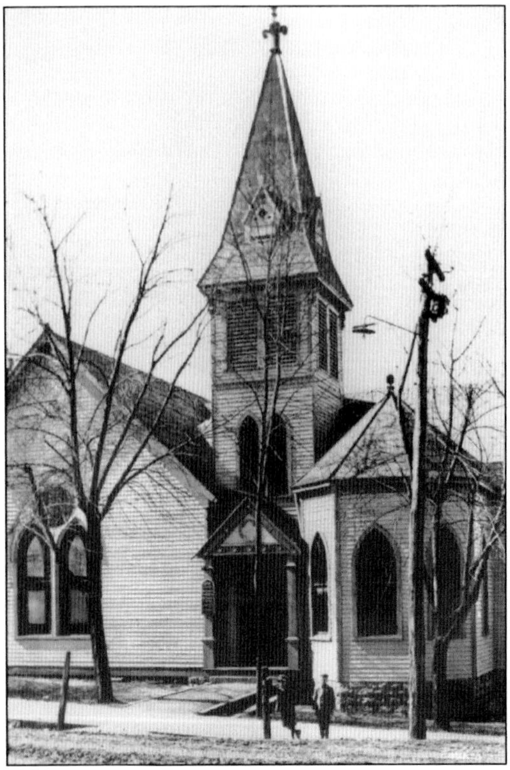

The Old Presbyterian Church was built in 1891. The congregation built the church on Main Street north of the General Burnside House. Members of all faiths were allowed to hold their services in the building until they could build their own churches. In 1915, a Christian church was also built in "Lower" Burnside. However, the First Baptist and Burnside Methodist congregations built their churches in "Upper" Burnside. (Courtesy of Rogers Photography.)

A young Thomas Moody stands in front of the lion cage at the Cincinnati Zoo. Moody recalls a couple who entered his father's (Samuel Spencer Moody) store—the S. S. Moody Dry Goods Store. The Moody family showed the couple around Burnside. Upon their leaving, they asked Thomas to go home with them. S. S. and Edna Moody agreed, and Thomas was treated to all the sites of Cincinnati. Several days later, Thomas boarded a train back home to Burnside. (Courtesy of Tom Moody.)

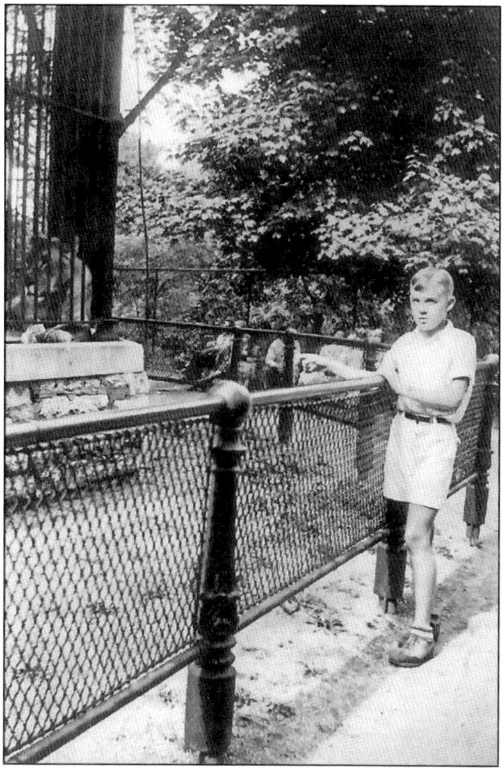

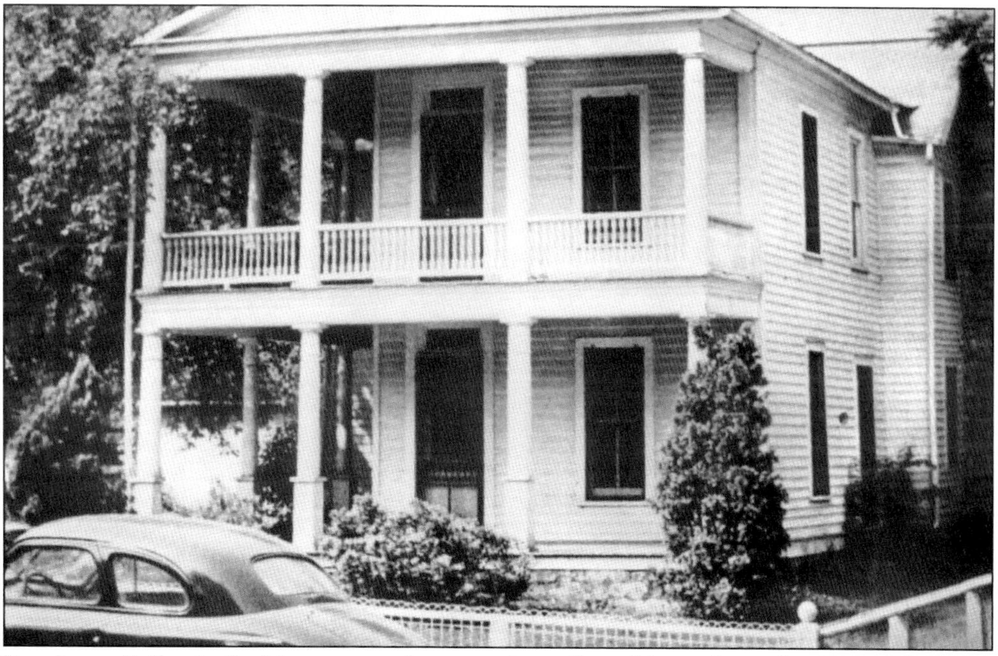

Rev. James Ballou built this two-story home in the valley of Burnside in the 1800s. The home was used by Gen. Ambrose Burnside as his headquarters during the Civil War. The house was sold several times and became known as the Duncan House. Later the home was used as a bed-and-breakfast. In 1945, it was the oldest house in Burnside. (Courtesy of Tom Moody.)

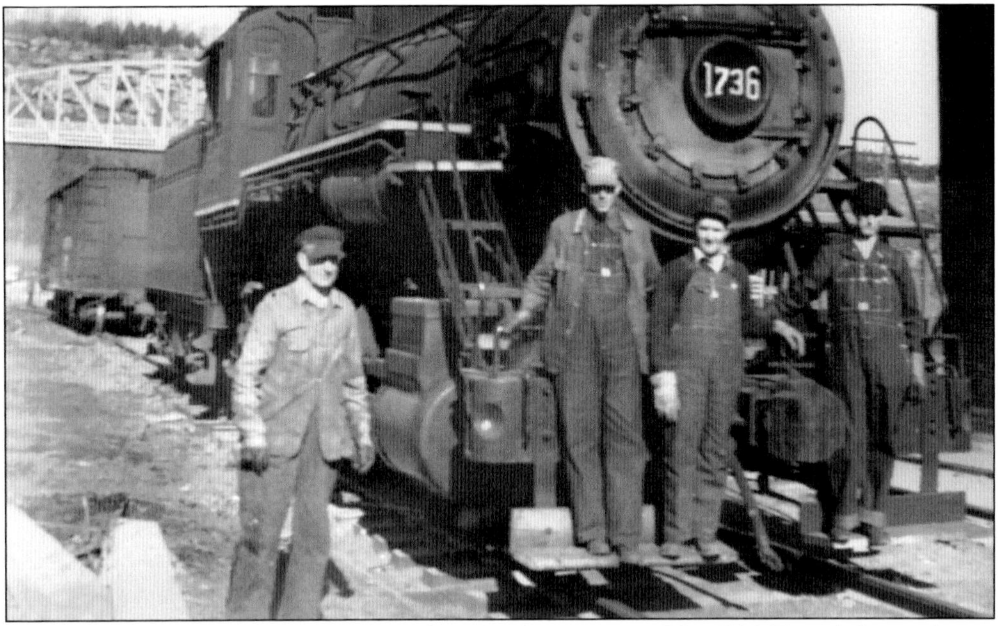

This photograph shows the crew of Southern Railway's engine No. 1736. From left to right are A. C. Cameron, Carl Bryant, Bob Mays, and C. H. Baugh. Eight northbound and eight southbound trains stopped in Burnside each day. Engineers became well known in town, and one of the most recognized was Charlie "Dutch" Eiford. Dutch was well known for his ability to play "Oh, How I Love Jesus" on the train engine whistle. (Courtesy of Tom Moody.)

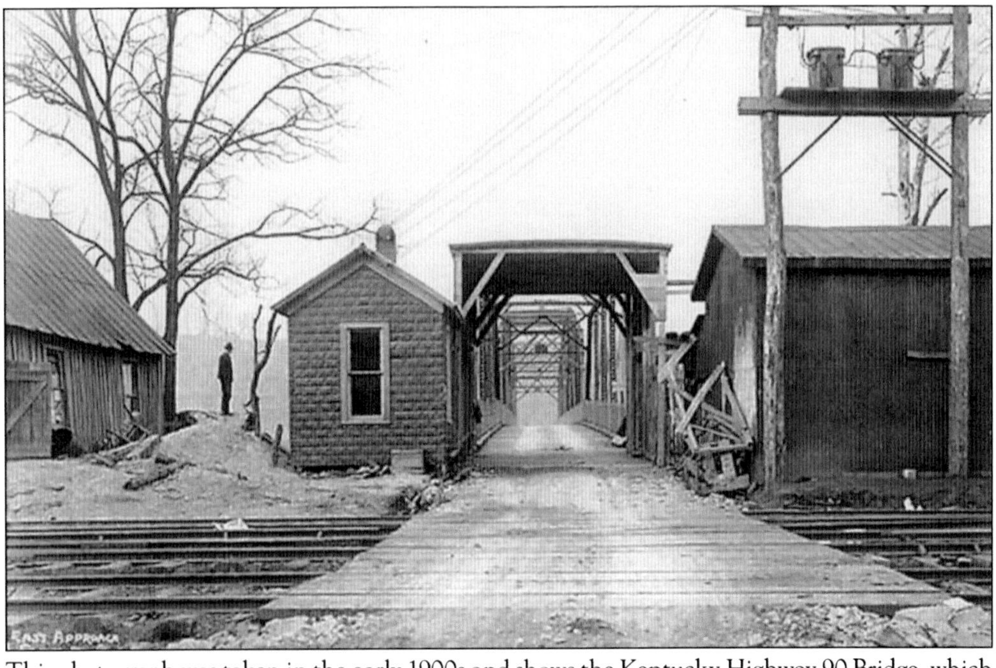

This photograph was taken in the early 1900s and shows the Kentucky Highway 90 Bridge, which led to Bronston. The structure was a swing bridge and crossed 50 feet above the South Fork River. A swing bridge has a deck that rotates around a center point. While in service, the bridge opened to allow steamboats easy passage into Burnside. (Courtesy of John T. Carter.)

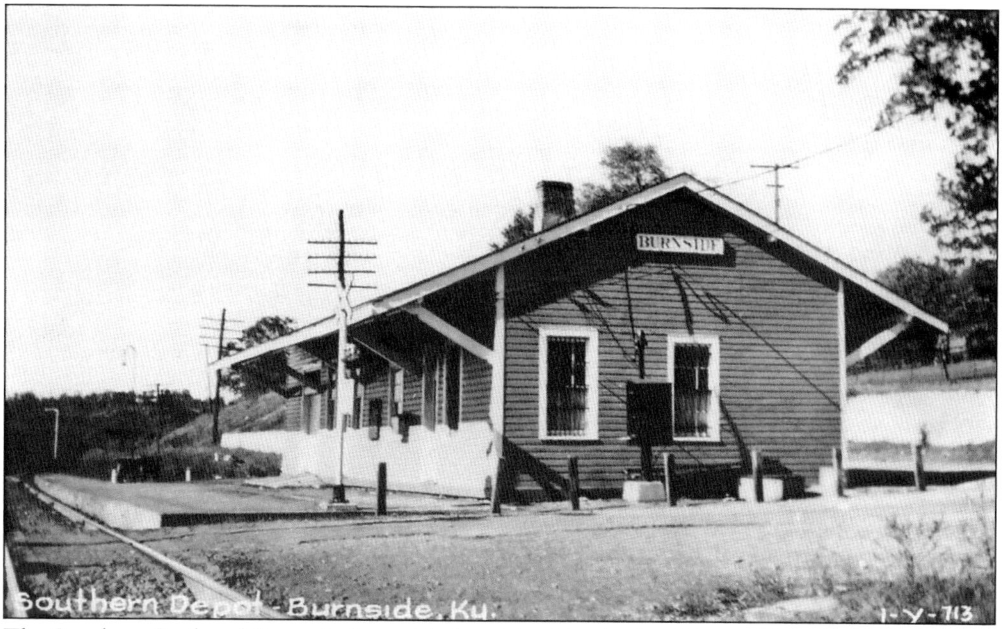

The Southern Railroad Depot in Burnside faced the Cumberland River. This photograph shows the old Burnside Depot as it was prior to 1950. (Courtesy of Tom Moody.)

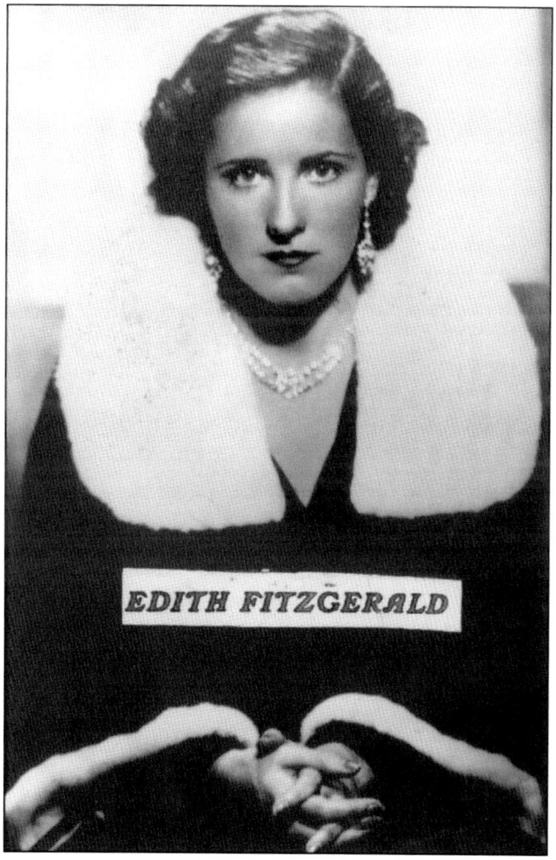

Edith Fitzgerald (January 23, 1897–February 4, 1968) started her career as an actress on Broadway. She became a proofreader for a Broadway producer and wrote short stories for the *Saturday Evening Post*. Fitzgerald became a scenario and dialogue writer for Metro-Goldwyn-Mayer and Columbia Studios, writing motion picture scripts for Greta Garbo. (Courtesy of Judith Waddell.)

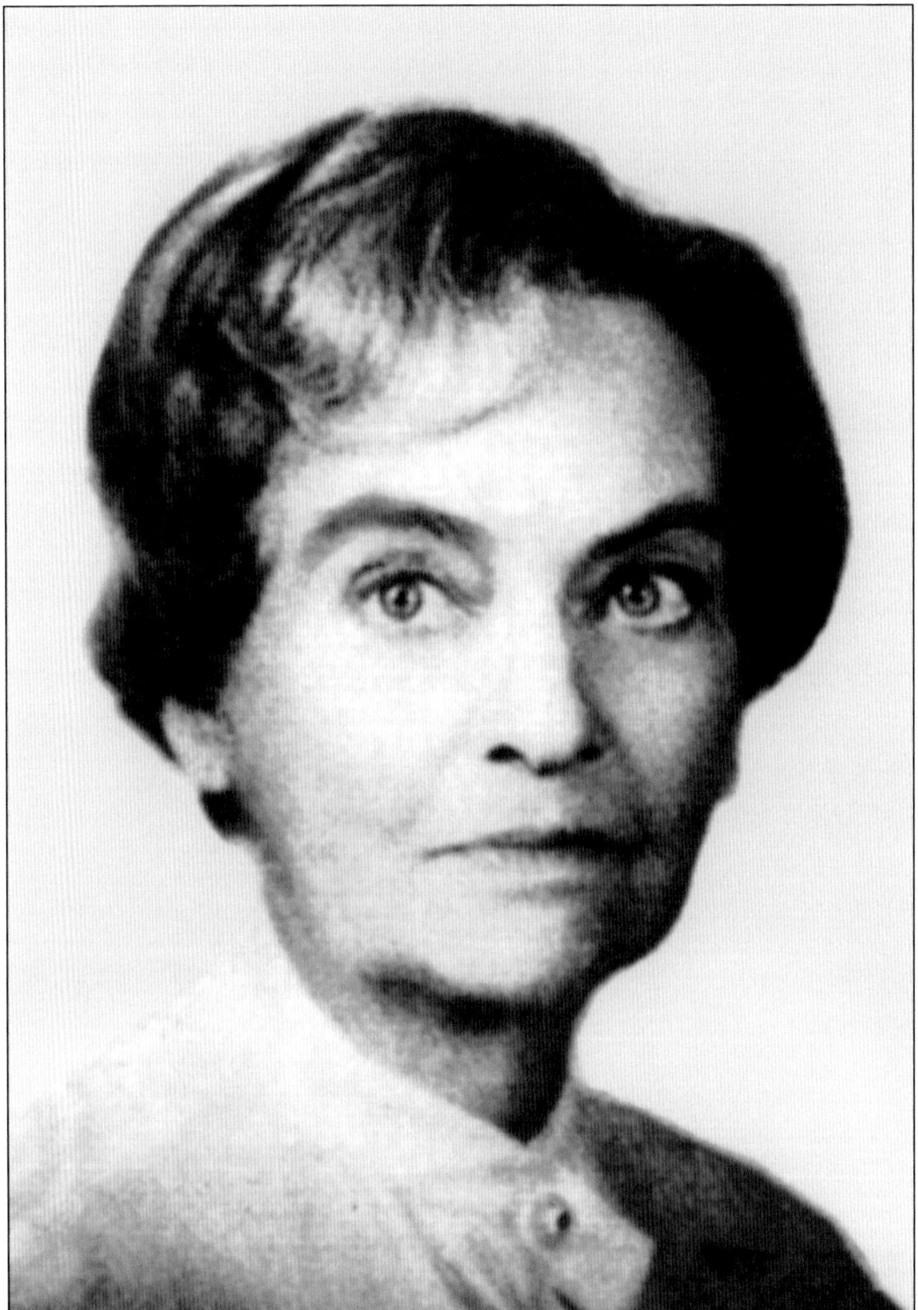

Harriette Simpson Arnow (July 7, 1908–March 22, 1986) was called a brilliant female writer and spent much of her childhood in Burnside. As a girl, Arnow repeatedly asked for a typewriter. Her mother bought her a cow instead. Harriette sold the cow's milk and eventually purchased a secondhand typewriter. Arnow's first book, *Mountain Path*, was published in 1939. *Hunter's Horn* (1949) was a best seller that received critical acclaim. *The Dollmaker* (1954) won the National Book Award of 1955 and was later made into a movie starring Jane Fonda. Her last book was her memoir, *Old Burnside* (1977). (Courtesy of Rogers Photography.)

Five

Building Wolf Creek Dam

The Wolf Creek Dam and Reservoir were authorized for construction by the Flood Control Act of 1938. The dam was constructed across the Cumberland River in Russell County, approximately 10 miles southwest of Jamestown and 12 miles north of Albany. Originally to be placed at Wolf Creek farther up river, its site was changed, but the name Wolf Creek remained.

The primary purpose of the dam was flood control and the production of hydroelectric power. The contract for construction of the dam was awarded on July 21, 1941, to the S. A. Healy Company from White Plains, New York, on a bid of $15,803,690.

Ground-breaking ceremonies were held on September 1, 1941, in Rowena, Kentucky, with an estimated crowd of 7,000 to 10,000 people. Residents from all over the region turned out alongside dignitaries and government officials for the official start of the project. The main speaker was the chief of U.S. Army Corps of Engineers, Maj. Gen. Julian L. Schley, but a young Tennessee congressman named Albert Gore was well received by the crowd.

Construction was barely underway when the United States entered World War II. With less than 8 percent of the project completed, the War Production Board suspended all activity in August 1943. After the war ended, J. A. Jones and Wright Construction Companies resumed work on the dam in August 1946.

The E. J. Albright Company began the construction of the powerhouse in 1949. The first of six generators, each rated 45,000 kilowatts, came online in October 1951. The final unit was placed in operation on August 20, 1952. In 1953, the Wolf Creek Power Plant generated more than 650 million kilowatt hours of hydroelectric power. The dam is capable of supplying the needs of an average city (population of 375,000) via 270 megawatts of electricity.

On September 1, 1951, ten years after the ground-breaking, a crowd of 2,000 gathered to see and hear Vice President Alben Barkley dedicate the Wolf Creek Project.

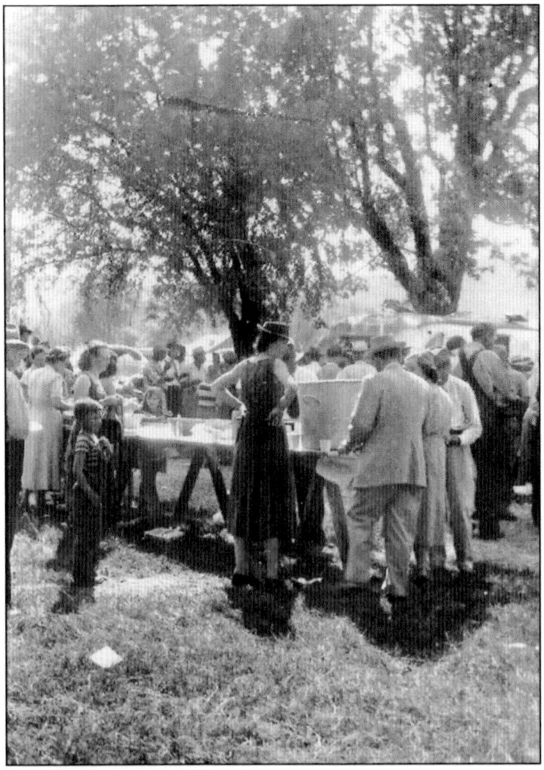

On September 1, 1941, a groundbreaking ceremony was held near Rowena, Kentucky. Between 7,000 and 10,000 people showed up for the celebration. The hungry crowd devoured 50 cases of bread and 900 gallons of Kentucky burgoo. The ingredients used that day in the traditional stew included 650 pounds of beef, 88 hens, 8 bushels of onions, 16 bushels of potatoes, and 80 dozen ears of corn. This photograph shows a man helping himself to a cool drink. (Courtesy of John T. Carter.)

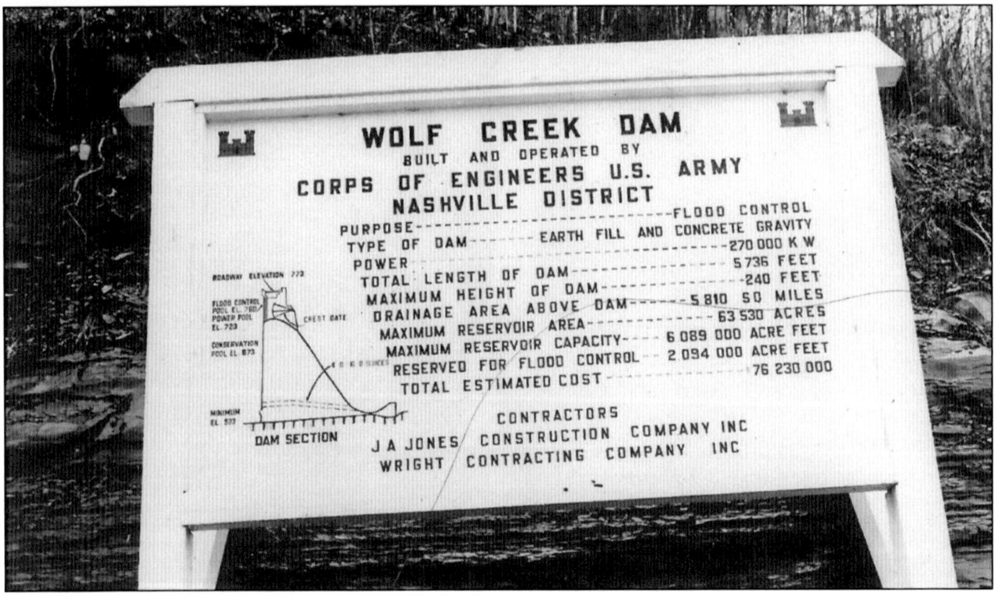

This sign was posted near the construction entrance of Wolf Creek Dam to give visitors information about the dam. The sign gives all the basic information pertaining to the dam. Wolf Creek Dam is a combination concrete gravity and earth-fill structure located at mile 460.9 of the Cumberland River near Jamestown, Kentucky. A gravity dam is a concrete dam that relies on its mass for stability. U.S. Highway 127 traverses the top of the mile-long Wolf Creek Dam. (Courtesy of Randolph Smith.)

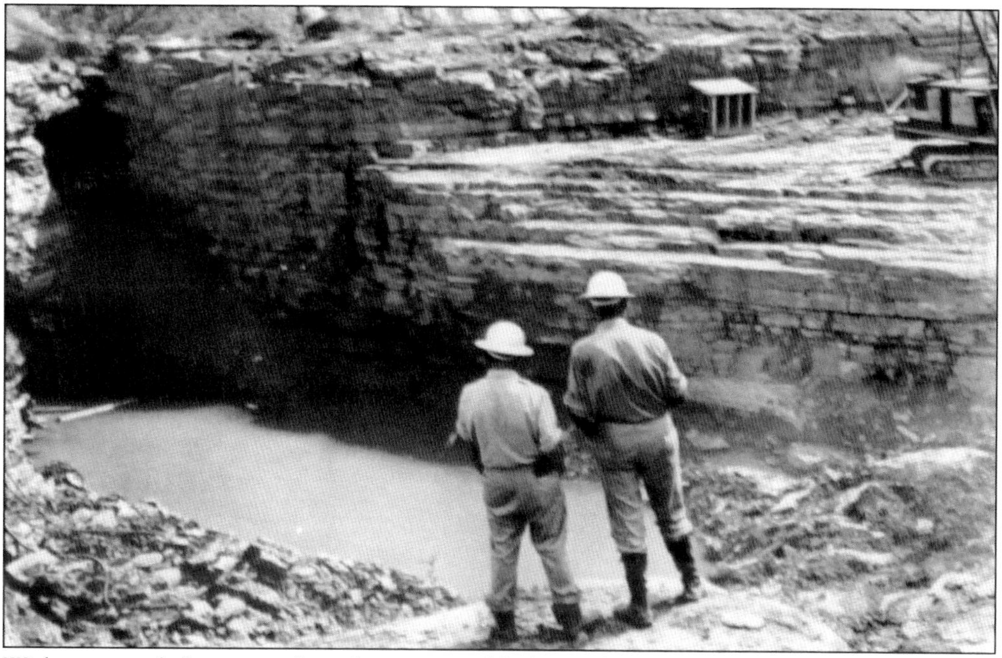

With an overwhelming number of caverns, sinkholes, and underground passages underlying the dam site, engineers soon realized the enormous task ahead of them. Building the dam would be a massive undertaking. Large cave openings such as the one in this photograph had to be filled in with concrete before construction of the dam could progress. (Courtesy of Judy and Floyd.)

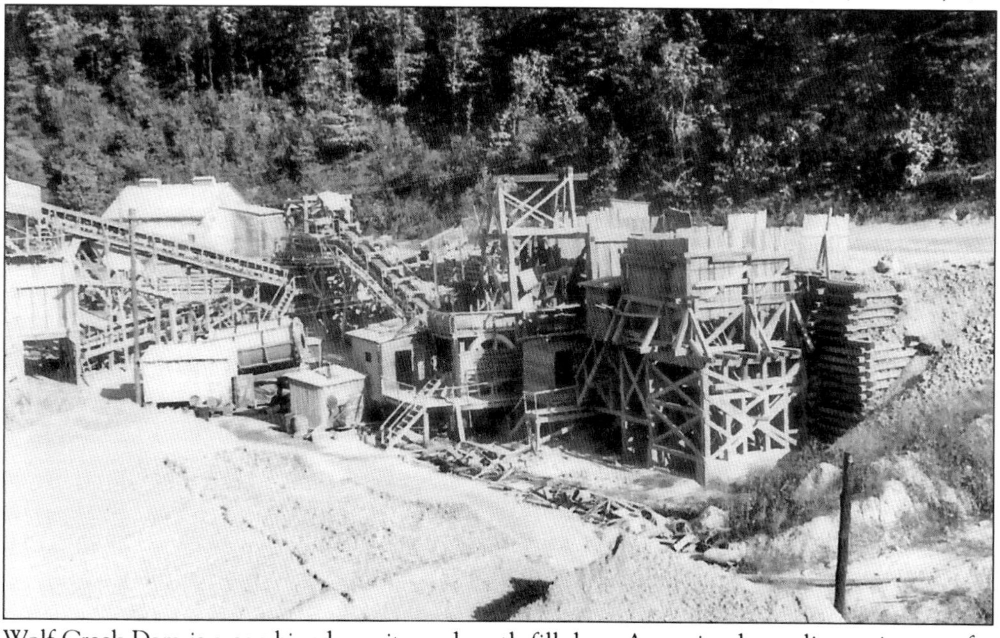

Wolf Creek Dam is a combined gravity and earth-fill dam. A gravity dam relies on its mass for stability. An earth-fill dam has more than 50 percent of its total volume formed of compacted material taken from a nearby source, such as a quarry or excavation pit. This photograph shows a plant where quarried stone was crushed and processed into fine aggregate. Aggregate consists of sand, gravel, and rock fragments. (Courtesy of Randolph Smith.)

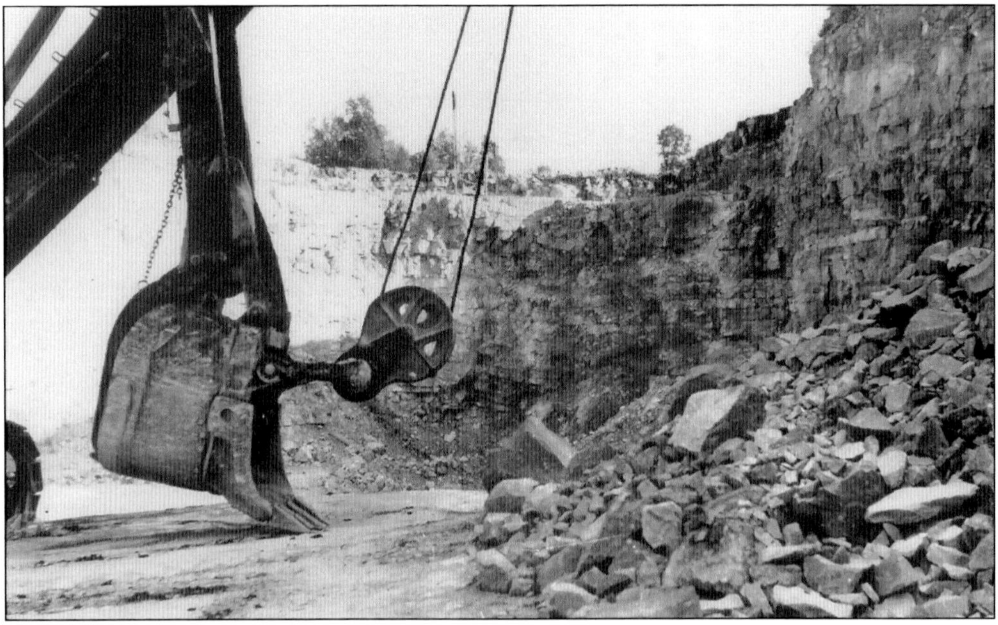

This photograph shows a rock quarry near Wolf Creek Dam. There were many such rock quarries supplying stone and aggregate for the construction of the dam. To obtain the rock, it had to first be blasted loose from the earth. Holes were drilled into the rock. The holes were charged with an explosive and detonated. Stone was then collected and either sent directly to the site in a dump truck or sent to the crusher to be broken down into aggregate. (Courtesy of Randolph Smith.)

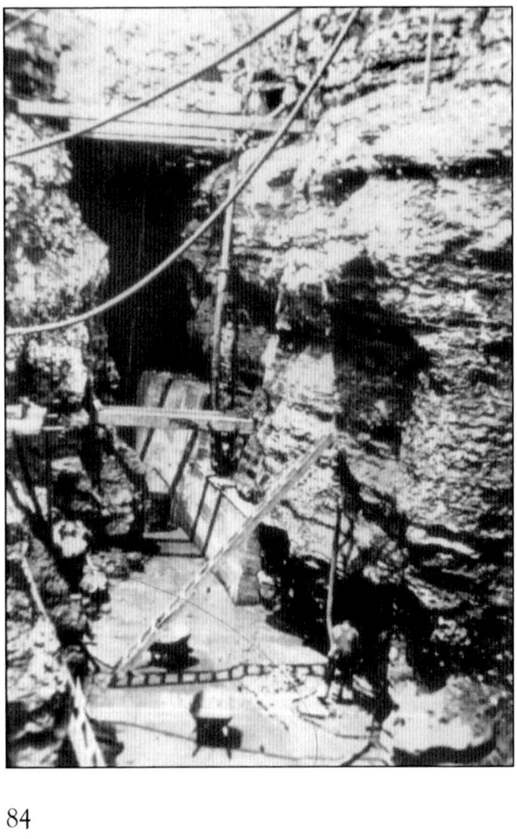

Workers had an enormous task of filling in caverns and sealing off caves. In this photograph, a concrete wall is being built to seal off the monstrously sized opening of a cave. Kentucky has a number of catacombs, or cave networks. Kentucky is home to the world's largest cave—Mammoth Cave. Mammoth Cave has more than 360 explored miles. (Courtesy of Carole Tupman.)

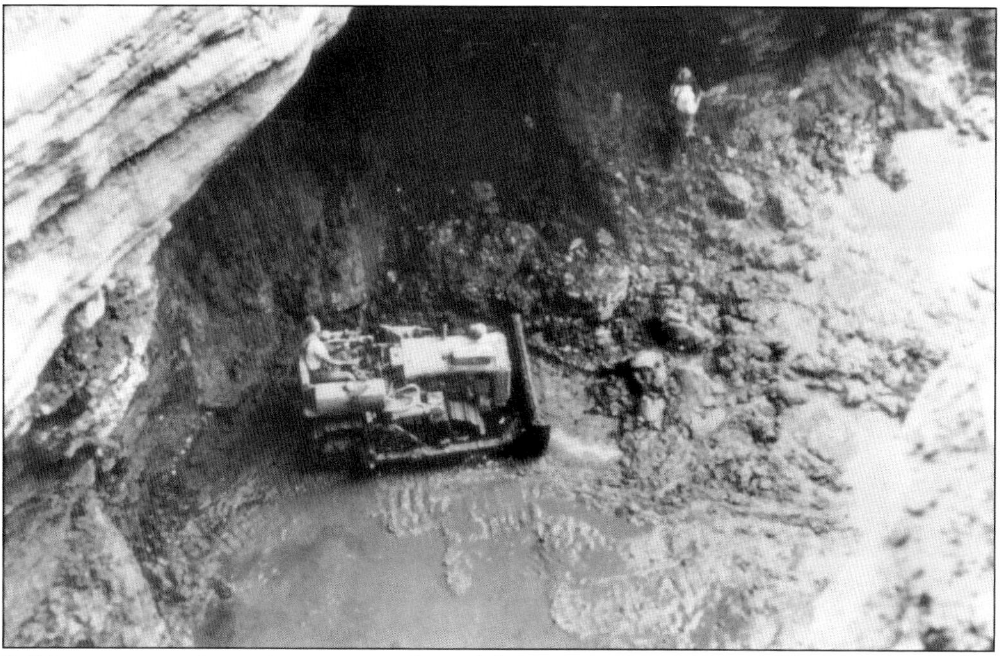

Bulldozers were used to push concrete, rocks, and dirt into caverns, crevices, and sinkholes. Sinkholes link with a subterranean passage and occur in limestone regions. Limestone, a sedimentary rock mainly composed of calcium carbonate, is an important resource in Kentucky. It is the principal source of crushed stone used in construction. (Courtesy of Carole Tupman.)

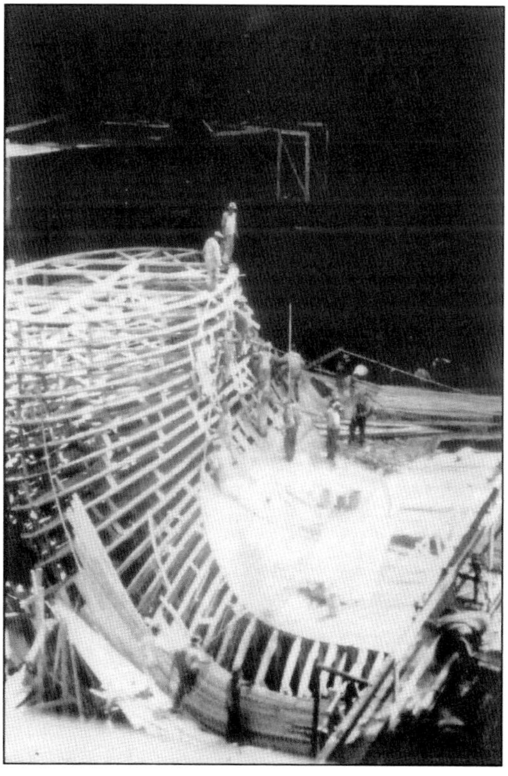

This photograph shows the construction of the form work in the water discharge area. Forms were built in gravity dams to increase the strength and quality of the concrete in the dam. Gravity dams required large amounts of concrete for their construction. (Courtesy of Carole Tupman.)

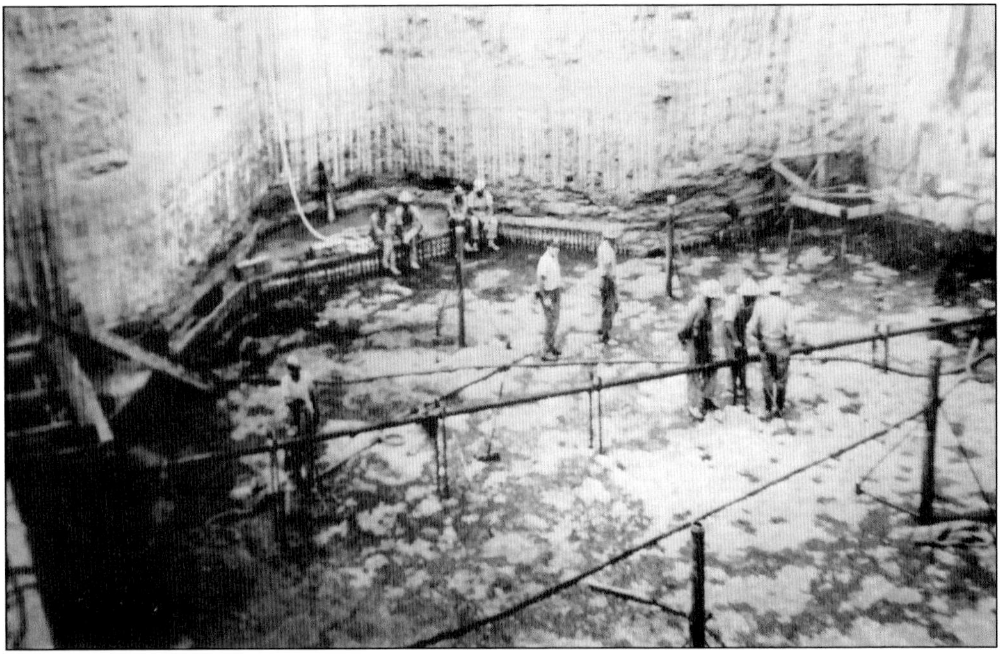

Generators are machines that change water power, steam power, or other mechanical energy into electricity. A total of six large generators were placed inside Wolf Creek Dam. In this photograph, the foundation is being prepared for the installation of the generators. Poor foundation conditions are associated with the fracture or failure of the dam. (Courtesy of Carole Tupman.)

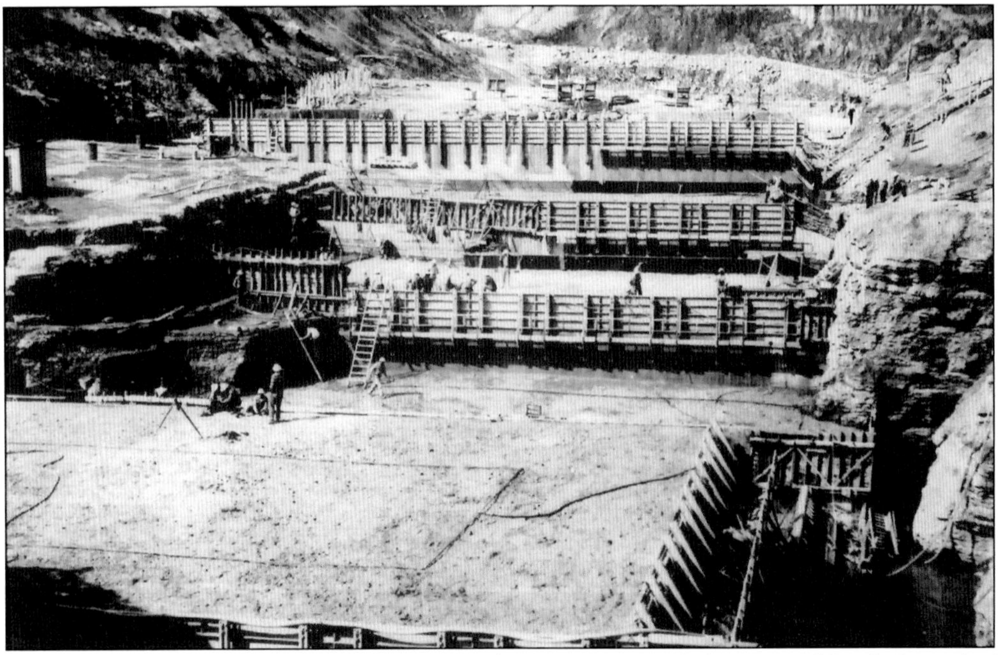

This photograph shows the early stages of the dam construction below ground level. A total of 60 percent of the dam is belowground. Gravity dams need an enormous amount of concrete, which has to be cooled once it is poured. The cables on the ground in this image are actually cooling the concrete. Cool concrete reduced the risk of cracking. (Courtesy of Carole Tupman.)

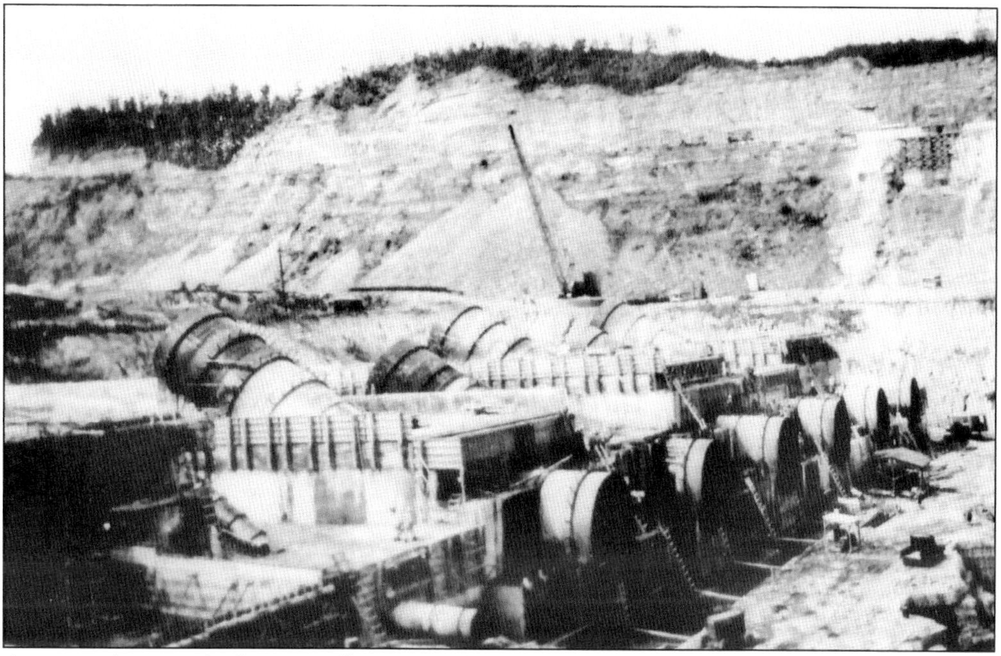

A penstock controls the water flow into a hydroelectric generator. It is generally a steel pipe that takes the water from the reservoir to the power generating plant. This photograph shows construction of the penstocks leading to the six power generators. Gates on the penstocks allow operators to control the amount of water entering the penstock. (Courtesy of Carole Tupman.)

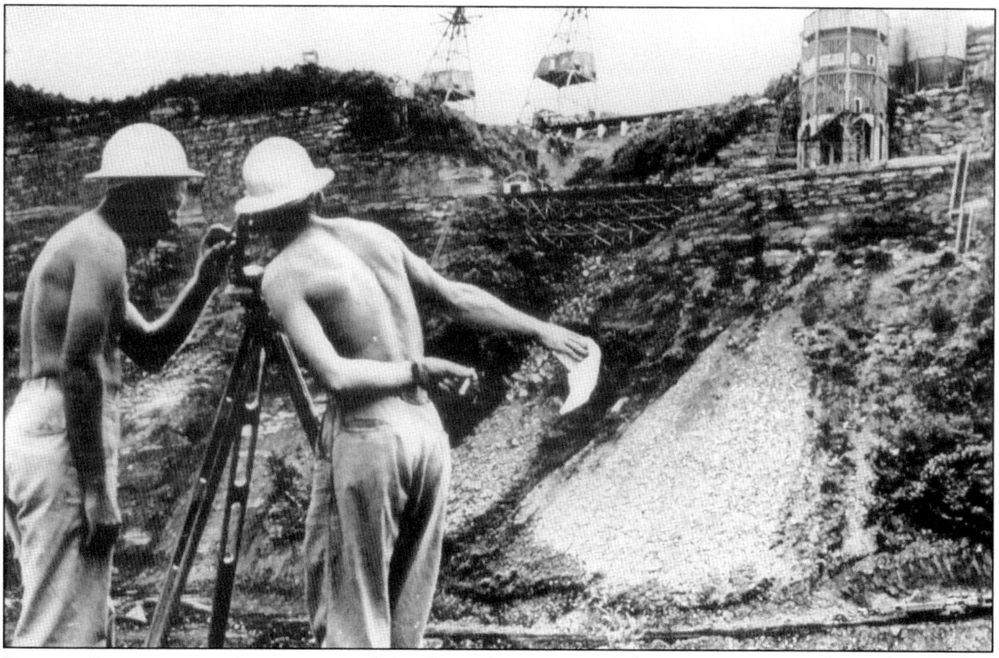

Two engineers survey the progress of the dam. An engineer's first priority was safety. They had to keep the end product in mind as well as the safety of the employees. At the same time, they were legally responsible to the community for the cost of the structure and keeping it within budget. (Courtesy of Carole Tupman.)

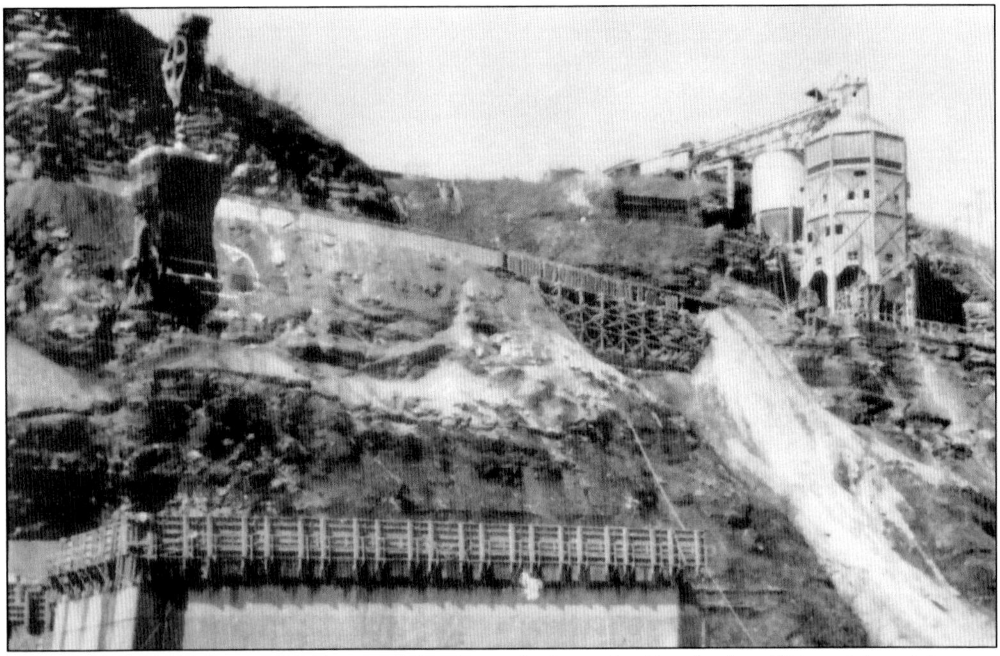

A concrete batch plant sat on the south bank overlooking the Cumberland River. Materials were delivered from quarries and loaded into a mixer. When mixed with water, cement turns into a binding agent that glues sand and aggregate into a hard, solid mass called concrete. This batch plant could produce 400 cubic yards of concrete an hour. (Courtesy of Carole Tupman.)

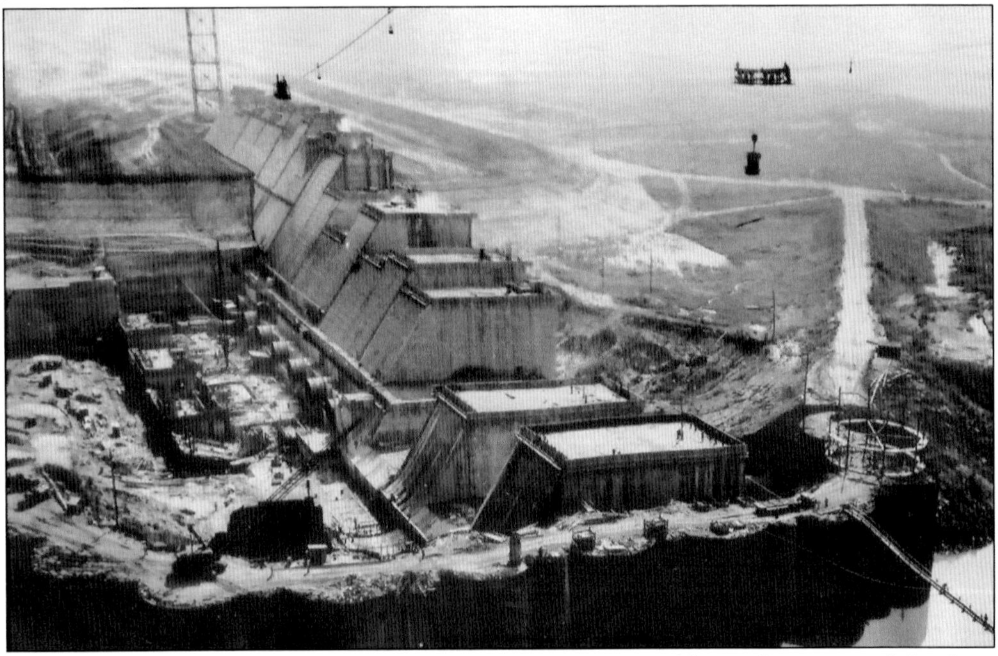

Towers were built, and cables were used to move concrete quickly to all sections of the dam. Concrete begins to harden as soon as it is created, so engineers needed a fast way for the concrete to be delivered. In this photograph, huge buckets of concrete are being pulled along the cable system. Concrete work was challenging and dangerous. (Courtesy of Carole Tupman.)

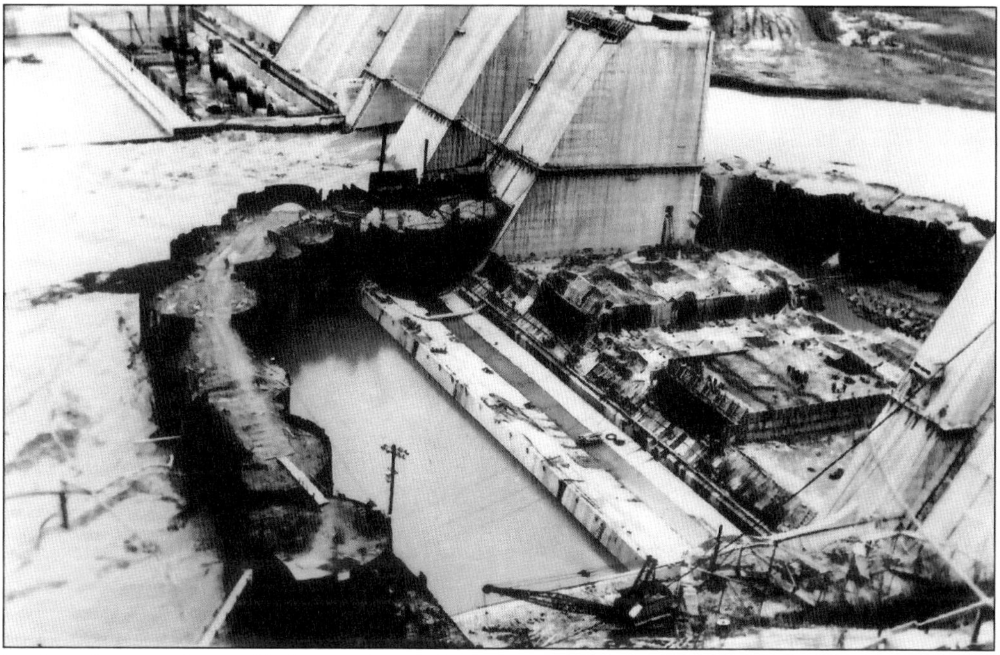

In this photograph, a cofferdam is shown diverting the Cumberland River away from the area of construction. A cofferdam is a temporary dam designed to contain and divert water away from the section of the dam being worked on. Notice the turbulent water swirling around the cofferdam. Floodwaters rampaged across the area in December 1949. (Courtesy of Carole Tupman.)

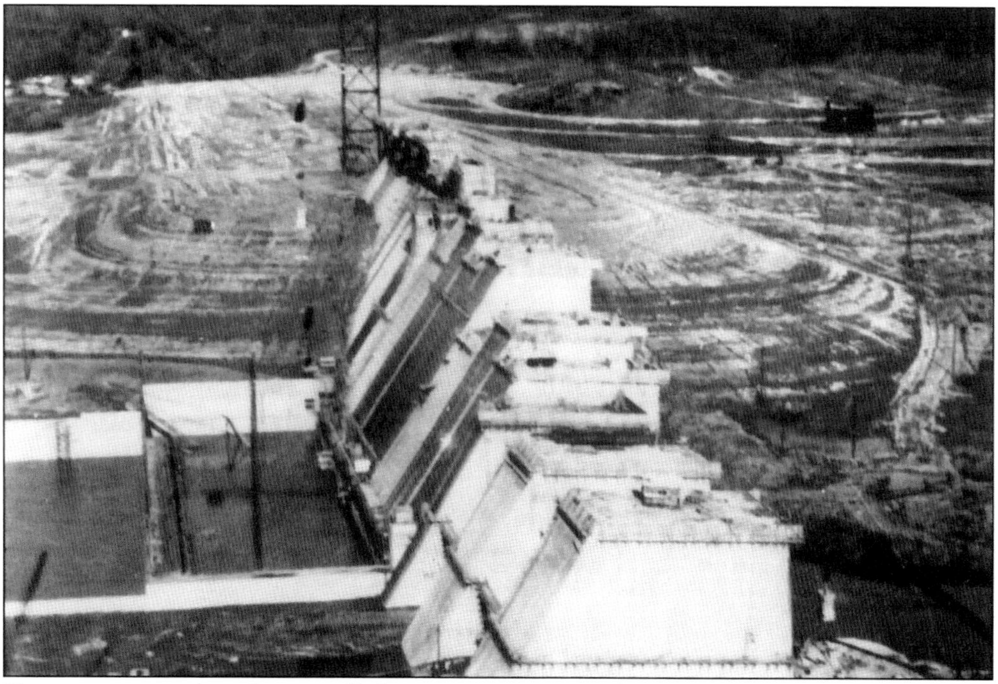

Huge concrete and steel gates called Tainter gates are used to regulate water flow. Wolf Creek Dam has 10 Tainter gates. They each stand 37 feet high and are 50 feet wide. This photograph shows the construction of the Tainter gates is nearly complete. (Courtesy of Carole Tupman.)

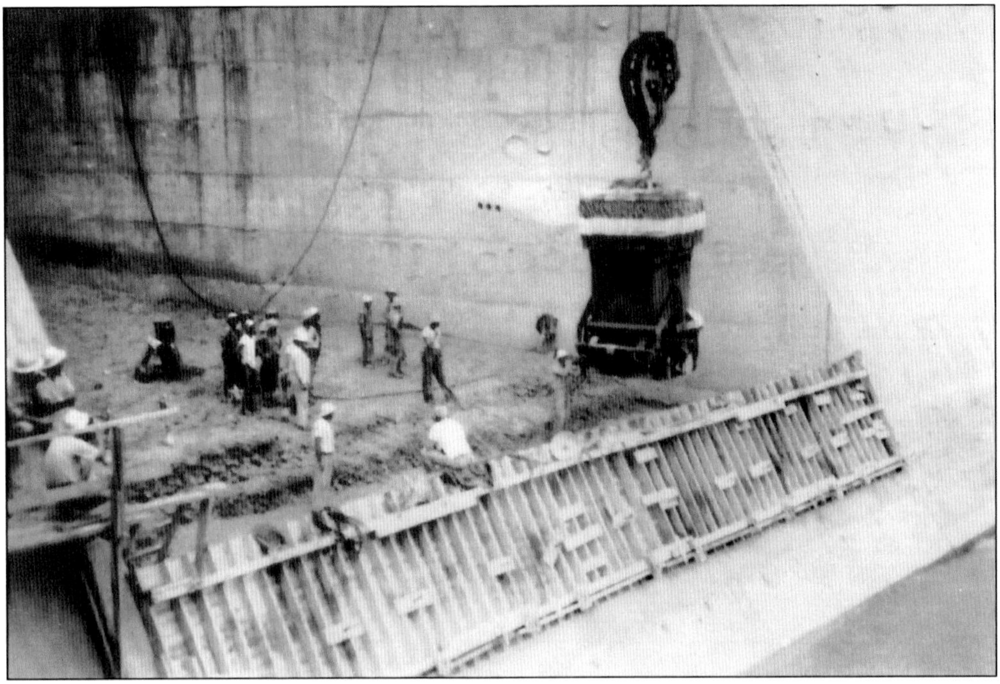

This photograph shows one of the last buckets of concrete being delivered by the cable system to workers on the dam. Once concrete was placed, large vibrating devices made the concrete more compact, which increased its strength. (Courtesy of Carole Tupman.)

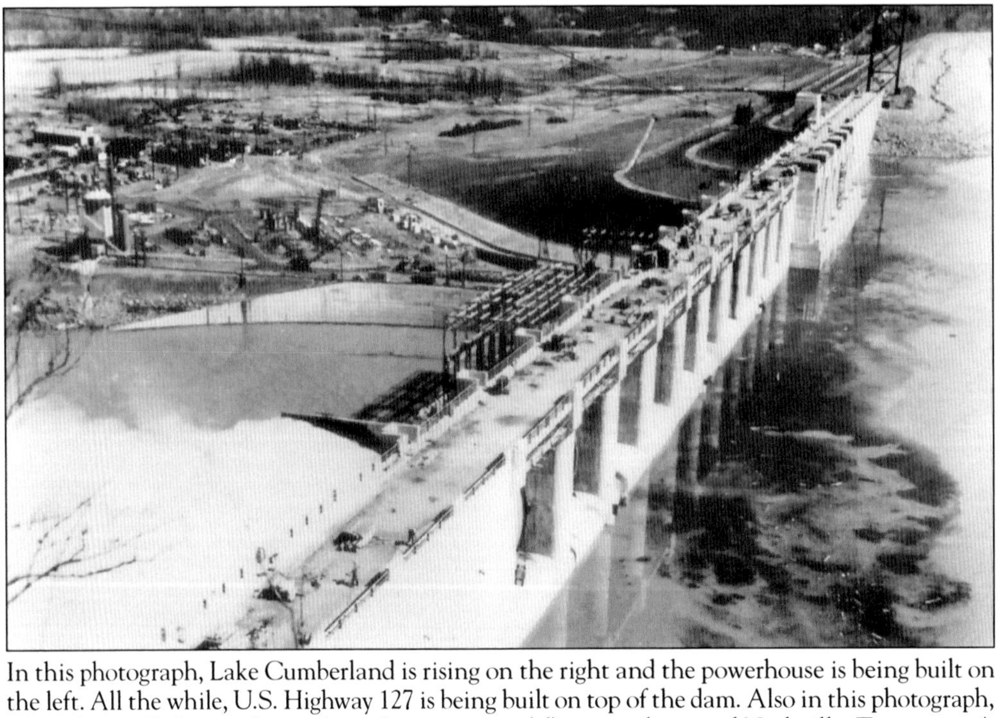

In this photograph, Lake Cumberland is rising on the right and the powerhouse is being built on the left. All the while, U.S. Highway 127 is being built on top of the dam. Also in this photograph, water shoots 60 feet in the air from sluice gates and flows south toward Nashville, Tennessee. A sluice is a water channel that is controlled by a gate. (Courtesy of Carole Tupman.)

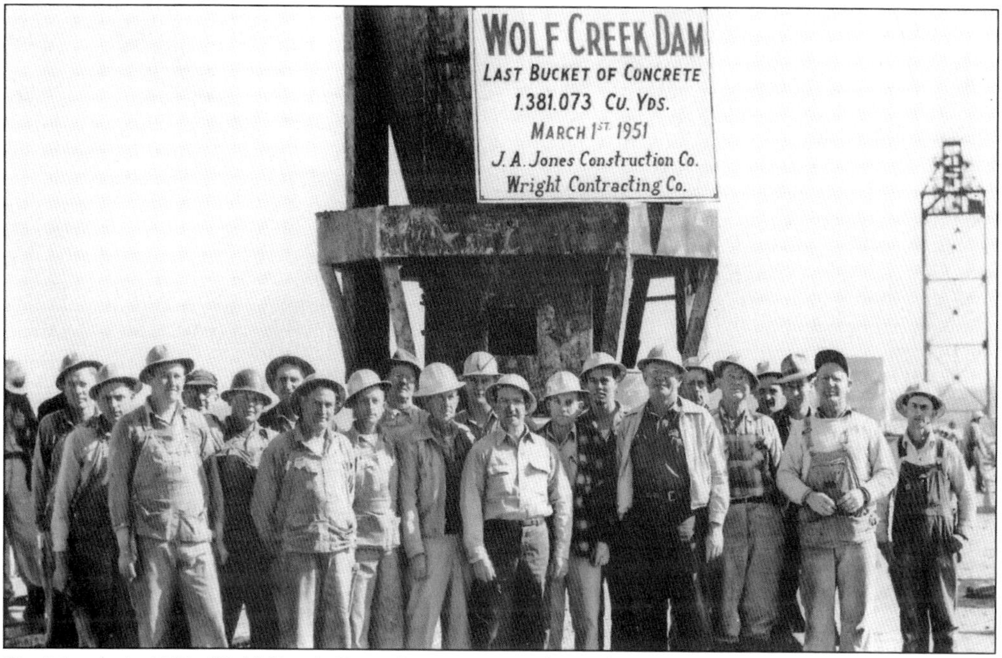

On March 1, 1951, Wolf Creek Dam foremen pose for a photograph taken with the last bucket used to carry concrete from the batch plant to the work site. During the construction of Wolf Creek Dam, 1,381,073 cubic yards of concrete was used. That is enough concrete to fill more than 69,000 concrete-mixing trucks to capacity. (Courtesy of Debbie Lake.)

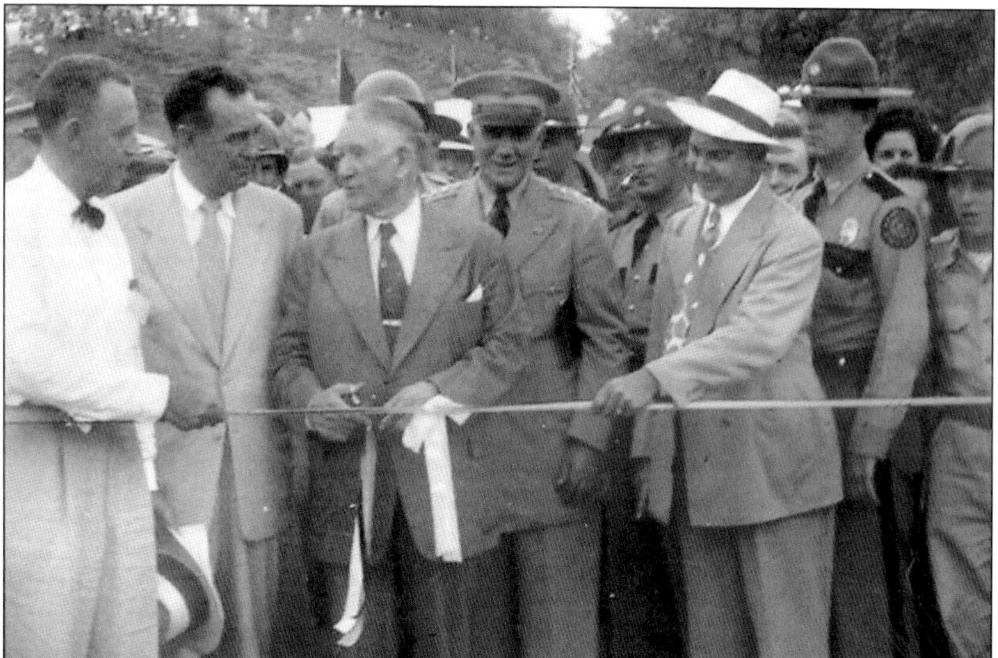

Ten years after the initial kick-off ceremony, Wolf Creek Dam was dedicated on September 1, 1951. Alben Barkley cut the ceremonial ribbon. Barkley was the 35th vice president of the United States and was from Paducah, Kentucky. (Courtesy of John T. Carter.)

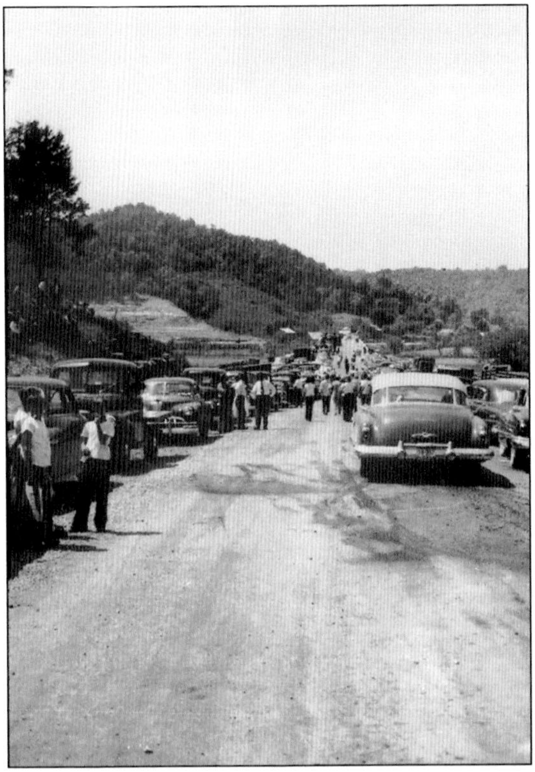

Two thousand people were present for the dam's dedication in 1951. Although the S. A. Healy Company of New York won the rights to the project on July 21, 1941, with a bid of $15,803,690; overall costs for land, damages, the powerhouse, and hydroelectric power production equipment were approximately $55 million. (Courtesy of John T. Carter.)

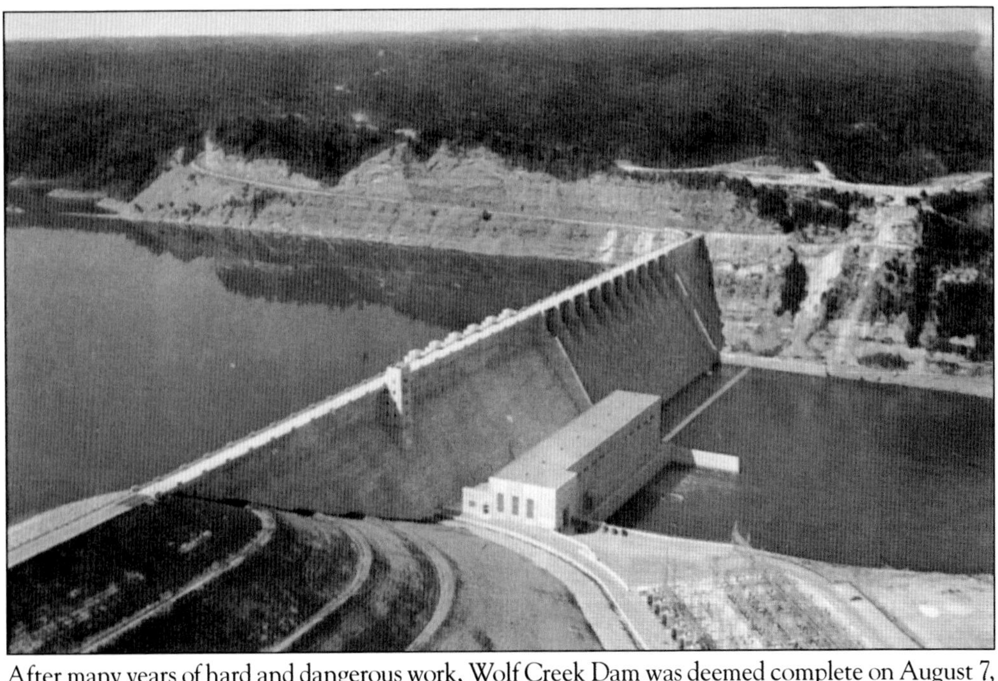

After many years of hard and dangerous work, Wolf Creek Dam was deemed complete on August 7, 1950. Turbines in the dam produce and send power to six states through the Tennessee Valley Authority system. At the end of the 1995 fiscal year, the dam produced 39,646,420,200 kilowatt hours of electrical power valued at $196,745,074. (Courtesy of the authors' collection.)

Six

Ill Effects of Wolf Creek Dam

Not everyone was happy about the building of the dam. Residents knew their lives would be forever changed when they were forced to move to higher ground and leave their lives and land behind. Before the dam could be built, property had to be seized, trees had to be cleared, temporary roads had to be created, and new bridges had to be constructed.

After World War II ended and construction resumed on the dam, reality called with notices from the War Department. The letters explained the intent to purchase properties. When property owners refused to sale, the land was condemned or taken by force. Second and third generations of families would be forced to move.

Relocating was not limited only to the living, but also to the dead. The remains of 2,800 people and 123 cemeteries would have to be moved to higher ground.

Communities such as Rowena, Horseshoe Bottom, Swan Pond Bottom, Lula, Long Bottom, Indian Creek, and Stokes would cease to exist once the lake filled. Residents in Long Bottom were the first to leave their homes, churches, and school. Shortly after, other communities were evacuated.

Burnside was more fortunate; the town would be moved to higher ground. Houses would have to be built and businesses relocated. Most of the businesses refused to relocate to "Upper" Burnside. Jobs were lost. Some residents, mostly the young, moved on to bigger towns and new jobs.

In 1948, the clearing of Burnside began, and 600 residents were forced to move to higher ground. The town was dismantled and cleared away.

In the spring of 1951, as the cold spring waters rose, the heart of Burnside was silenced as Lake Cumberland permanently flooded the area.

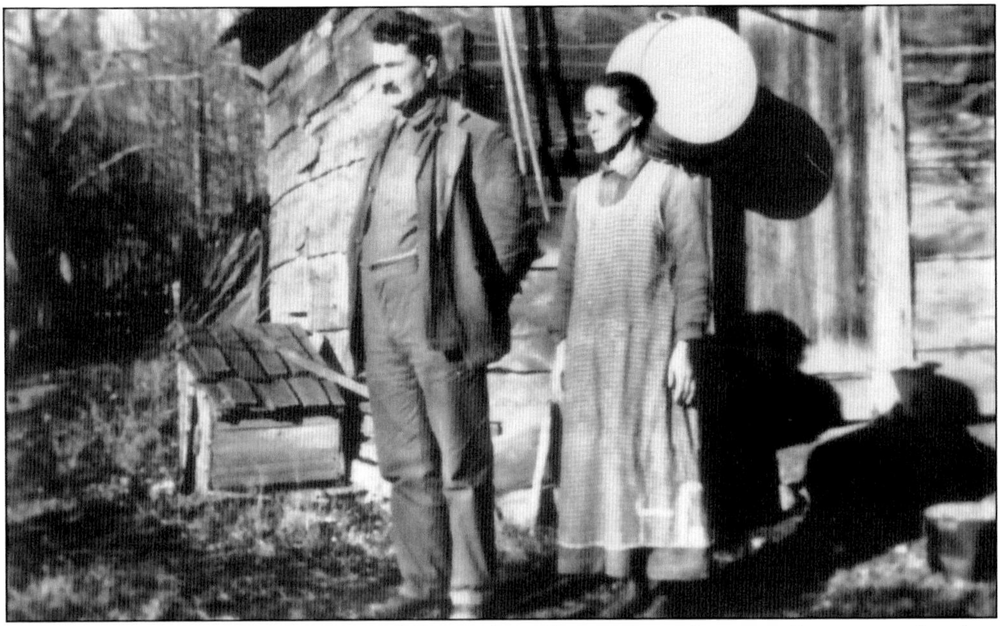

The future was unknown for many of the residents living along the river. One man refused to leave because burning embers in his fireplace had not been completely extinguished for more than 100 years. The Corps of Engineers agreed to help him. His hearth and embers were relocated to his new property. In this photograph, Willis and Addie Lee Robertson are shown standing outside their home. (Courtesy of Carole Tupman.)

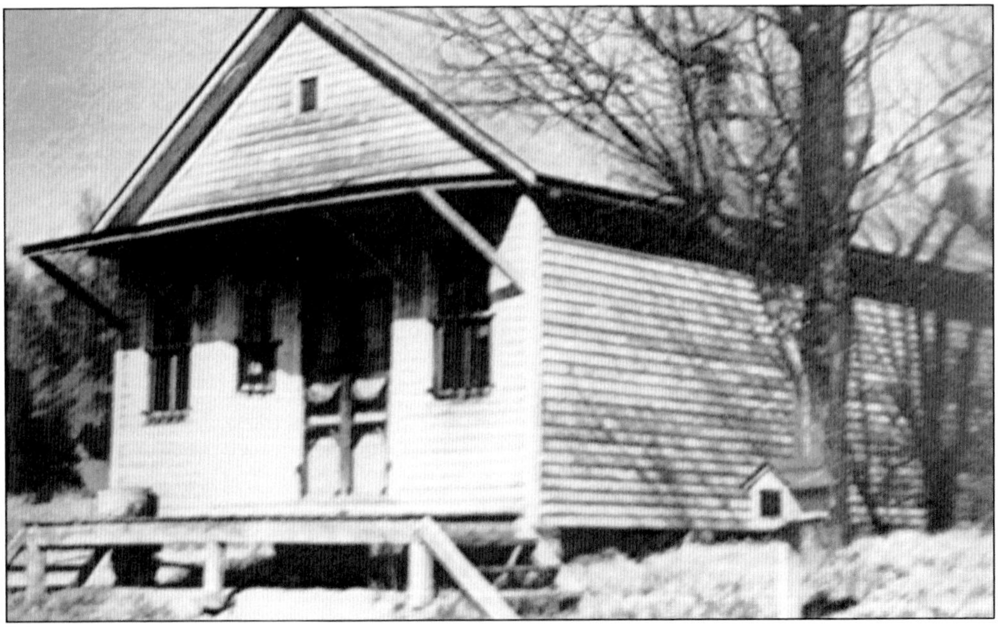

Horseshoe Bottom had the first post office in the area, established in 1822. There was a one-room school, a Methodist church, a gristmill, and a blacksmith shop. The name came about because the river flowed in the shape of a horseshoe. Horseshoe Bottom is currently under Jamestown Marina. This photograph shows the E. C. Kinnett Store and Post Office in Horseshoe Bottom shortly before being torn down. (Courtesy of Debbie Lake.)

Once the purchase price was agreed upon, home and landowners received a "Notice of Acceptance of Option for Purchase of Land" letter and a full copy of the accepted option from the U.S. Army Corps of Engineers. The letter shown here was sent to Claude Leveridge of Rowena, Kentucky. Leveridge was a ferryman for the Rowena Ferry. (Courtesy of Debbie Lake.)

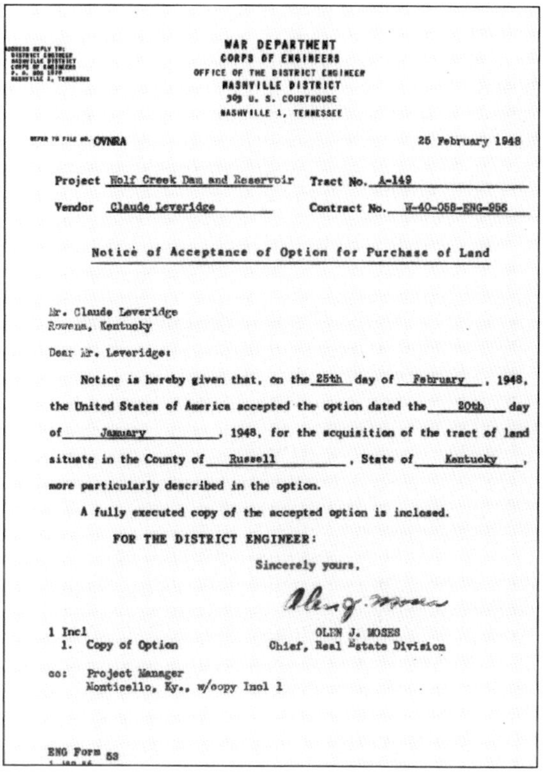

WAR DEPARTMENT
CORPS OF ENGINEERS
OFFICE OF THE DISTRICT ENGINEER
NASHVILLE DISTRICT
309 U. S. COURTHOUSE
NASHVILLE 1, TENNESSEE

OVNRA — 25 February 1948

Project Wolf Creek Dam and Reservoir — Tract No. A-149

Vendor Claude Leveridge — Contract No. W-40-059-ENG-956

Notice of Acceptance of Option for Purchase of Land

Mr. Claude Leveridge
Rowena, Kentucky

Dear Mr. Leveridge:

Notice is hereby given that, on the 25th day of February, 1948, the United States of America accepted the option dated the 20th day of January, 1948, for the acquisition of the tract of land situate in the County of Russell, State of Kentucky, more particularly described in the option.

A fully executed copy of the accepted option is inclosed.

FOR THE DISTRICT ENGINEER:

Sincerely yours,

OLEN J. MOSES
Chief, Real Estate Division

1 Incl
1. Copy of Option

cc: Project Manager
Monticello, Ky., w/copy Incl 1

ENG Form 53

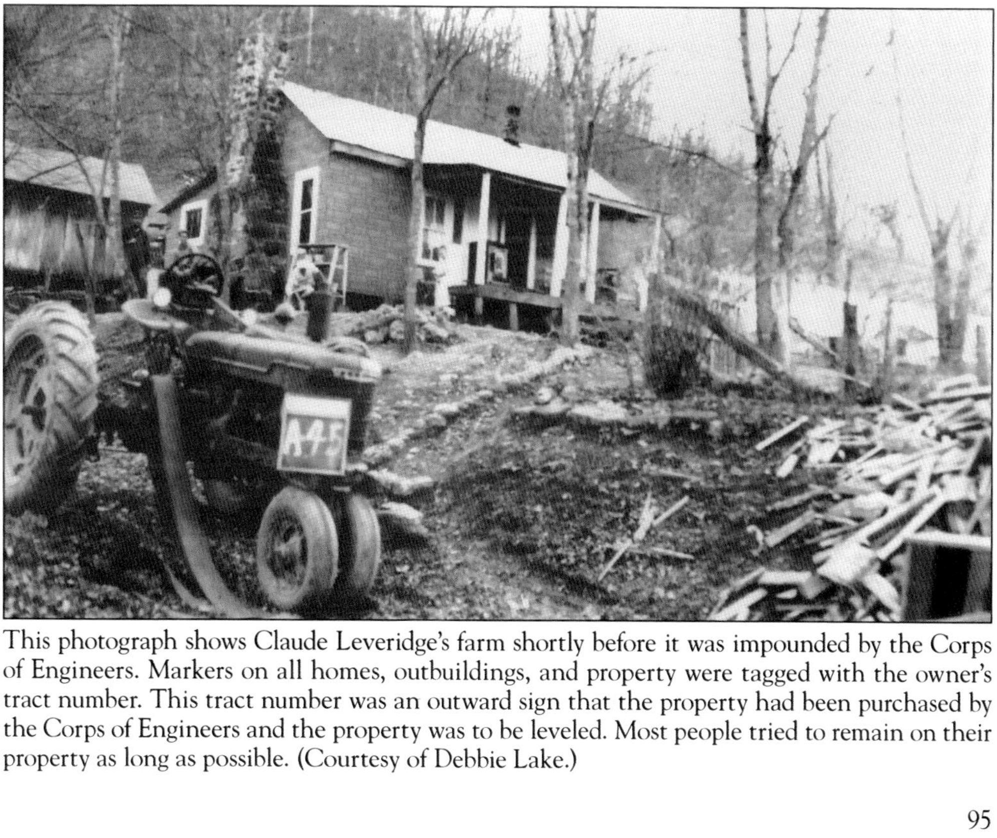

This photograph shows Claude Leveridge's farm shortly before it was impounded by the Corps of Engineers. Markers on all homes, outbuildings, and property were tagged with the owner's tract number. This tract number was an outward sign that the property had been purchased by the Corps of Engineers and the property was to be leveled. Most people tried to remain on their property as long as possible. (Courtesy of Debbie Lake.)

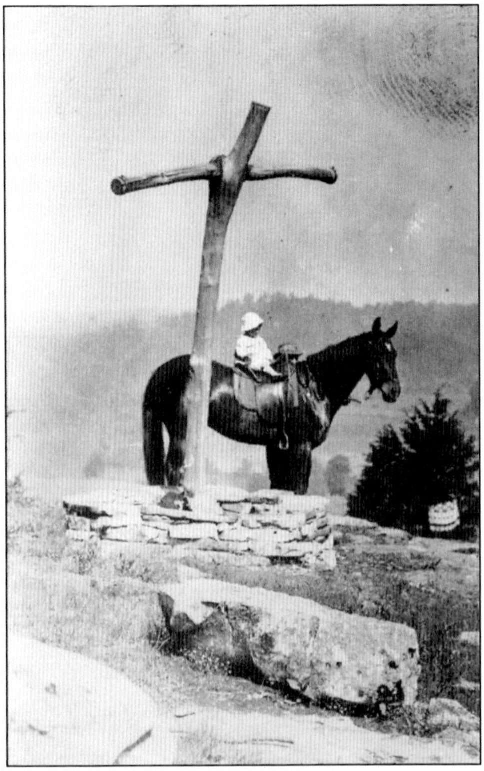

In this photograph, a small child sits atop a black horse near a grave on Bunker Hill. Remains of 2,800 people and 123 cemeteries were relocated because of the impoundment for Lake Cumberland. Headstones, coffin lids, and remains were removed and reinterred in cemeteries on higher ground. With the lowering of Lake Cumberland in 2007, several small cemeteries resurfaced, exposing empty coffins and burial vaults. (Courtesy of the PCHS.)

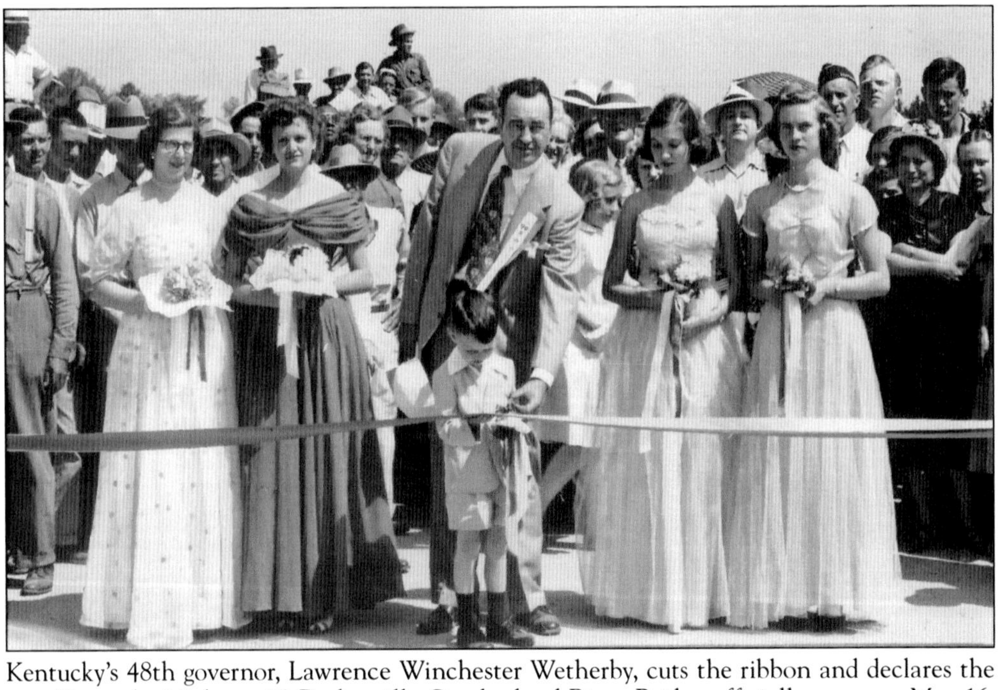

Kentucky's 48th governor, Lawrence Winchester Wetherby, cuts the ribbon and declares the new Kentucky Highway 90 Burkesville Cumberland River Bridge officially open on May 16, 1951. Governor Wetherby presided as William Young cut the ribbon. Wetherby was succeeded as governor by Happy Chandler in 1955. (Courtesy of Randolph Smith.)

Harold "Hank" Hardwick cuts the ribbon to officially declare the new Burnside railroad bridge open to north and southbound traffic on the Southern Railway. Hardwick's home was the only home moved from the valley to "Upper" Burnside. The house was cut into sections and moved up the hill by truck. The home was reassembled and for several years was occupied by Marguerite Dudley Sloan, who gave it the name Dudley Manor. The house remains intact on East French Avenue. (Courtesy of John T. Carter.)

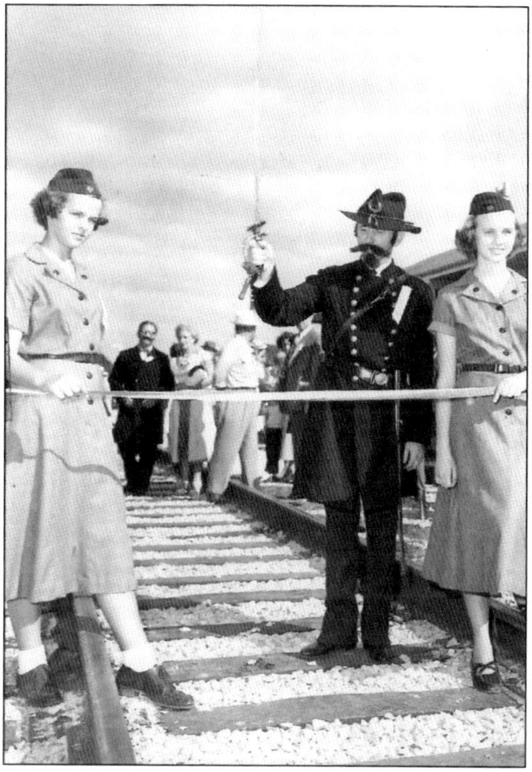

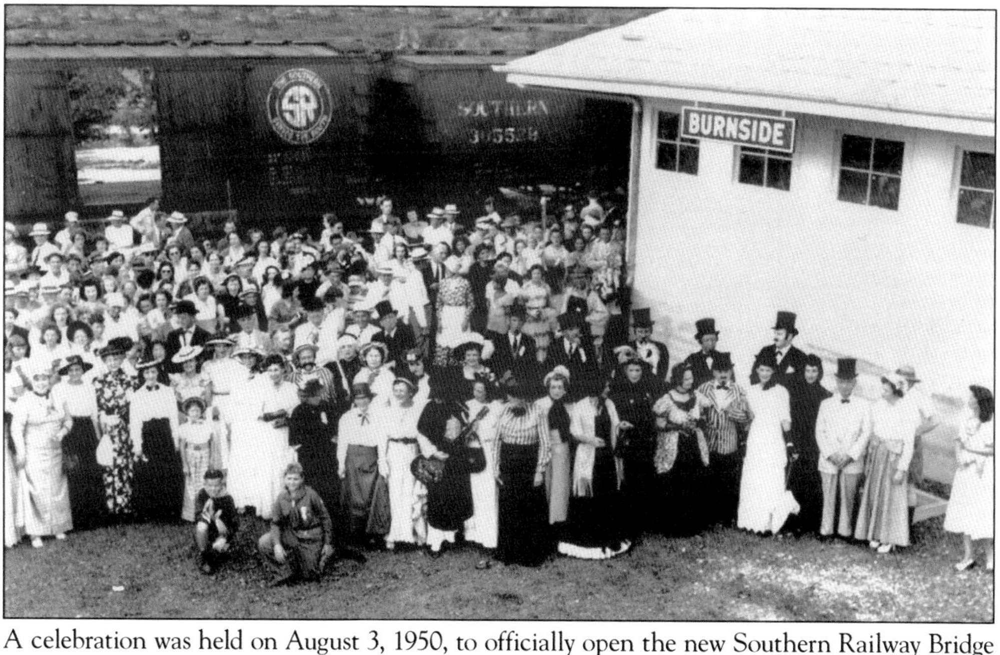

A celebration was held on August 3, 1950, to officially open the new Southern Railway Bridge in Burnside. Town residents dressed in festive "Gay Nineties" period costumes. At 4:47 p.m., they boarded Southern Railway train No. 4—the *Royal Palm*. The train carried them across the new bridge and into nearby Somerset. More than 500 people attended the event. (Courtesy of Rogers Photography.)

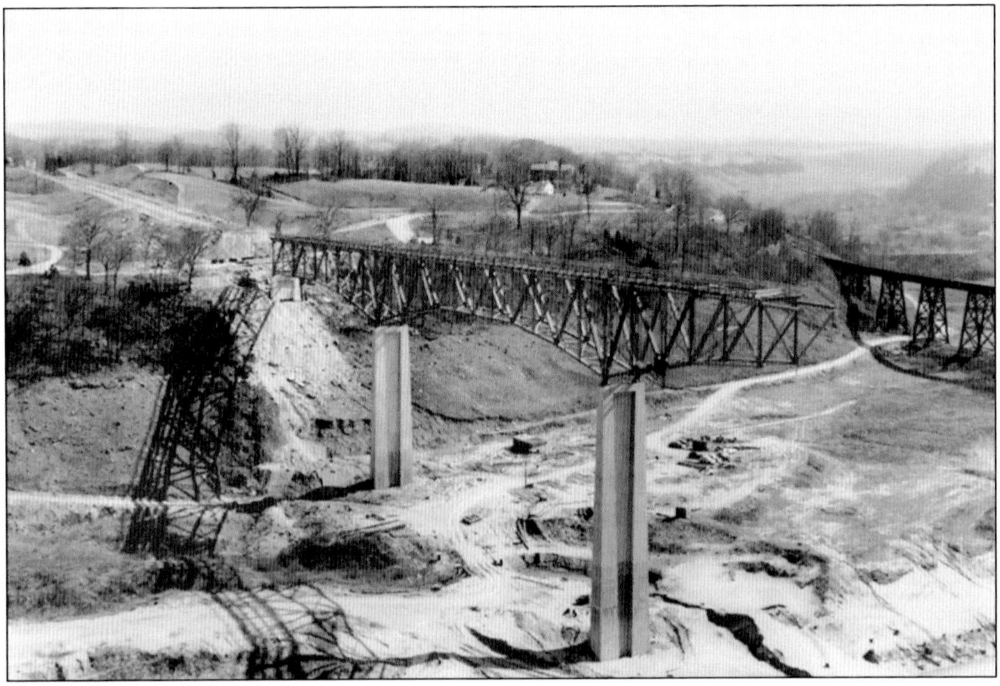

Once completed, the U.S. Highway 27 Cumberland River Bridge would span 1,390 feet, with the tallest pier height of 203 feet. The bridge was dedicated on March 31, 1951. Gov. Lawrence Wetherby addressed the audience. (Courtesy of Rogers Photography.)

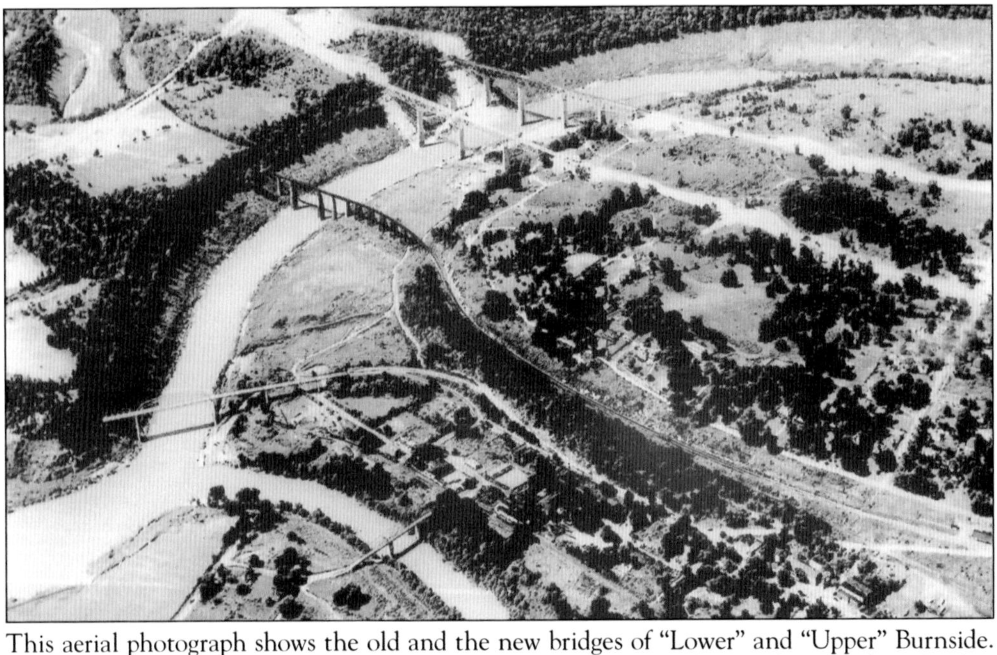

This aerial photograph shows the old and the new bridges of "Lower" and "Upper" Burnside. Starting at the top and working down to the left, the bridges are the Southern Railway Bridge, the new U.S. Highway 27 Bridge, the old railroad bridge, the old U.S. 27 Bridge, and the old Kentucky 90 Bridge. The three old bridges would be dismantled, and "Lower" Burnside would be cleared of homes and businesses. (Courtesy of John T. Carter.)

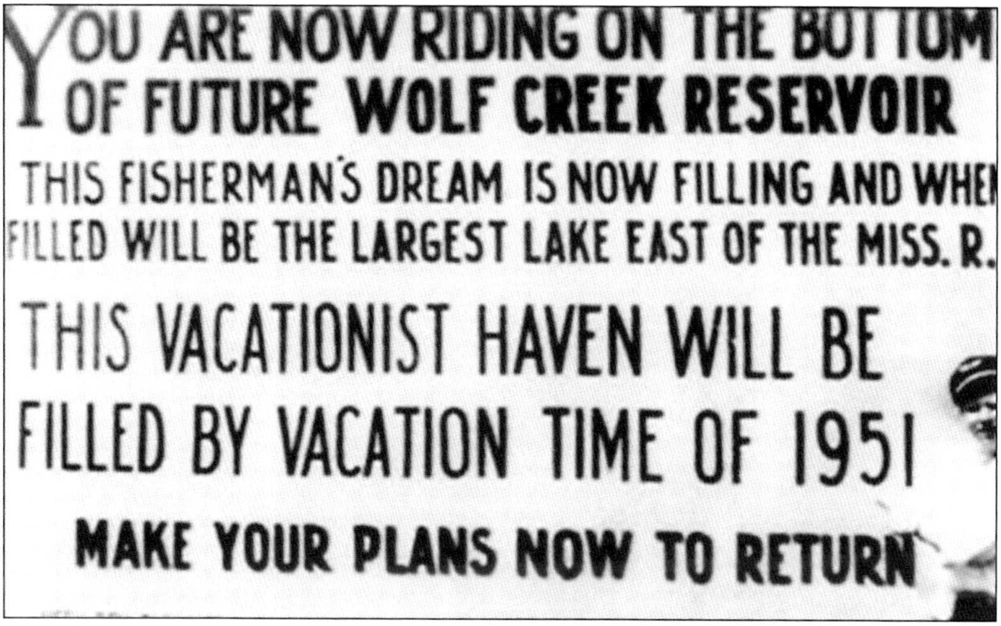

This photograph shows a sign placed on the west side of the Cumberland River of "Lower" Burnside. The sign makes promises of things to come. Residents were told Lake Cumberland was going to be a huge tourist location. An increase in tourists would mean an increase in jobs and revenue for the area. Some residents thought Lake Cumberland would become the "Great Lake of the South." (Courtesy of the PCHS.)

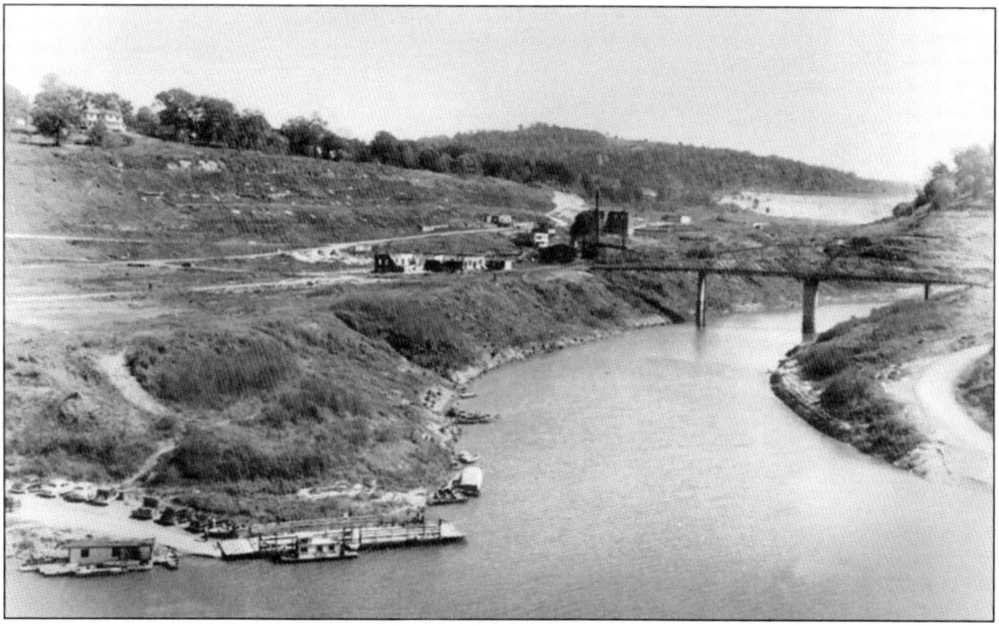

There were mixed emotions when town residents learned that "Lower" Burnside would be moved onto the hill of "Upper" Burnside. More than 600 residents would be displaced, and many complained they were not offered a fair price for their property. In 1948, the town began its move. In this photograph, only a few building foundations, the old Kentucky 90 Bridge, and the ferry remain. (Courtesy of Rogers Photography.)

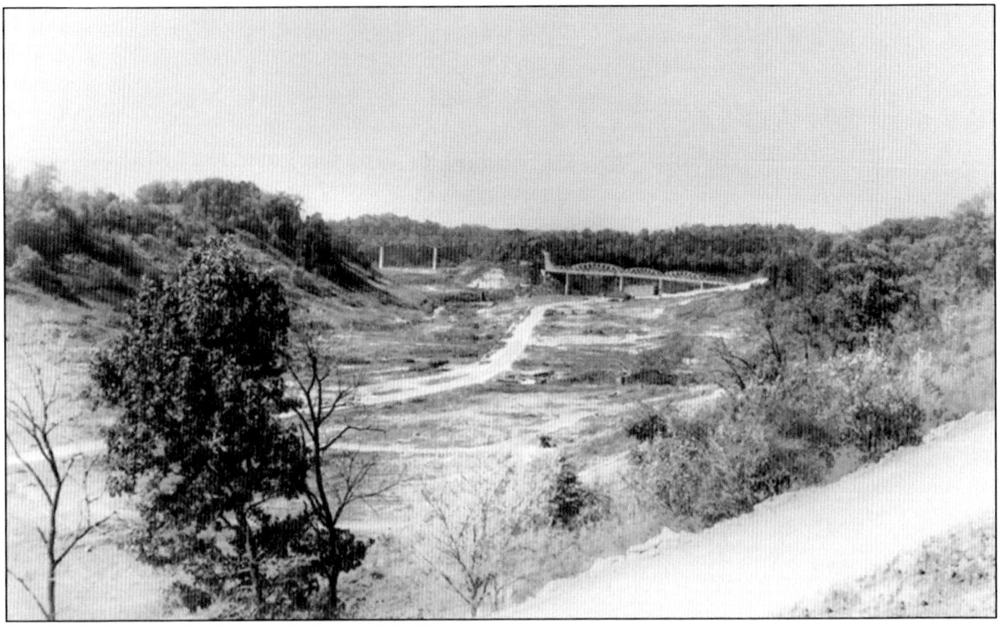

Once businesses and homeowners were evacuated, all buildings were dismantled, and all trees were cut down. Bernice Mitchell said, "Many tears were shed as people saw their old homes torn down." This photograph was taken from the causeway connecting Bunker Hill with the new U.S. Highway 27. The new Highway 90 Bridge is seen in the distant left while the old U.S. Highway 27 Bridge is on the right. (Courtesy of Rogers Photography.)

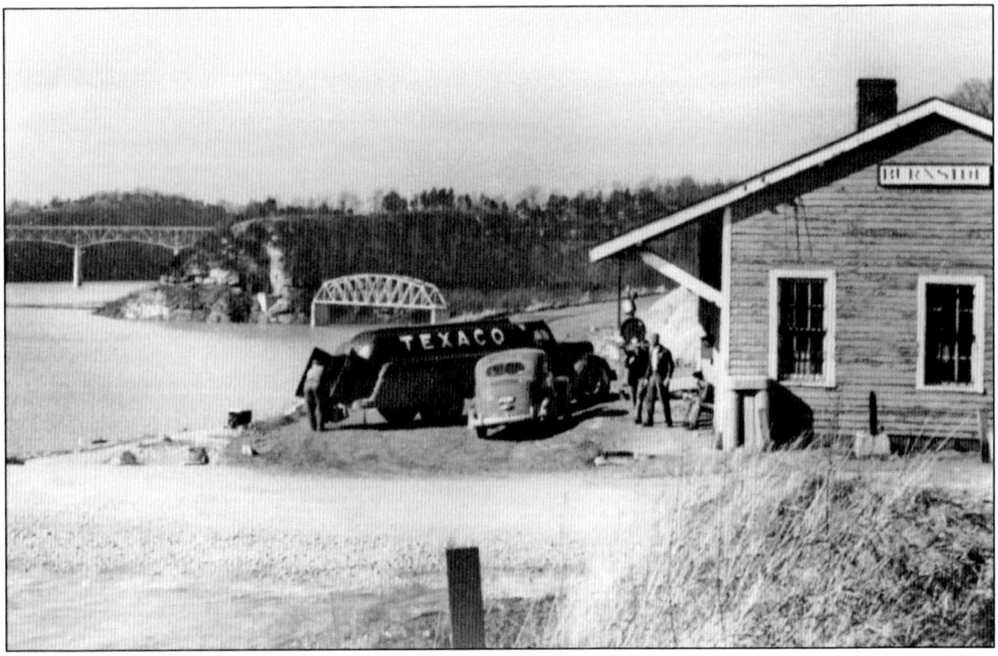

In the early months of 1951, heavy rains inundated the area. When asked what the lake looked like in 1951, longtime resident Thomas Moody said if he had not known better, he would have thought a spring flood had hit. Only this time, the water was not going to go back down. In this photograph, the old Burnside train depot is soon to be dismantled. (Courtesy of the authors' collection.)

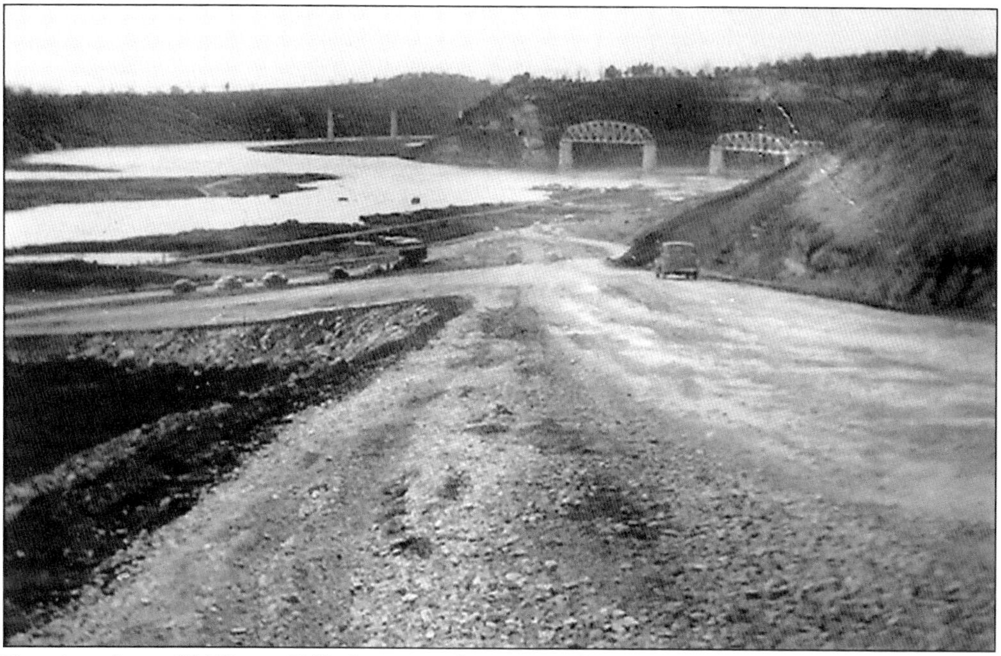

Traveling down Old Depot Hill, this car makes its way down to the Bronston Ferry. The ferry to Bronston made its last run on February 10, 1951. This photograph also shows the lake beginning to fill. Engineers said it would take the lake two to three years to reach maximum capacity. It only took about six months. (Courtesy of Tom Moody.)

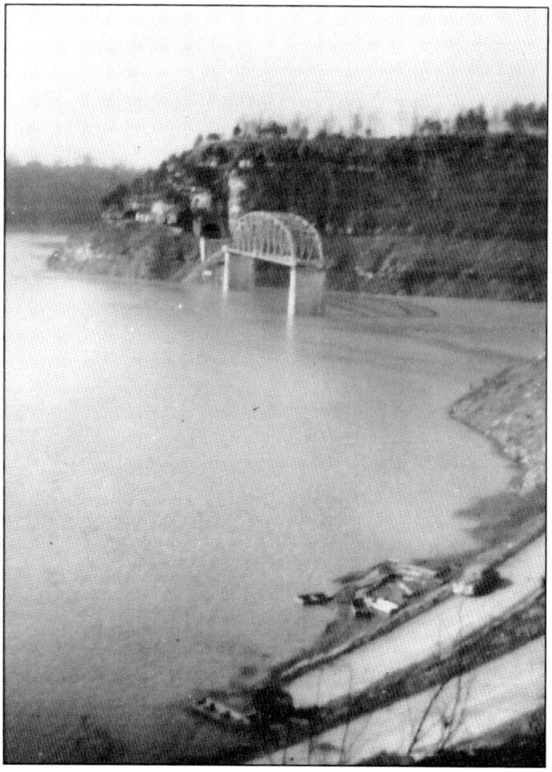

On January 18, 1951, the lake level was 73.5 feet according to the old Burnside river gauge on the side of the U.S. Highway 27 Bridge. The bridge was in the process of being dismantled, but the water rose much quicker than expected. The last span was left in the water and was used to determine the depth of the lake. (Courtesy of Tom Moody.)

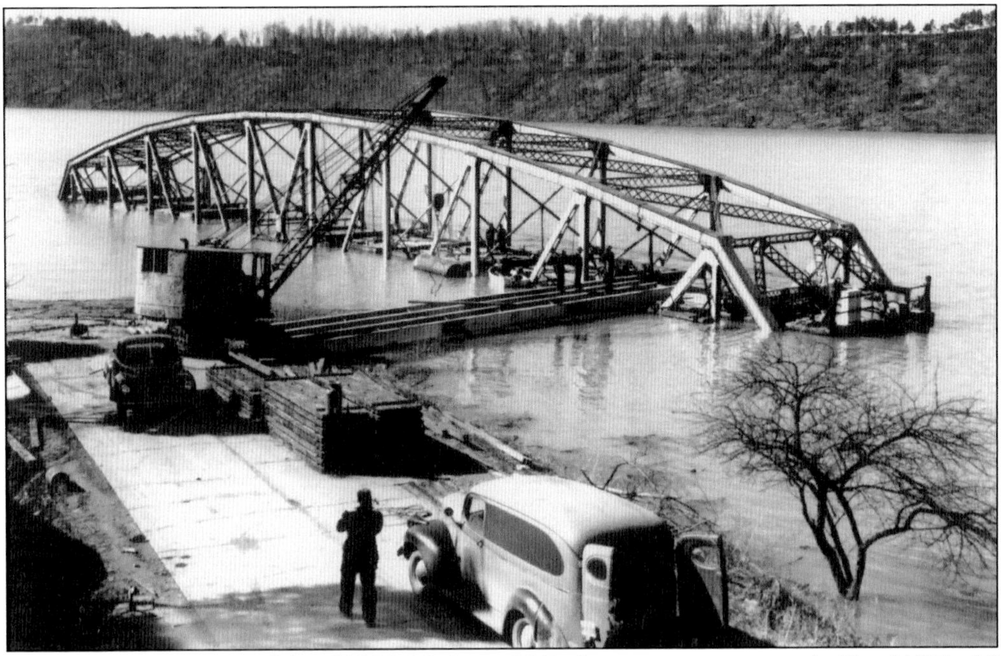

Removing the last span of the old U.S. Highway 27 Bridge was not an easy task. Harold "Hank" Hardwick estimated the weight of the span and secured barges under it. The two remaining piers were blasted loose. As the water rose, the barge lifted the span and carried it to Waitsboro, where it was dismantled. (Courtesy of Rogers Photography.)

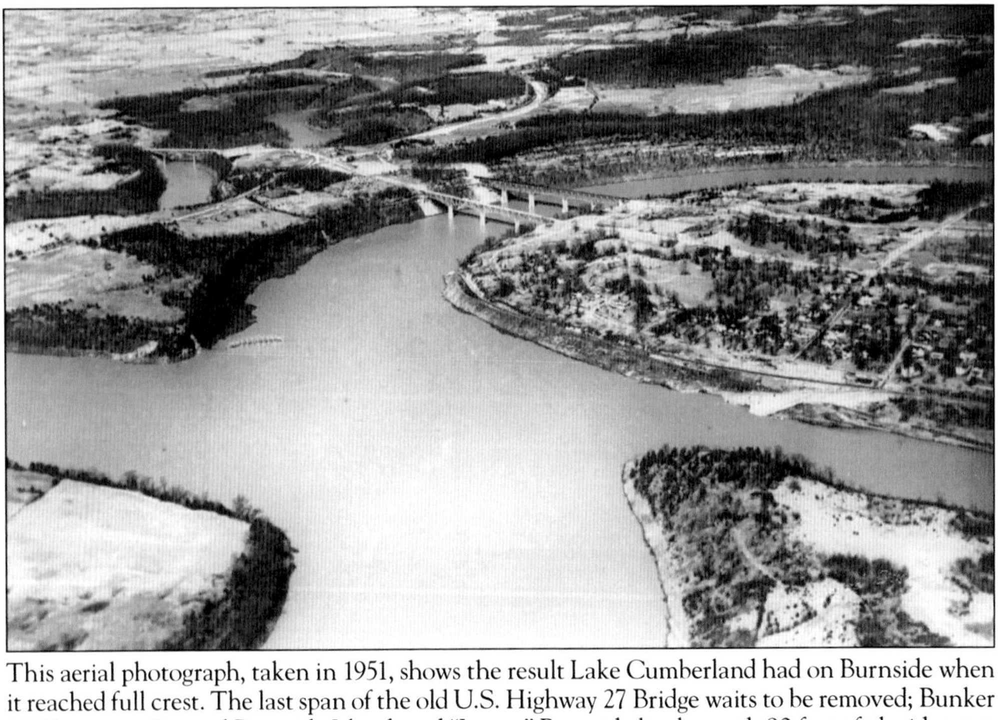

This aerial photograph, taken in 1951, shows the result Lake Cumberland had on Burnside when it reached full crest. The last span of the old U.S. Highway 27 Bridge waits to be removed; Bunker Hill becomes General Burnside Island; and "Lower" Burnside lies beneath 90 feet of placid water. (Courtesy of the authors' collection.)

Seven

Lake Cumberland Is Born

Engineers predicted it would take Wolf Creek Reservoir two to three years to fill to capacity. Local residents who understood the unpredictable nature of the Cumberland River predicted otherwise.

In January and February 1951, unusually heavy rains inundated the area. The reservoir filled to spillway crest in March and to maximum capacity by April 1951.

One year later, on April 17, 1952, an Act of Congress officially changed the name of the Wolf Creek Reservoir to Lake Cumberland.

When Wolf Creek Dam was planned, recreation was almost an afterthought. No one could have imagined the impact Lake Cumberland would have on the economy of south-central Kentucky. In 1999, approximately 4.75 million visitors added more than $152.4 million to the local economy.

Although tourism started slowly in the area, it grew steadily over the years. Early boat docks were primitive and were basically boat liveries. Over the years, marinas grew to serve the needs of recreation enthusiasts and boaters alike.

Early houseboats were simply travel trailers attached to a steel hull—humble beginnings for the luxurious houseboats now seen floating on Lake Cumberland. Today thousands of houseboats ply the waters of the lake. For that reason, Lake Cumberland has been deemed "the Houseboat Capital of the World."

Lake Cumberland is also known as an unsurpassed fishing location. From the early days of the lake's creation, it was advertised as one of Kentucky's premier year-round fishing destinations. Over the years, Lake Cumberland has continued to provide fishers walleye, striper, and bass.

But tourists do not have to be water recreation lovers to enjoy the lake. Many vacationers visit Lake Cumberland for the privacy and tranquil vistas. Still others enjoy playing golf or camping with family along the shores. Overall, Lake Cumberland has been the backdrop to magical moments for visitors for more than 50 years.

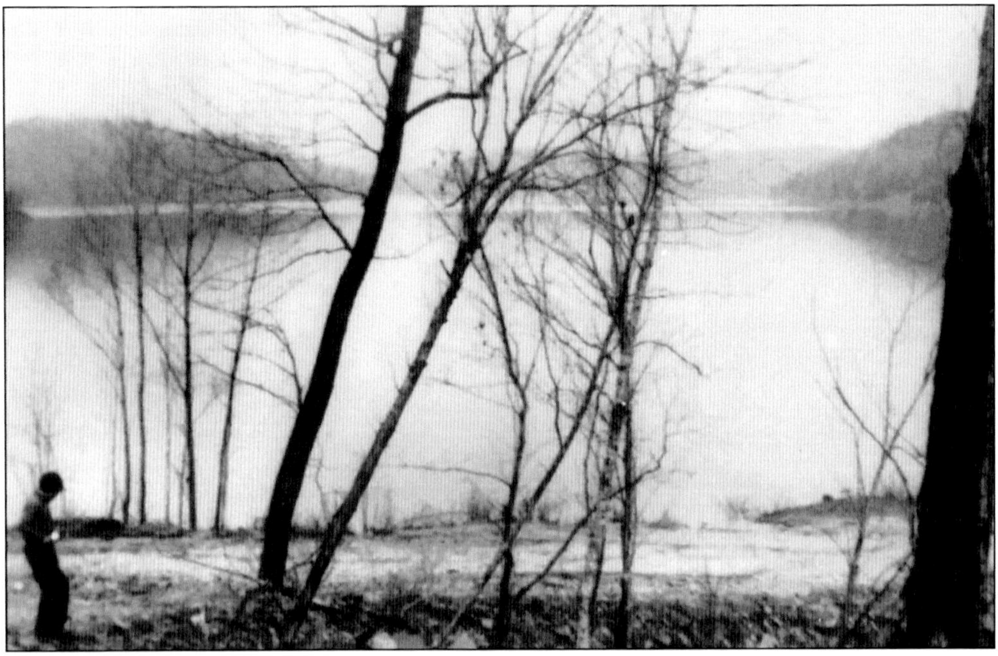

This photograph was taken in February 1951 from what would become Grider Hill Dock. Bruce Sloan had the foresight to place a bid for the land offered by the U.S. Army Corps of Engineers. His dream was to build one of the first boat docks on Lake Cumberland. (Courtesy of Grider Hill Dock, Brian King, and Stacy Grafton.)

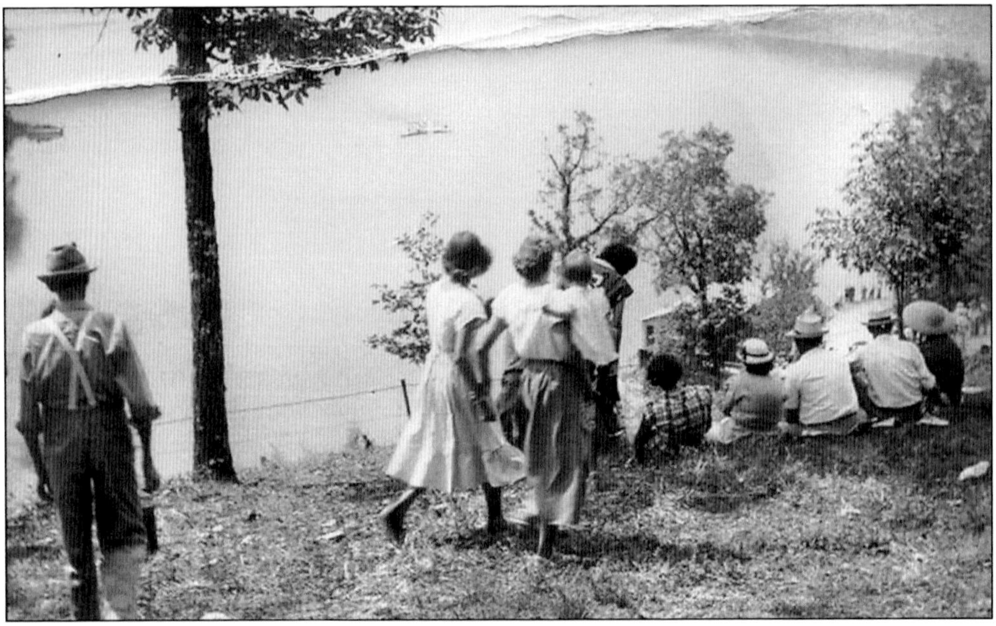

This photograph shows a boat race at Waitsboro in the early 1950s. Today the most popular activity on Lake Cumberland is the Poker Run. The Poker Run is a contest involving high-performance boats racing to five different sites on the lake. At every stop, racers collect a sealed envelope with a playing card inside. At the end of the race, the envelopes are opened, and the boat with the best poker hand wins. (Courtesy of John T. Carter.)

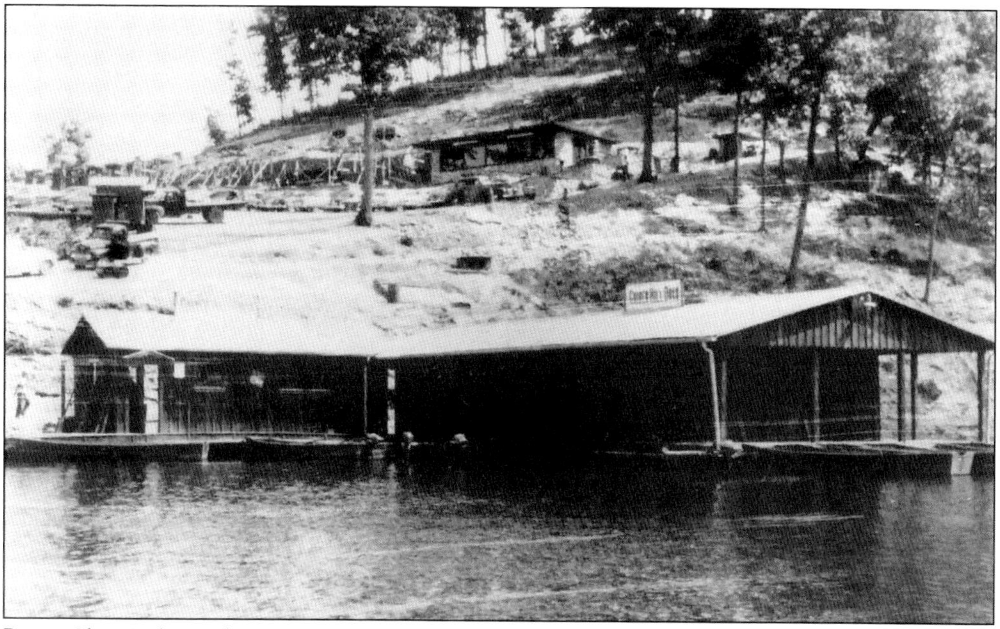

Bruce Sloan's dream became a reality when he opened Grider Hill to the public in the spring of 1951. He and his wife, Gay, managed the dock. Their sons, Tony, Ned, and Bruce, helped. In this photograph, taken in the late summer of 1952, the dock and restaurant are complete, and construction is underway on the lodge. (Courtesy of Grider Hill Dock, Brian King, and Stacy Grafton.)

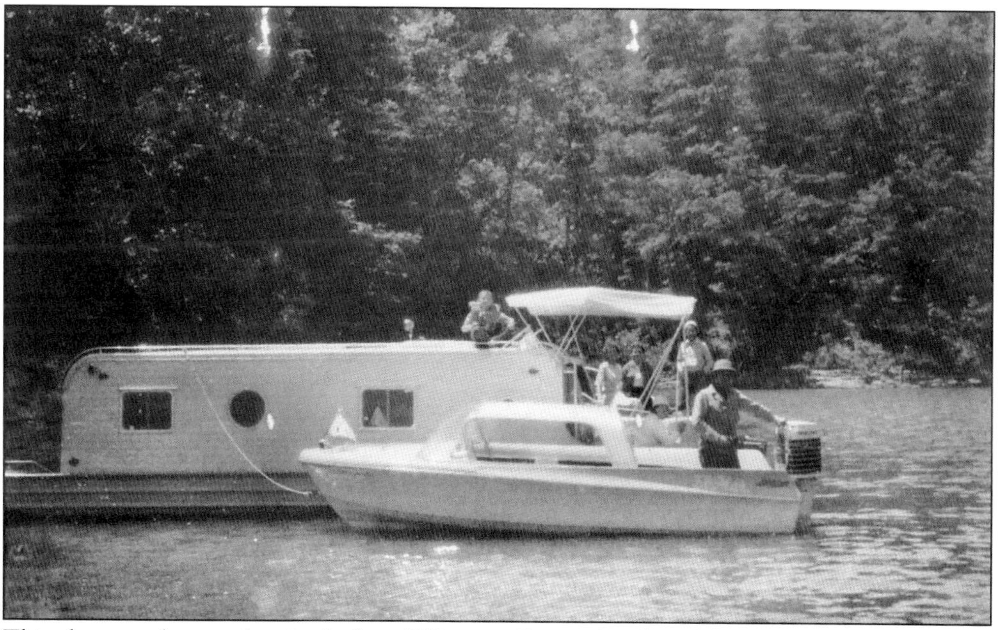

This photograph was taken in the late 1950s near Greasy Creek and shows the Lawrence family's Terra Marina houseboat. The boat was designed to be a combination houseboat/RV. When launched, the wheels stayed on the boat. These days, houseboats are more like floating condominiums with central air, bedrooms, bathrooms, kitchens, hot tubs, stereos, satellite televisions, washers and dryers, grills, and more. (Courtesy of James Lawrence.)

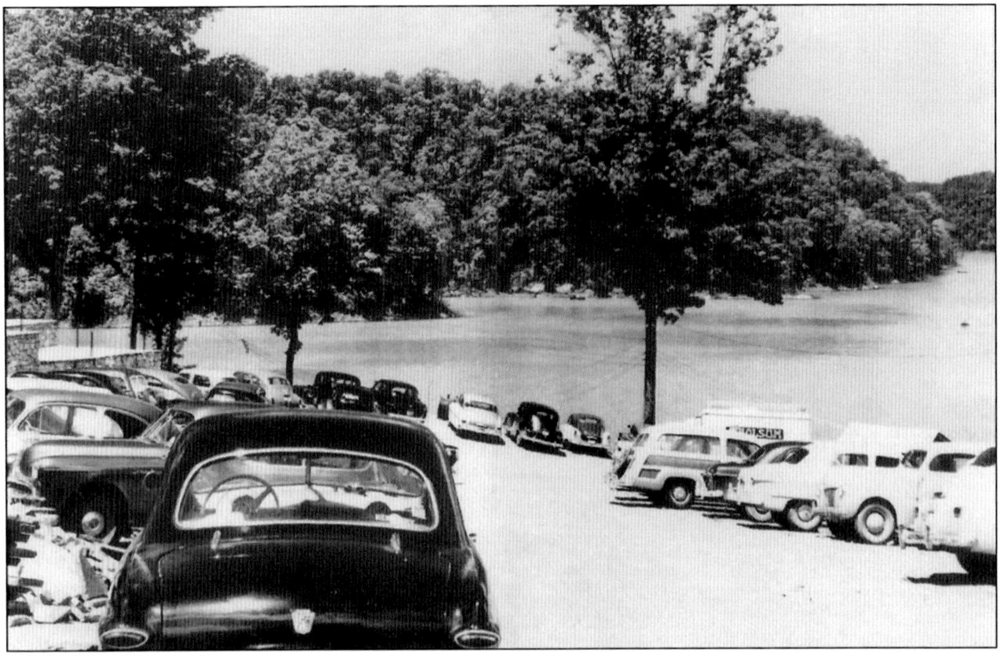

Visitors came from miles around to see the new Lake Cumberland. In the summer of 1952, cars parked wherever they could find a spot in Grider Hill's parking lot. Bruce Sloan had a vision of creating a marina and resort that was more than a fishing camp; a place people would want to return to year after year. (Courtesy of Grider Hill Dock, Brian King, and Stacy Grafton.)

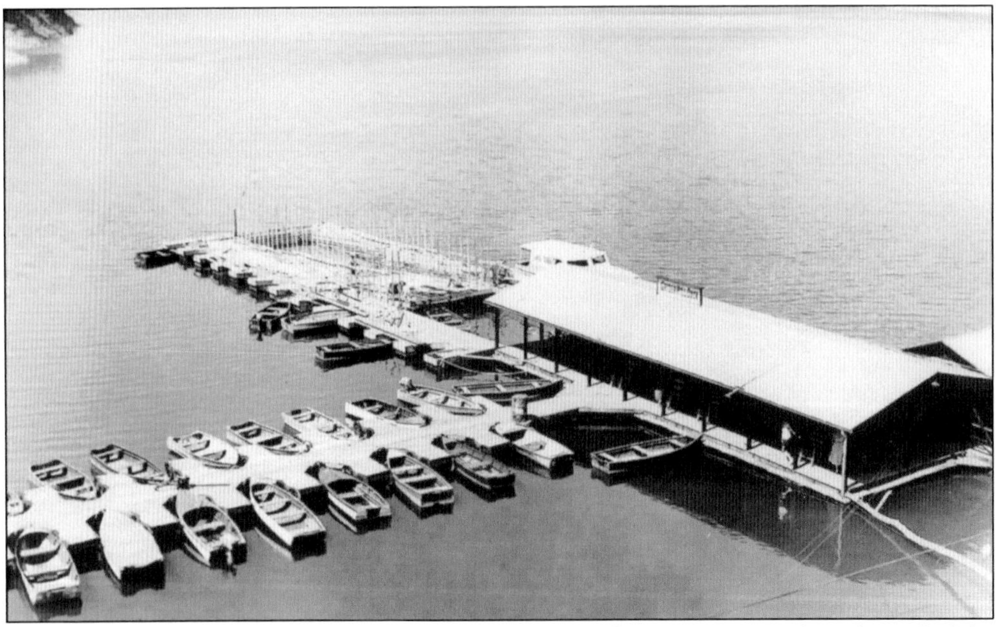

This photograph was taken at Grider Hill Dock in 1954. The swimming pool on the end of the dock is nearly complete. Tony Sloan said there were three types of visitors to the lake in the early days—those who could afford a motorboat, those who could afford to rent a motorboat, and those who could only afford to rent a wooden fishing boat. He said they were all equally lucky in fishing. (Courtesy of Grider Hill Dock, Brian King, and Stacy Grafton.)

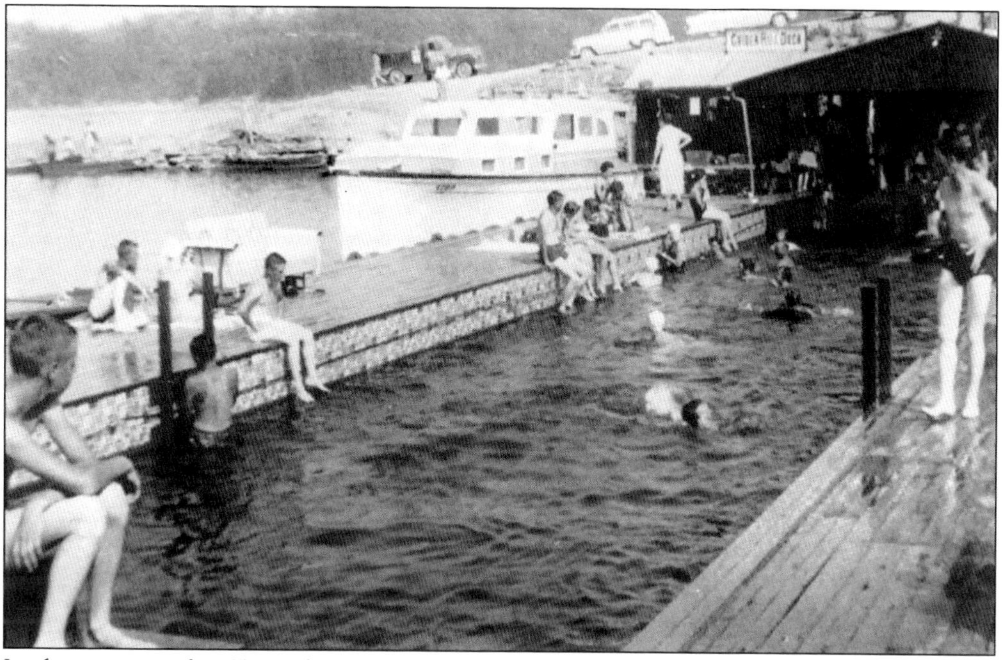

In the summer of 1955, Grider Hill Dock visitors enjoy their time swimming and playing in the new pool, which was a safe place to swim with boats pulling in and out of the dock. Lake Cumberland's average water temperature in July is 82 degrees Fahrenheit. (Courtesy of Grider Hill Dock, Brian King, and Stacy Grafton.)

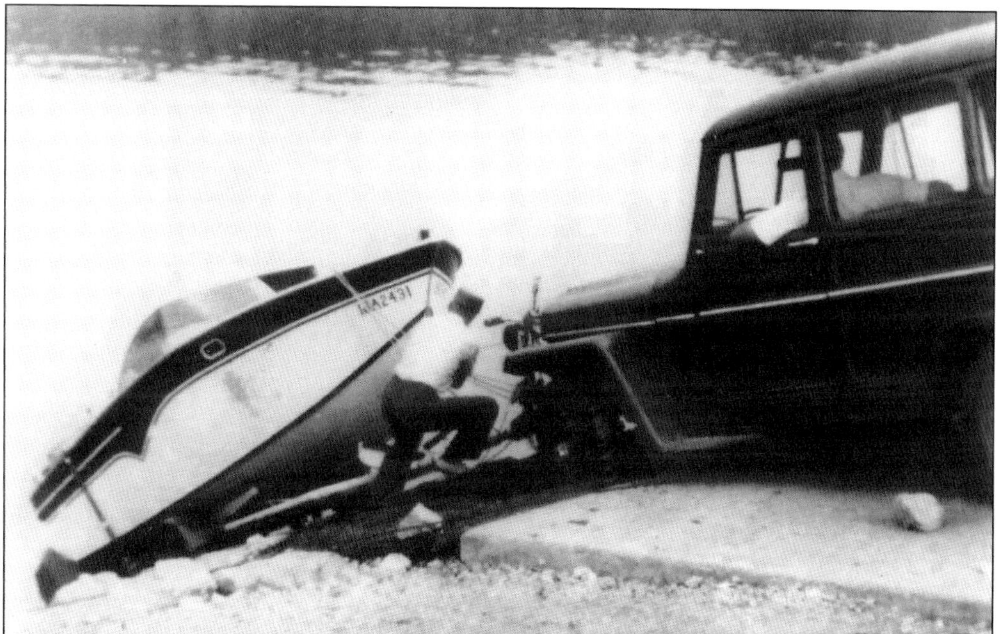

Launching a boat is not an easy task, as shown in this photograph taken at Grider Hill Dock in 1962. At the time this photograph was taken, the elevation of the lake was approximately 695 feet. There are currently 51 boat docks around Lake Cumberland. (Courtesy of Grider Hill Dock, Brian King, and Stacy Grafton.)

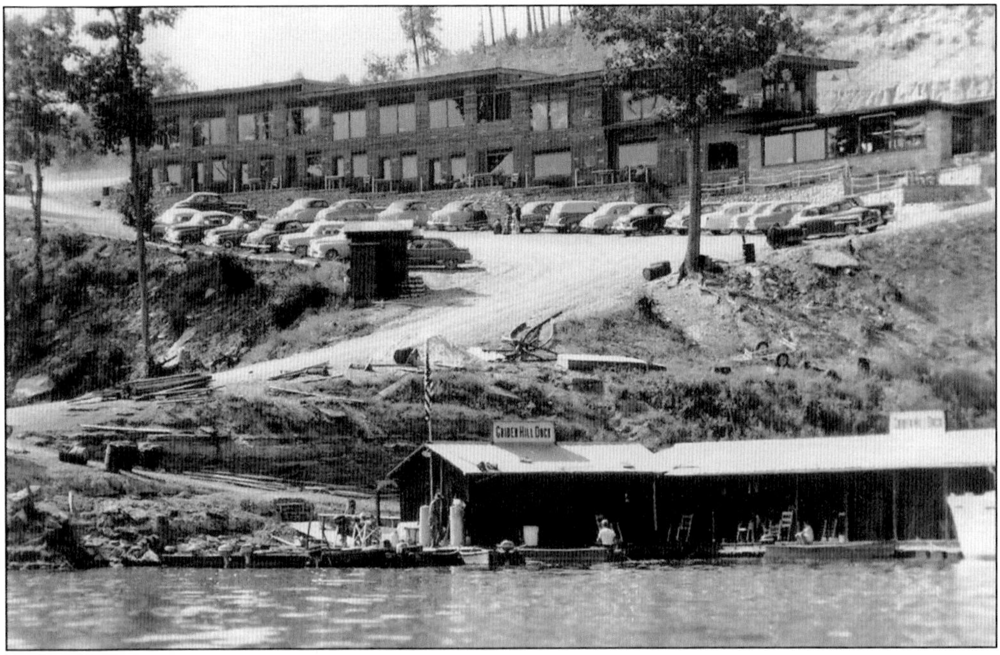

Bruce Sloan was inspired by architect Frank Lloyd Wright when he built the lodge at Grider Hill Dock. He used native stone and wood, both of which were mined and cut from his own land. The lodge and restaurant offered panoramic views of the lake. This photograph was taken in 1954. (Courtesy of Grider Hill Dock, Brian King, and Stacy Grafton.)

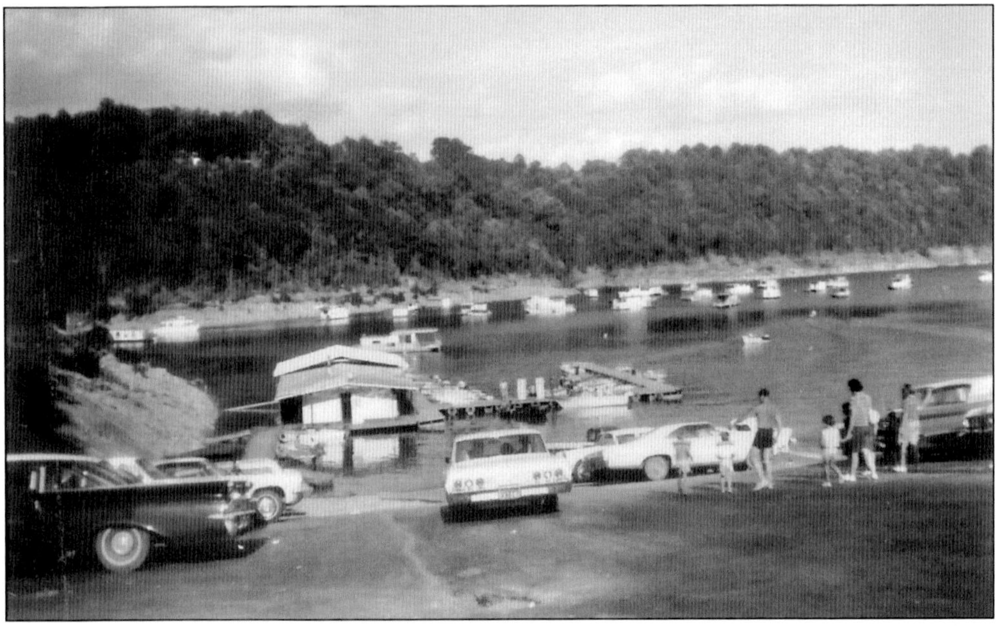

In this photograph, taken in the summer of 1966, a family walks toward Jamestown Dock to spend an afternoon swimming in Lake Cumberland. The continually growing number of people enjoying the lake encouraged many marinas and docks to expand their size in the 1960s. Today many visitors come from Ohio and have become referred to as the "Ohio Navy." (Courtesy of Debbie Lake.)

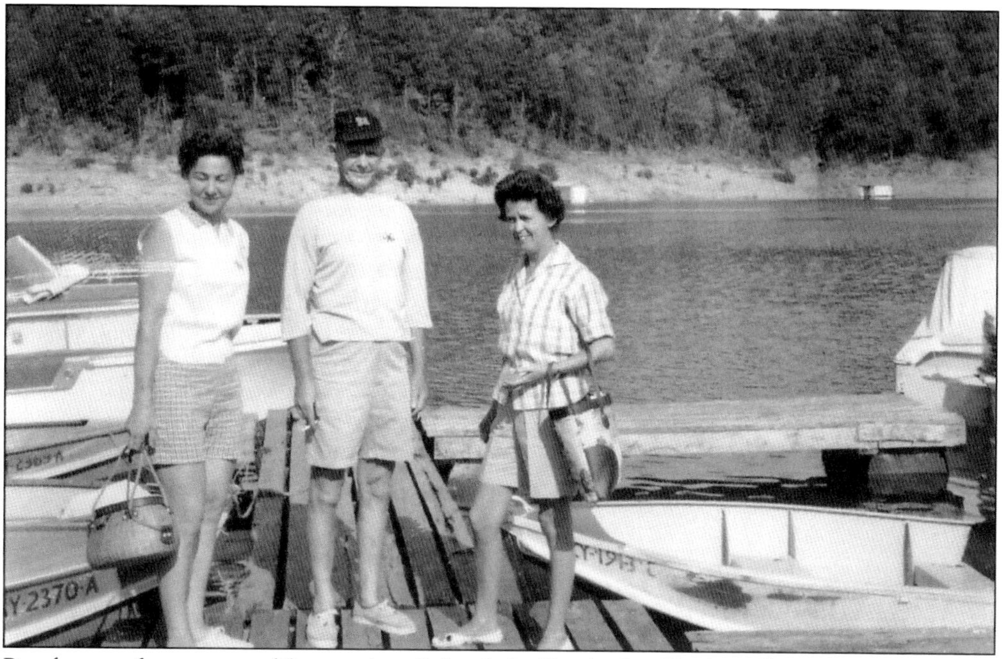

People came from near and far to enjoy all that Lake Cumberland had to offer. In this photograph, Martha Lawrence (far right) and her friends from Columbia, Kentucky, are anxious to spend the day in a boat on the lake. The image was taken by Eb Lawrence in the late 1950s. (Courtesy of James Lawrence.)

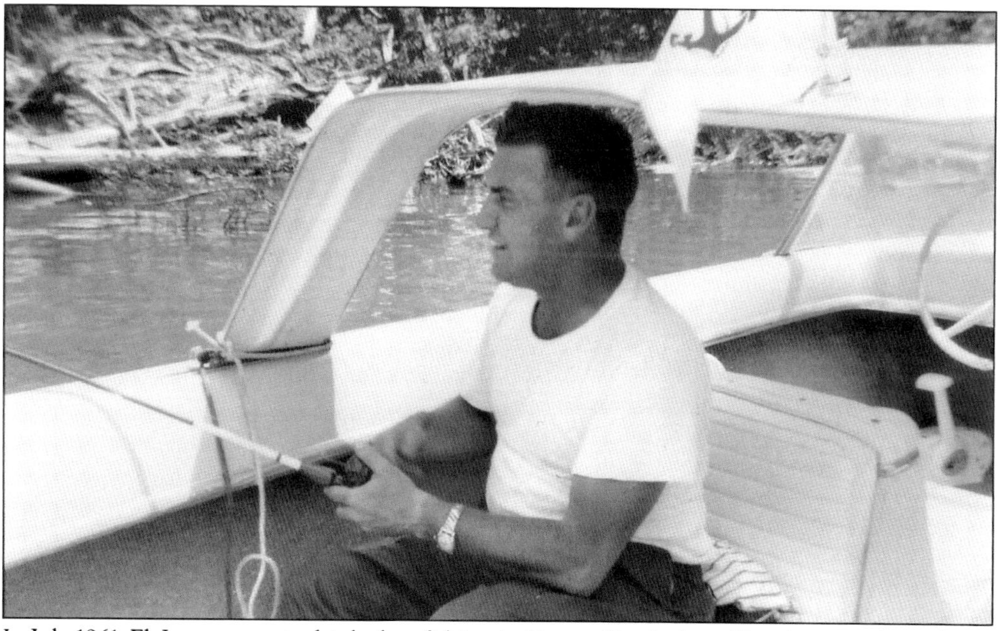

In July 1961, Eb Lawrence tries his luck at fishing in Greasy Creek aboard his Aristocraft runabout. Lake Cumberland is known for its varied stock of fish, including largemouth bass, smallmouth bass, white bass, Kentucky bass, bluegill, crappie, catfish, walleye, and striped bass. The lake is filled with private coves and creeks. Several creeks to explore for private fishing are Pitman Creek, Fishing Creek, and Beaver Creek. (Courtesy of James Lawrence.)

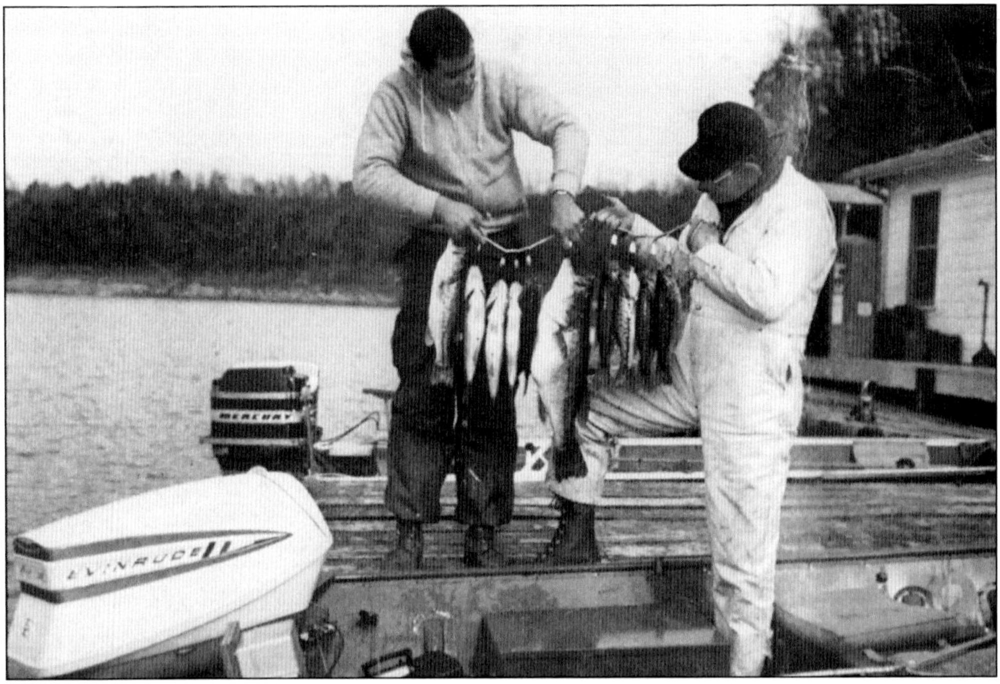

In this photograph, two men show off their bountiful catch of the day. In 1951, Lake Cumberland was stocked with 20 fingerlings per acre of largemouth bass, smallmouth bass, spotted bass, and striper. Many of those fingerlings are now averaging 10 to 20 pounds. (Courtesy of Phil Ruchka.)

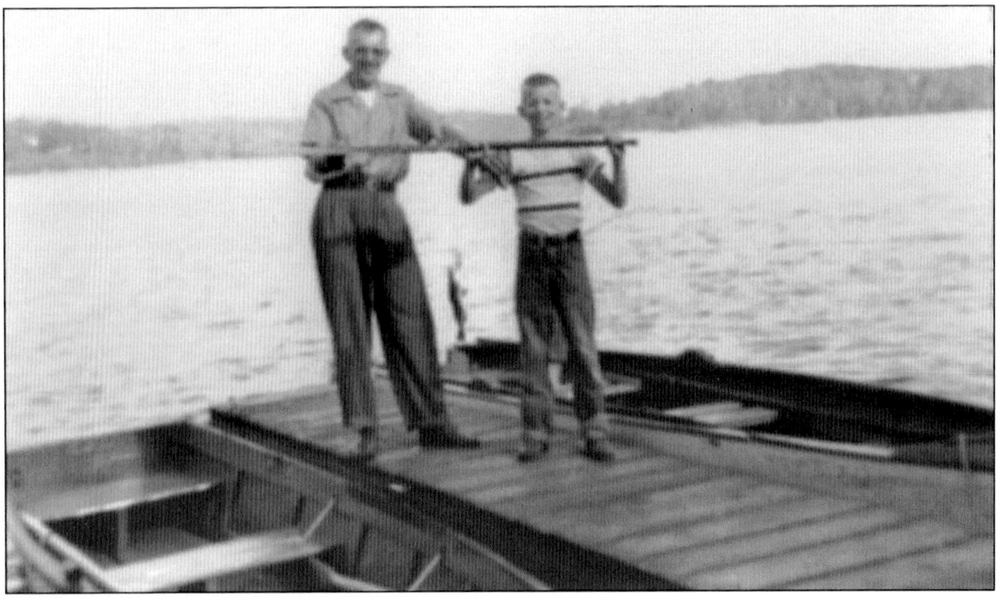

A father and son show off their catch of the day. Many state fishing records have been set at Lake Cumberland. Records include a 36-pound, 8-ounce sturgeon on October 3, 1954; a 7-pound, 7-ounce sauger on April 28, 1983; a 21-pound, 8-ounce walleye on October 1, 1958; a 58-pound, 4-ounce striped bass on December 11, 1985; a 21-pound brown trout on April 30, 2000; a 5-pound, 5-ounce lake trout on April 4, 1983; and a 14-pound, 6-ounce rainbow trout on September 10, 1972. (Courtesy of the Varland family.)

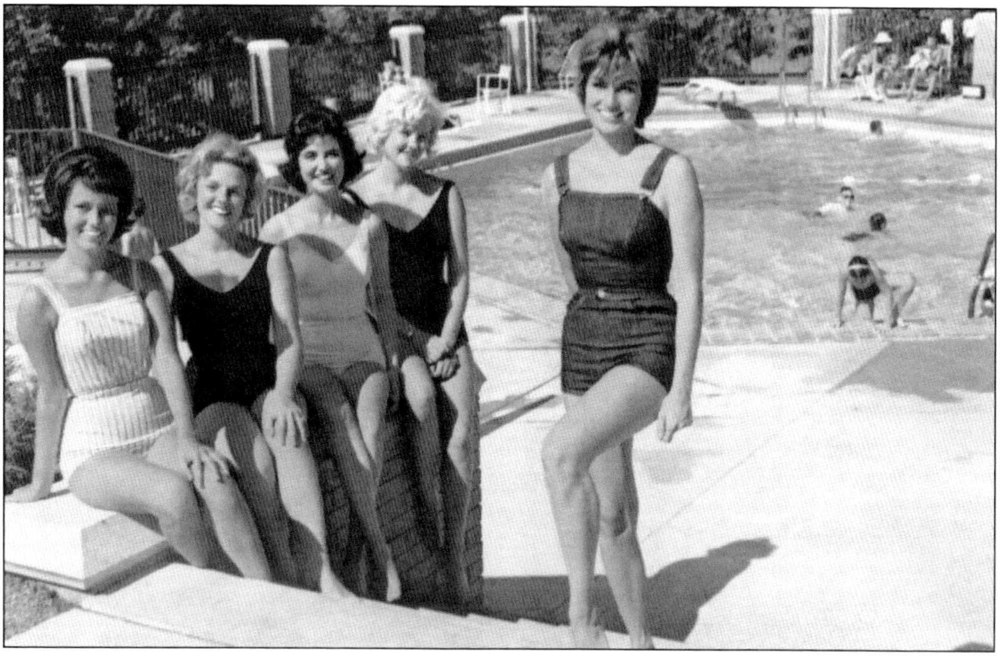

These bathing beauties show off the latest swimsuit fashions in this 1960s advertisement. Resort swimming pools added to the recreational activities and appeal of Lake Cumberland. The swimming pool, unlike the dock pool, was built of concrete and filled with chlorinated water. (Courtesy of the authors' collection.)

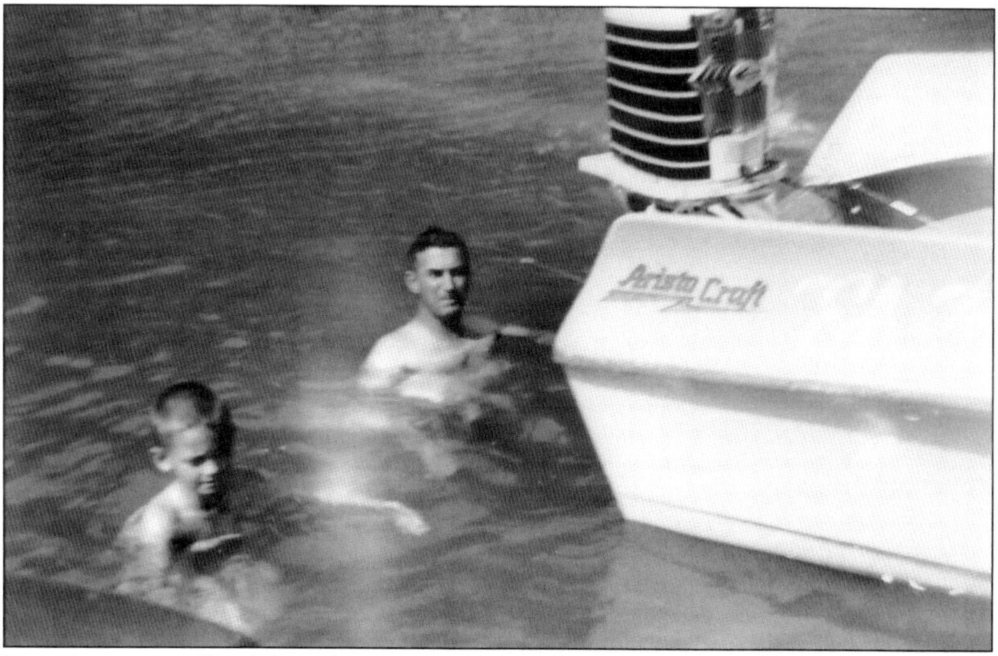

James Lawrence and his father, Eb Lawrence, swim in the warm summer water of Lake Cumberland near Greasy Creek. Lake Cumberland's average water temperature in August is 84 degrees Fahrenheit. The average water temperature for St. Petersburg Beach, Florida, in August is 86 degrees Fahrenheit. (Courtesy of James Lawrence.)

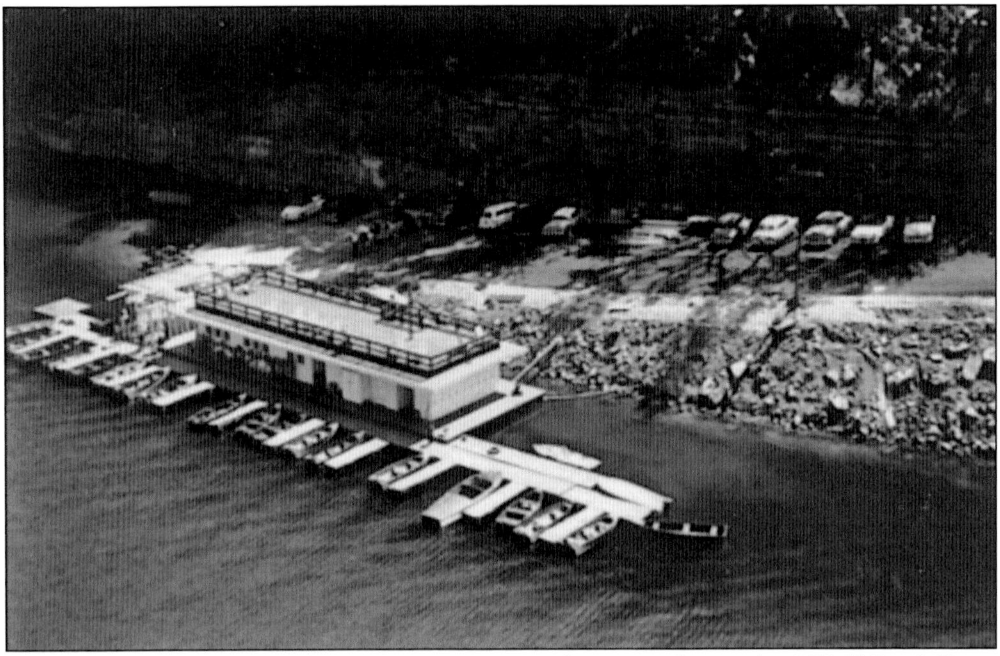

Lake Cumberland State Dock in Jamestown, Kentucky, is 8 miles north of Wolf Creek Dam. Contrary to belief, the dock is not a state-run operation. It is a privately owned business, and the dock is a licensee of the Kentucky Department of Parks. This photograph shows the State Dock in the mid-1950s. (Courtesy of James Sears and the Lake Cumberland State Dock.)

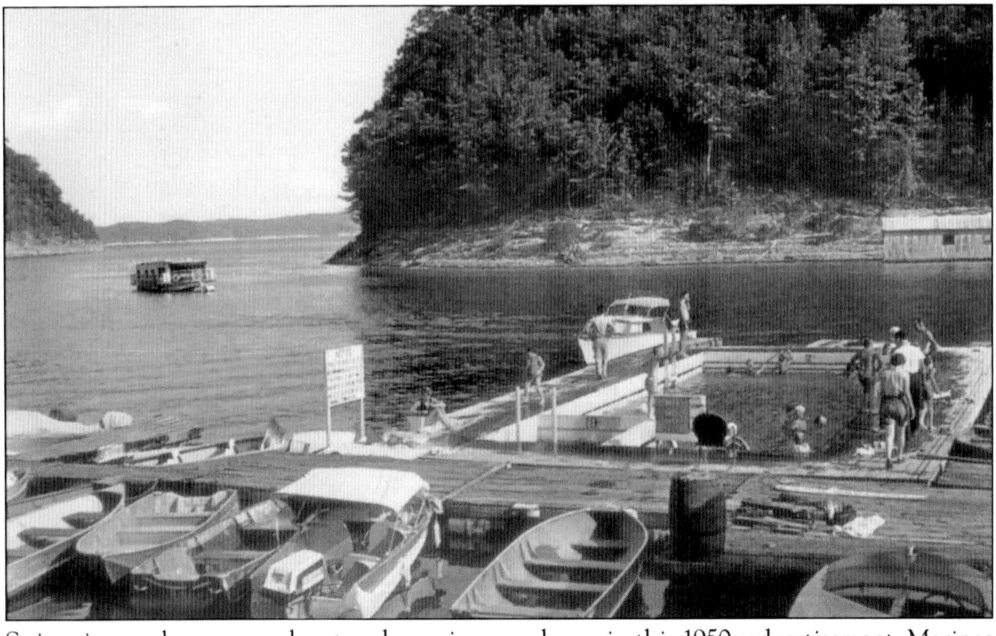

Swimming pools were popular at early marinas, as shown in this 1950s advertisement. Marinas and docks on Lake Cumberland include Alligator I Marina, Alligator II Marina, Beaver Creek Resort Marina, Buck Creek Boat Dock, Burnside Marina, Cave Springs Marina, Conley Bottom Resort, Grider Hill Resort, Jamestown Resort and Marina, Lake Cumberland State Dock, and Lee's Ford Marina Resort. (Courtesy of Phil Ruchka.)

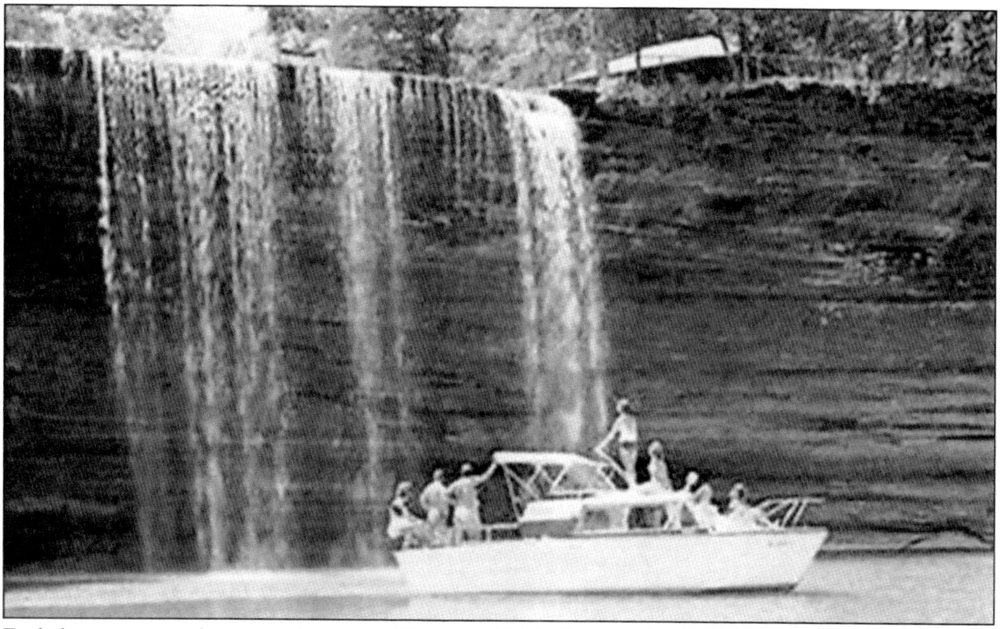

Early boaters were drawn to the natural beauty of 76 Falls near Grider Hill Dock. Seventy-six Falls was named in the early days of Clinton County. As a survey of the area was being made, members of the surveying team built a shop and lodging quarters near the falls. The station number was 76, and the falls became known as 76 Falls. The falls were 83 feet in length before the lake was filled. (Courtesy of the authors' collection.)

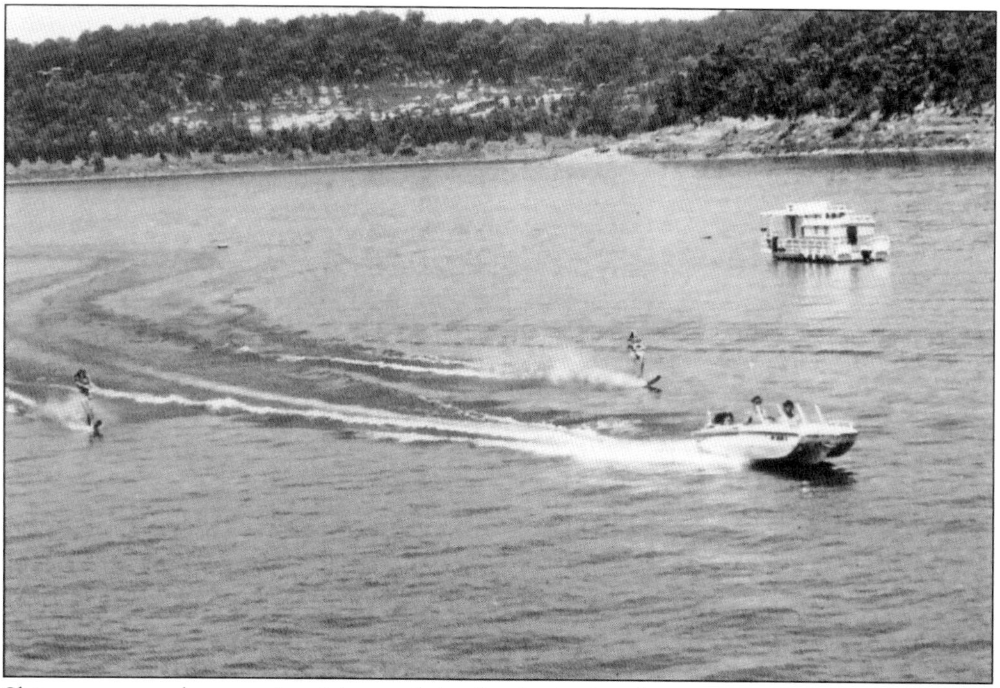

Skiing was an early recreational draw to Lake Cumberland and continues to be a popular activity. Water-skiing is a sport where an individual is pulled behind a motorboat on a body of water wearing skis. Skiers hold onto a rope and skim across the water. (Courtesy of Phil Ruchka.)

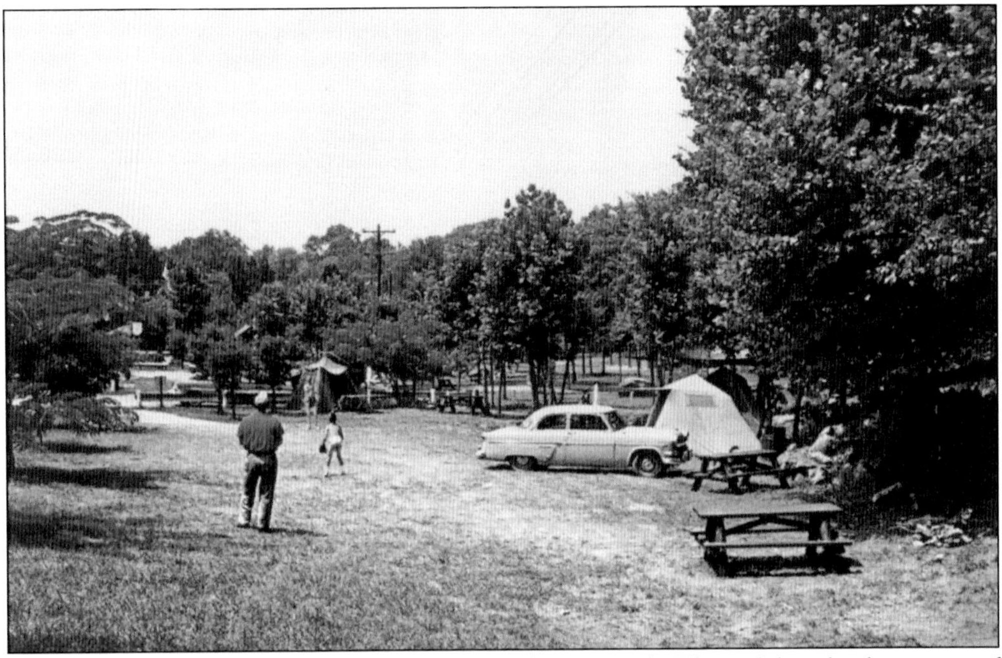

Campers enjoy a game of catch at General Burnside State Park. The park has the distinction of being the only island park in Kentucky and covers 390 acres. Formerly known as Bunker Hill, the park became a Kentucky state park on February 3, 1958. Recently, the 18-hole golf course was completely renovated. (Courtesy of Dawn Garvin.)

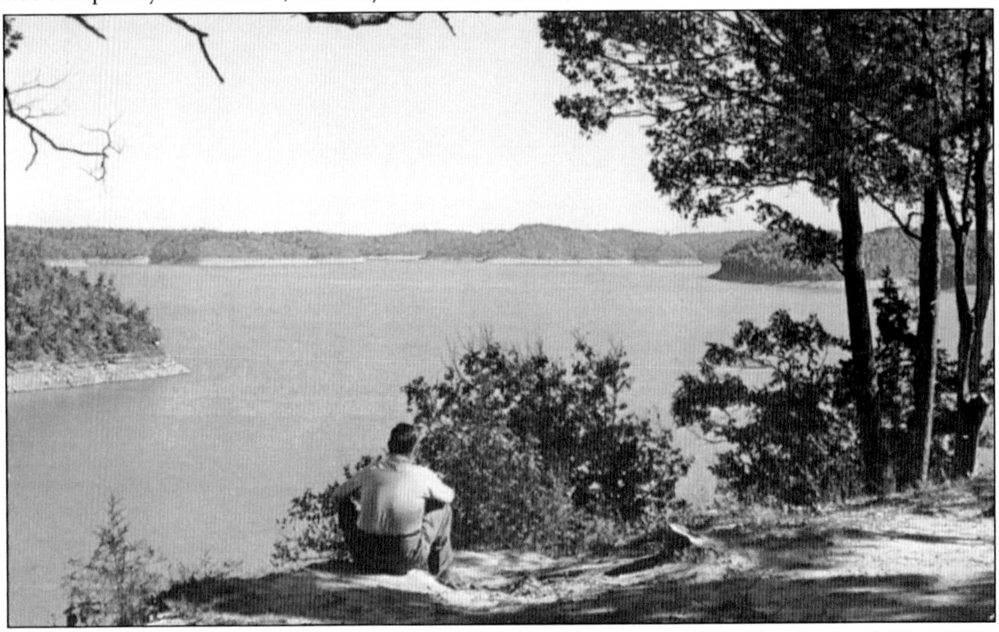

A postcard from the 1960s shows a gentleman enjoying the vistas of Lake Cumberland. The 1960s proved to be a period of increased popularity for Kentucky state parks. Facilities added at Lake Cumberland State Park during this time included a nine-hole golf course, ranch cottages, riding stables and trails, tennis courts, playgrounds, a community swimming pool, a grocery store, and a gift shop. (Courtesy of the authors' collection.)

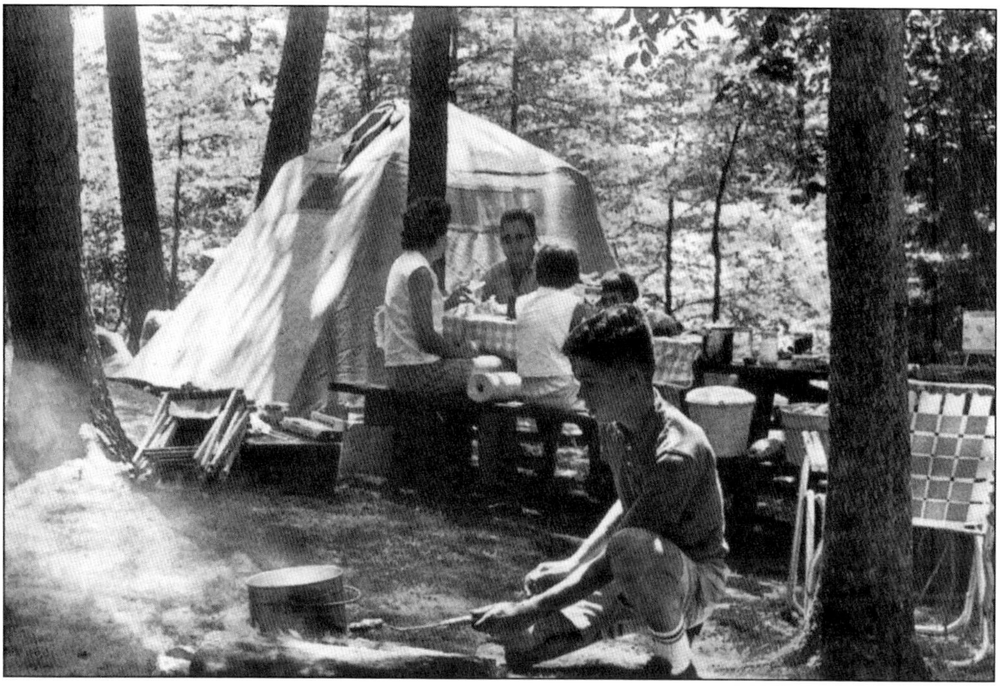

Camping is a family affair at Lake Cumberland. This photograph appeared in an advertisement brochure in the early 1960s. Families enjoyed camping beginning in the late 1800s. Despite the comforts of home, many enjoyed being close to nature. (Courtesy of Phil Ruchka.)

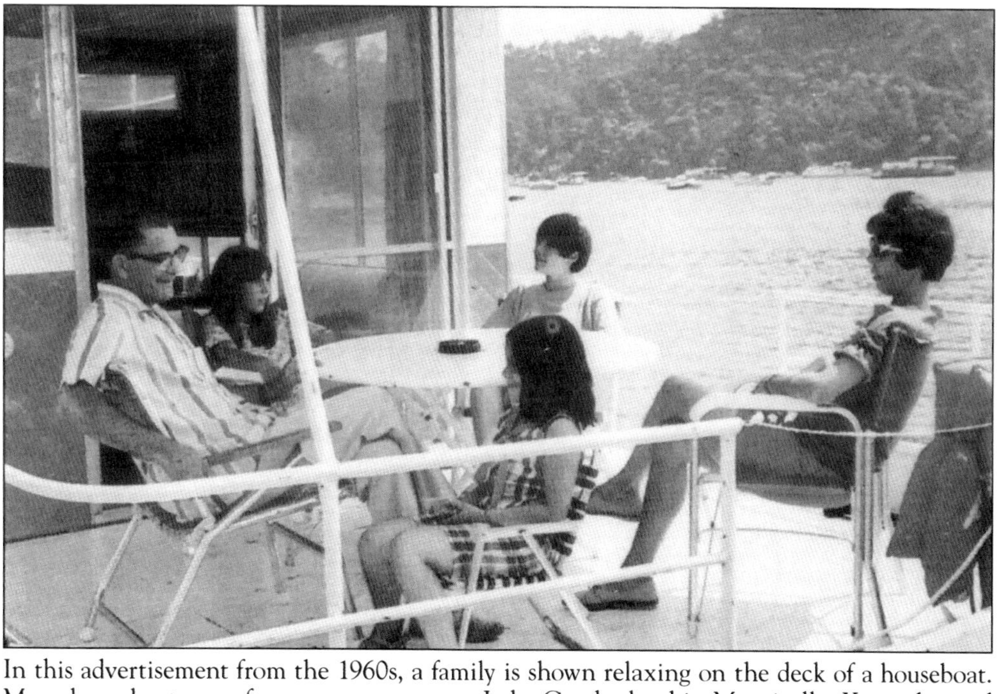

In this advertisement from the 1960s, a family is shown relaxing on the deck of a houseboat. Many houseboat manufacturers operate near Lake Cumberland in Monticello, Kentucky, and Somerset, Kentucky. Monticello claims to be the "Houseboat Manufacturing Capital of the World." (Courtesy of Phil Ruchka.)

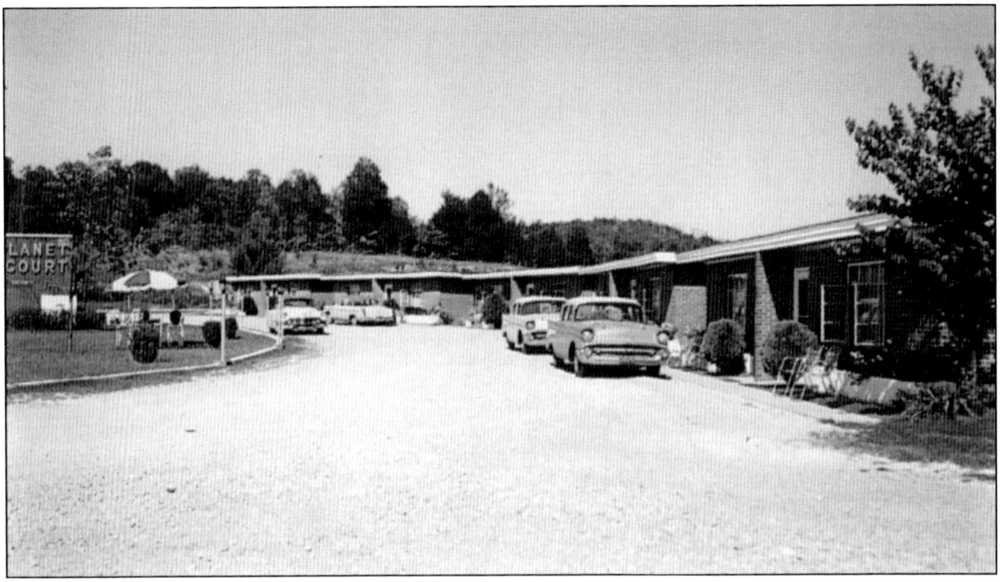

This postcard shows the Planet Court Motel. The back of the postcard reads, "On scenic Lake Cumberland. QUIET REST, 400 yards off US 27 on West Ky. 90. Phone 9103. Air Conditioning, window fans, television, and kitchenettes optional. Central heat, recreation area and family rates." (Courtesy of the authors' collection.)

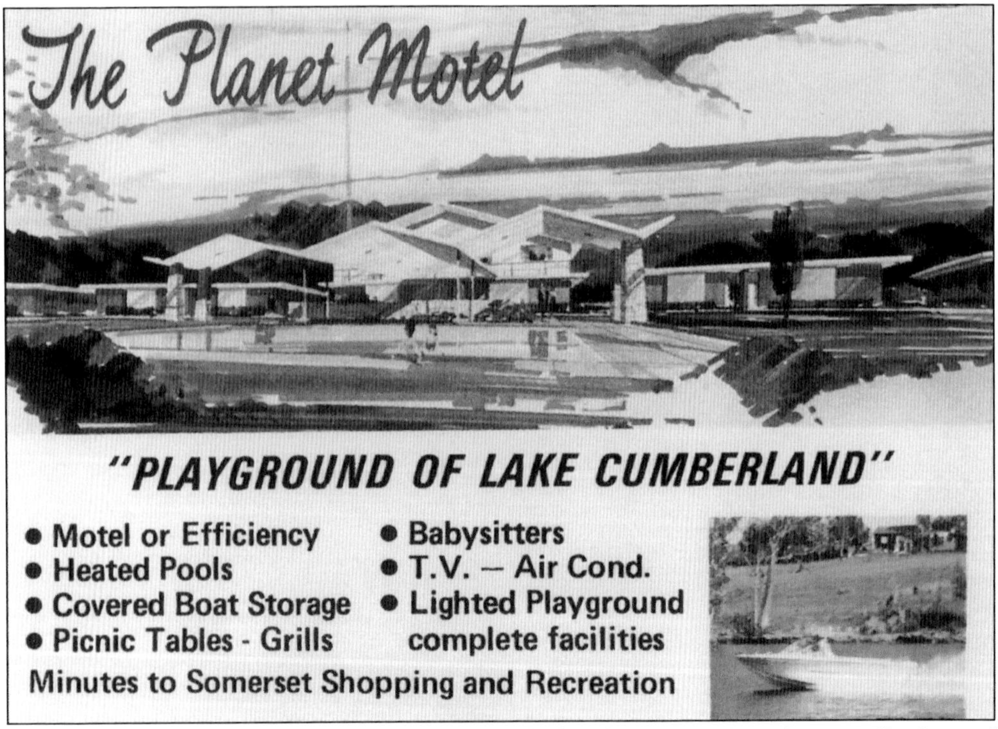

Self-touted as the "Playground of Lake Cumberland," the Planet Court Motel eventually changed its name to the Planet Motel. This photograph shows an advertisement from a 1960s Kentucky travel guide. The motel offers a heated pool, picnic tables and grills, a lighted playground facility, and even babysitting. (Courtesy of Phil Ruchka.)

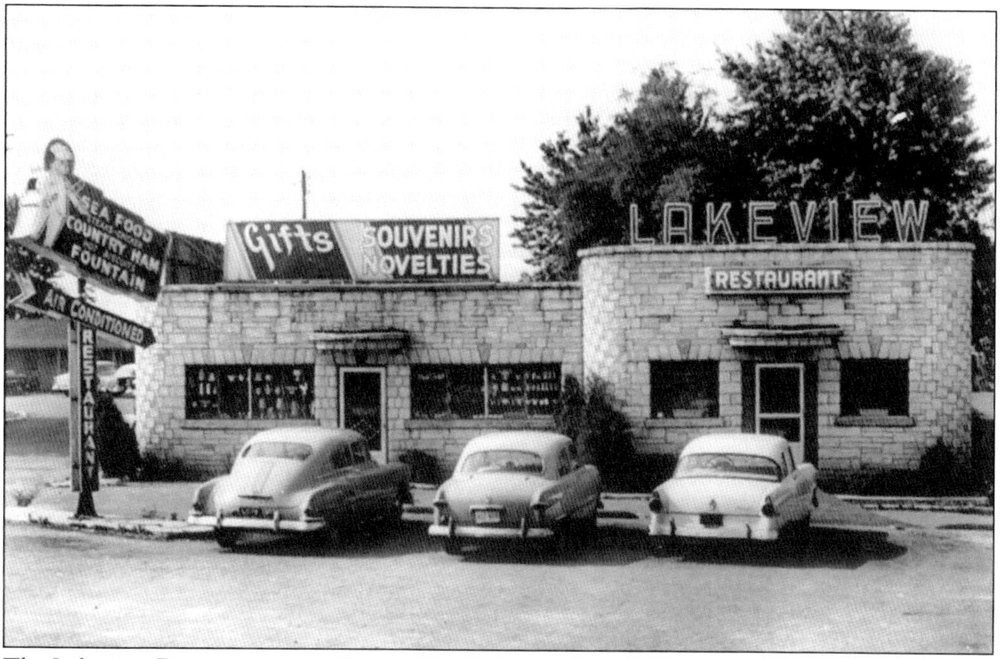

The Lakeview Restaurant sat in front of the Lakeview Motel. The term "motel" is derived from the term "motorist's hotel," which originally meant that the hotel provided parking. Most motels consisted of a building with connected rooms whose doors faced a parking lot. (Courtesy of the authors' collection.)

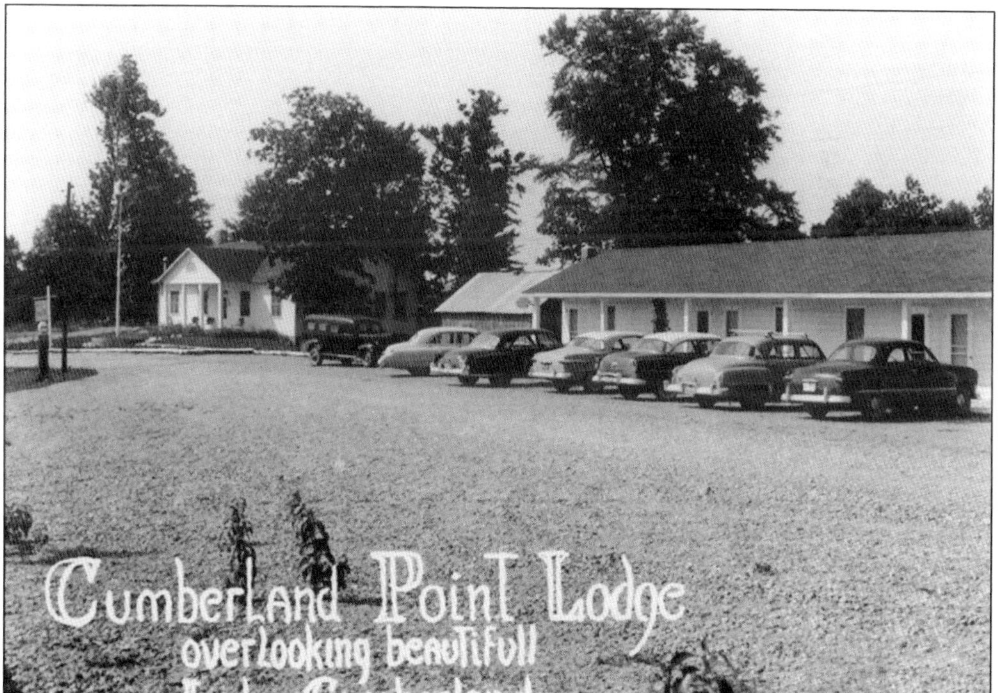

This photograph shows the Cumberland Point Lodge in Nancy, Kentucky, in the mid-1950s. The lodge no longer exists. (Courtesy of Rogers Photography.)

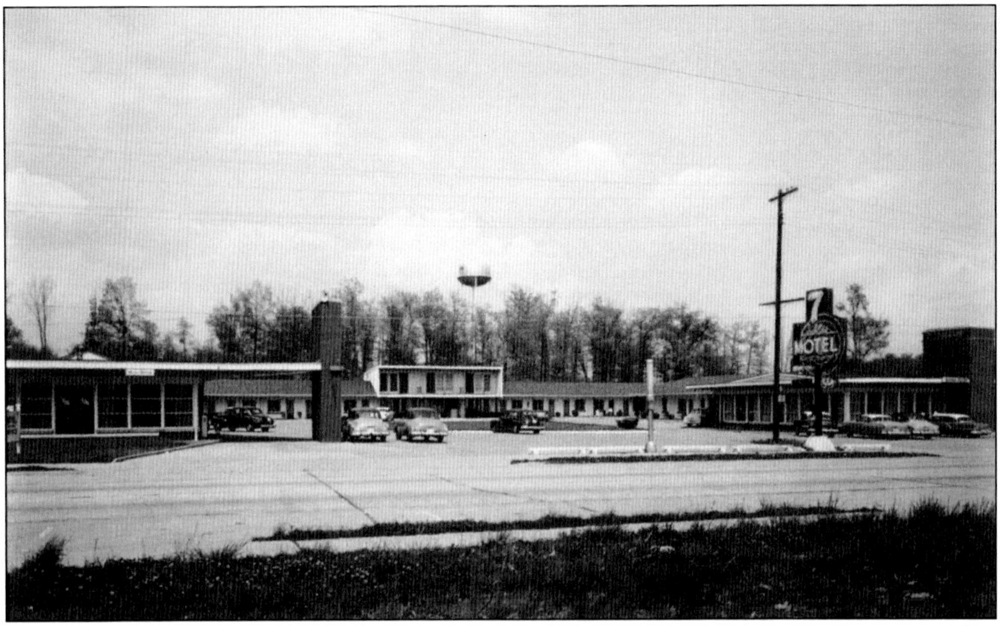

In this postcard from the 1950s, the new Seven Gables Motel and Restaurant are pictured in Burnside on U.S. Highway 27. The back of the postcard reads, "Outstanding accommodations. 35 Spacious rooms with private tile baths. Steam heat. Guest lounge. Air conditioned. Restaurant open 5 a.m. to 10 p.m. serving the finest food in the South. Gateway to Cumberland Falls. Phone 7." (Courtesy of the authors' collection.)

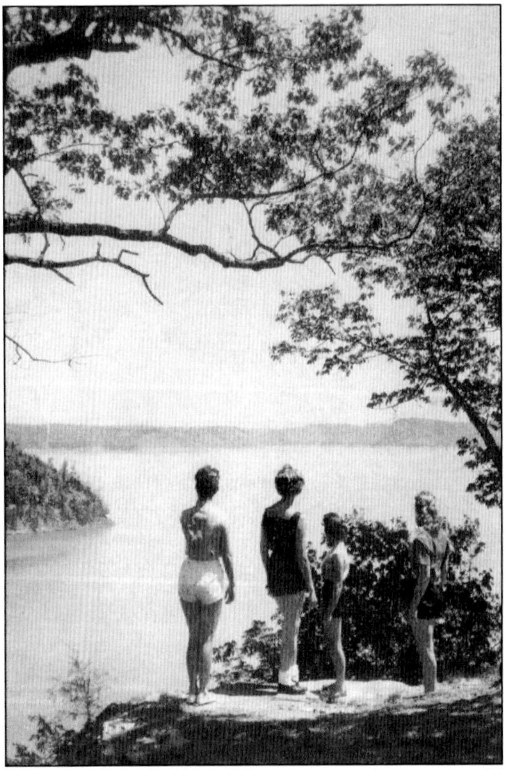

An advertisement from the early 1960s shows ladies enjoying the breathtaking views of Lake Cumberland. (Courtesy of Phil Ruchka.)

Eight

The Future of Lake Cumberland

Much has changed in the area since the wild Cumberland River ruled the land in south-central Kentucky. Several communities were born, thrived, and passed into memories. Lake Cumberland was created in 1951 and has offered a generation of new memories to countless visitors.

As spring arrives in south-central Kentucky, tourists flock to Lake Cumberland. A steady stream of automobiles towing boats of all sizes crowd Kentucky roadways. Tourists from all over the United States make their pilgrimage to the lake, despite lowered water levels caused by leaks in Wolf Creek Dam.

The first problems were noticed in 1962 when wet spots began to develop. Five years later, a sinkhole appeared. In March 1968, two sinkholes fell in, one of which measured 13 feet across by 40 feet deep. Further leaks were detected in the 1970s and the 1980s as a result of the porous limestone foundation.

In 2005, the condition of the dam deteriorated further. Sinkholes formed in the dam, and muddy discharge welled up in the river below the dam. The Corps of Engineers ranked the dam in the high risk of failure category and declared it in urgent need of repairs. In order to make repairs, the level of the lake had to be lowered.

Lowering the water level of Lake Cumberland would relieve pressure on the structure and reduce the risk of failure. Although failure of the dam would be catastrophic to areas downriver, the risk of this occurring has been reduced significantly with repairs.

Repairs to the dam are expected to be completed by 2012. In the meantime, the Corps of Engineers will keep the water level of Lake Cumberland at 680 feet. Once the repairs are made, the water level will return to normal at 723 feet in the summer and 695 feet in the winter.

The future of Lake Cumberland will not be a perfect one, but the lake will have a future. Each spring will bring vacationers and the customary stream of boat trailers. Just as generations of the past coexisted with the Cumberland River, the children and grandchildren of the river will coexist with the future of Lake Cumberland.

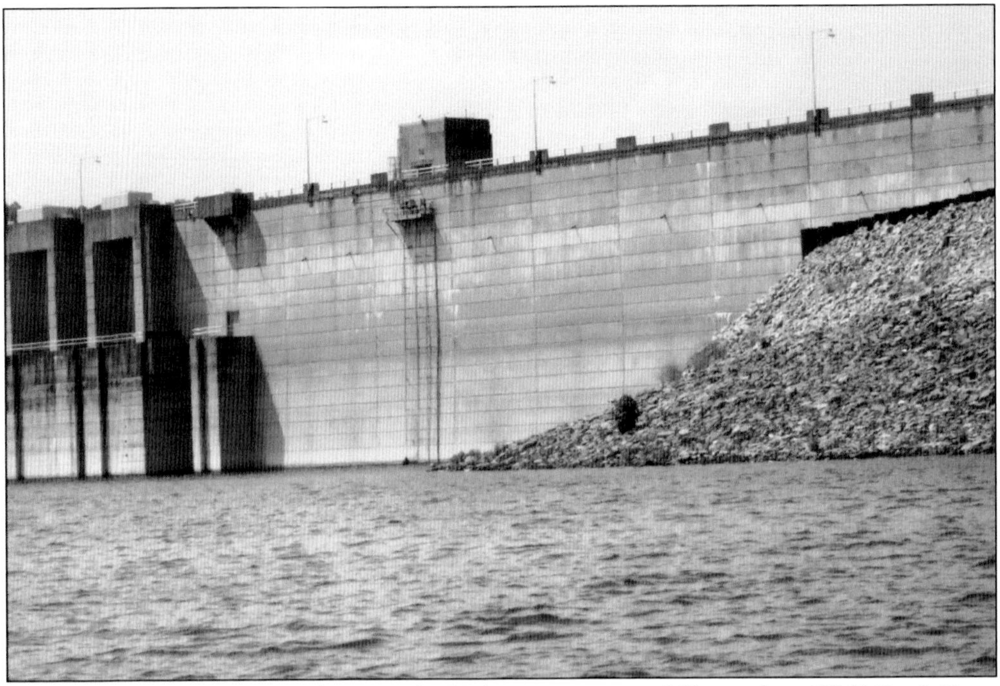

Lake Cumberland was lowered in 2007 by 50 feet so repairs could be made to Wolf Creek Dam. This photograph was taken in September 2008. The dark line on the dam and rocks serves as evidence that the water level has been lowered. (Photograph by Lucia Applegate.)

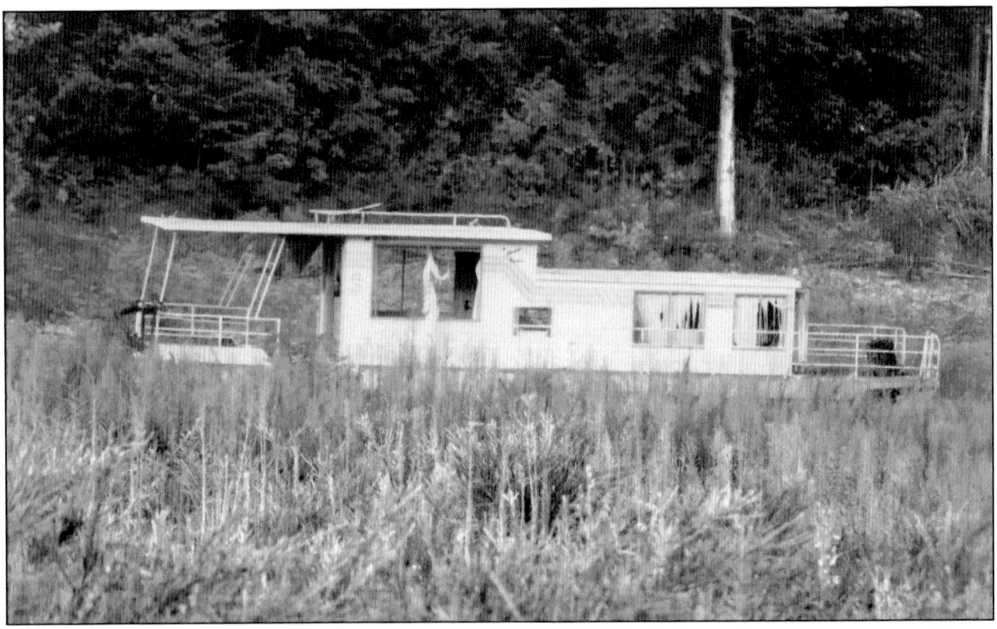

Lowered water levels caught this boat owner off guard, causing the houseboat to run aground near Burnside Marina. There are two basic categories of houseboats: non-cruising and cruising. Non-cruising houseboats are not meant for traveling out to sea. They spend most of their time moored, anchored, or tied up to a marina slip or dock. These are the most common type of floating home and can always be seen on Lake Cumberland. (Courtesy of the authors' collection.)

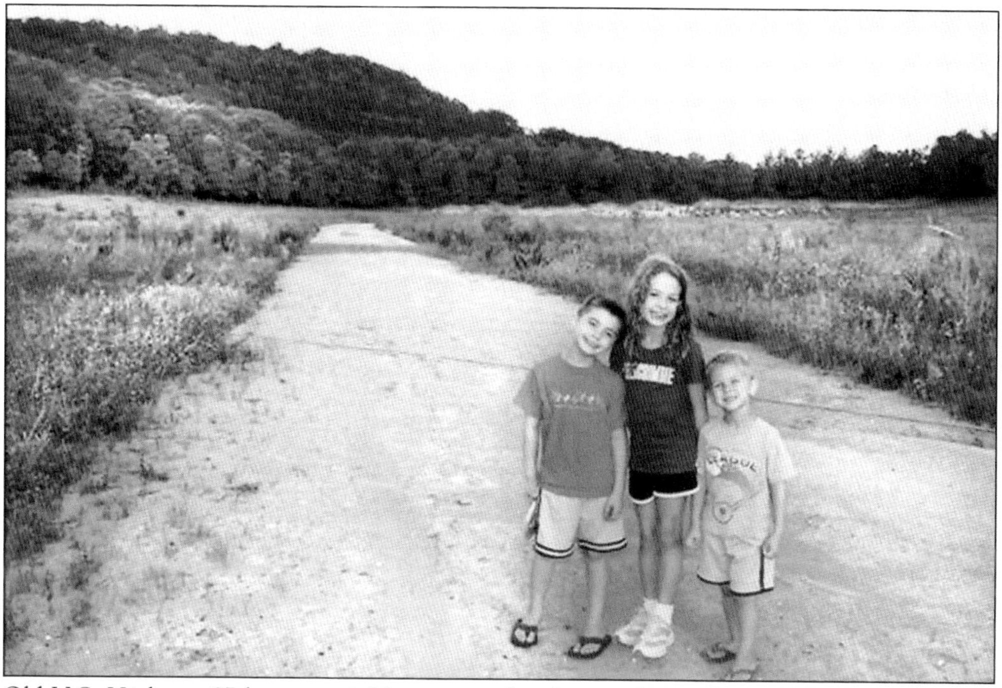

Old U.S. Highway 27 became visible as water levels were lowered in 2007. Along Old U.S. Highway 27, foundations of homes and businesses could be seen, while sidewalks could again be walked upon. (Courtesy of the authors' collection.)

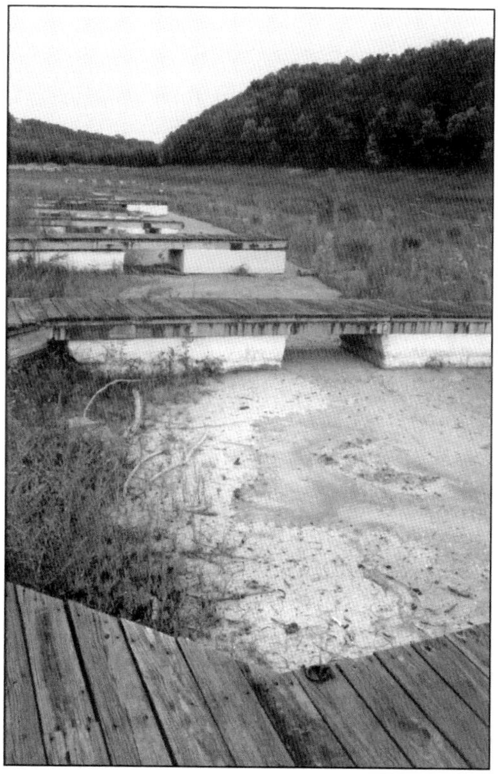

This once floating boat slip straddles old U.S. Highway 27 at Burnside Marina. Boat slips are found at marinas and docks. They allow boat owners or boat renters a way to keep their boat in one place. (Courtesy of the authors' collection.)

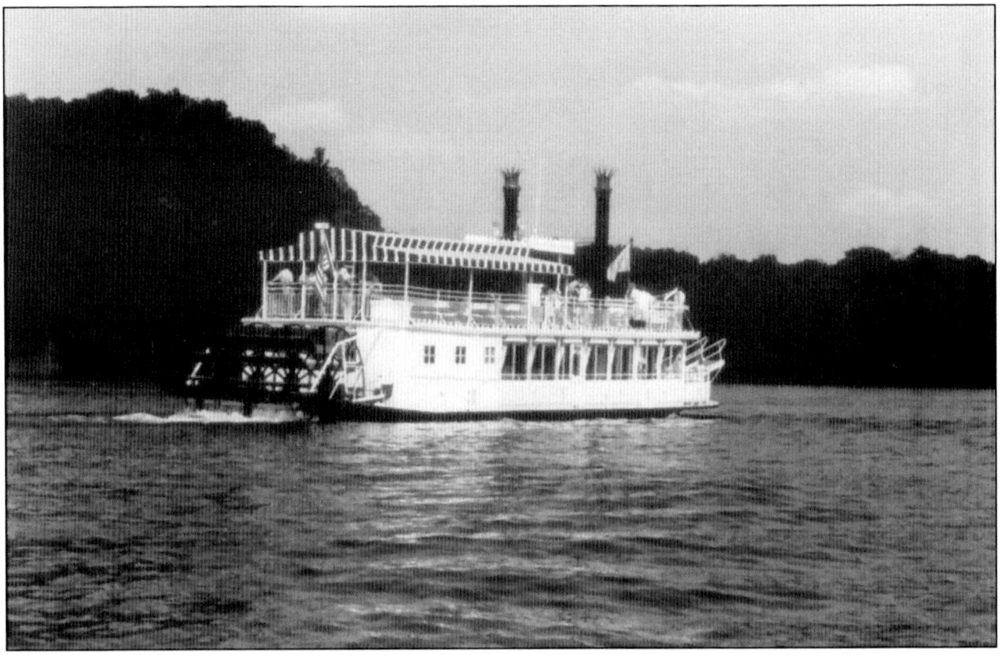

In the mid-1990s, a steamboat was brought up the Cumberland River from Nashville, Tennessee. The boat was lifted with cranes and placed into Lake Cumberland. The steamboat was used for dinner cruises, but it was not a successful venture. It was eventually taken out of Lake Cumberland. (Courtesy of Carole Tupman.)

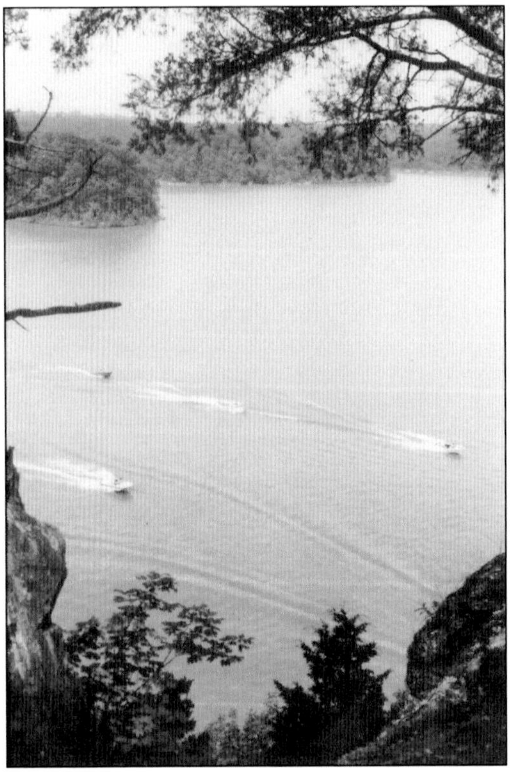

Viewed from along the rocky cliffs, boaters enjoy thousands of acres of a watery playground on Lake Cumberland. (Courtesy of Phil Ruchka.)

When Lake Cumberland is at full crest level, Burnside Marina offers 400 covered and uncovered slips. Burnside Marina is a public boat launch and offers a number of amenities, including a store and rentals of houseboats, fishing boats, Jet Skis, pontoon boats, and ski boats. (Courtesy of Jonathan Goforth.)

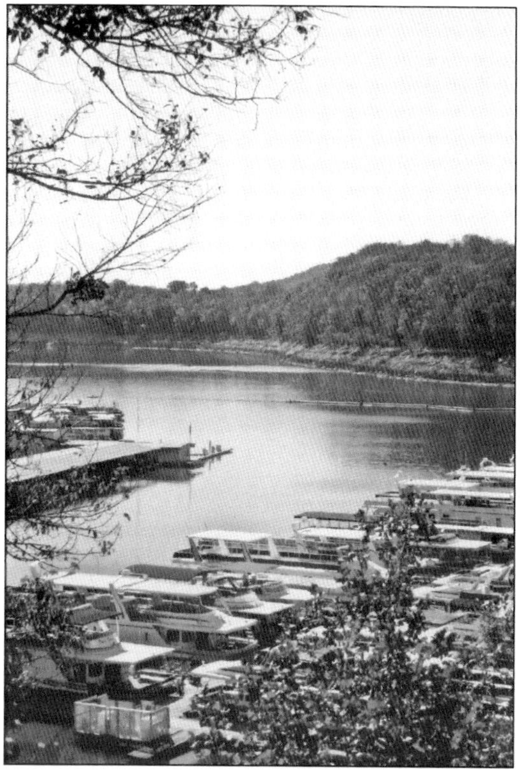

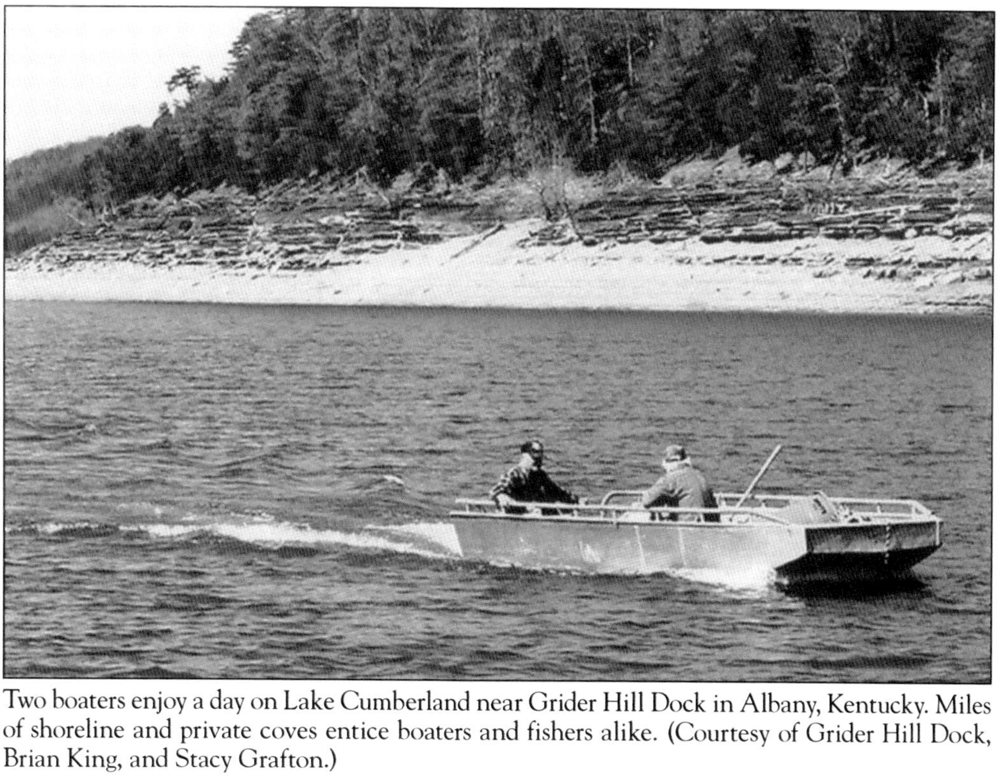

Two boaters enjoy a day on Lake Cumberland near Grider Hill Dock in Albany, Kentucky. Miles of shoreline and private coves entice boaters and fishers alike. (Courtesy of Grider Hill Dock, Brian King, and Stacy Grafton.)

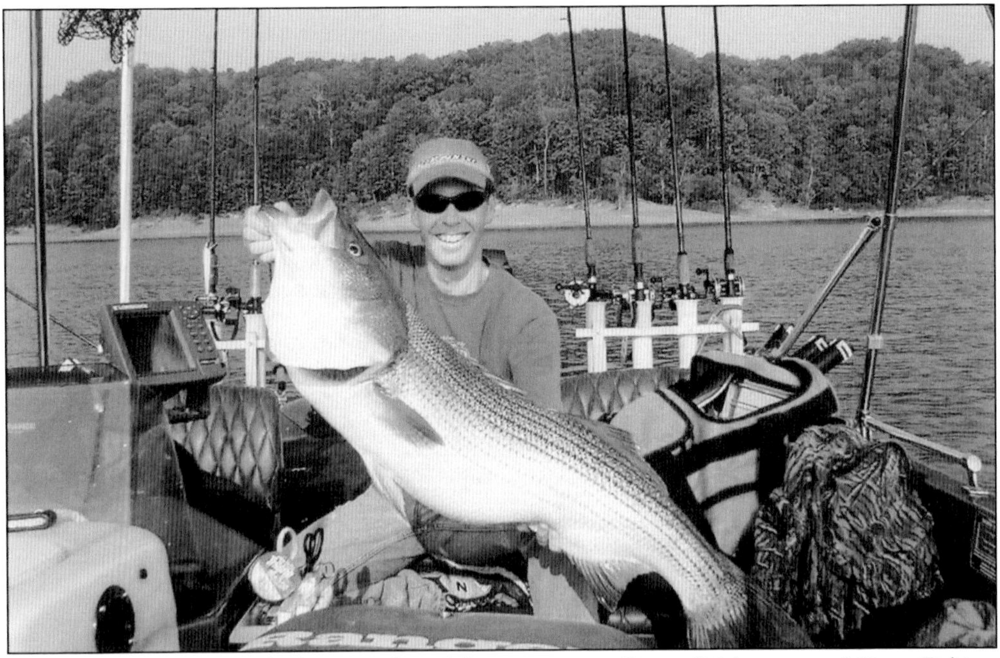

This photograph shows the big one that did not get away. Bryan Bihl, owner of Gone Fishing Guide Service, holds a massive striped bass that he pulled out of Lake Cumberland. The lake offers year-round fishing with multiple species of bass and trout. Lake Cumberland's striped bass average 12 to 15 pounds. (Courtesy of Bryan E. Bihl, Gone Fishing Guide Service.)

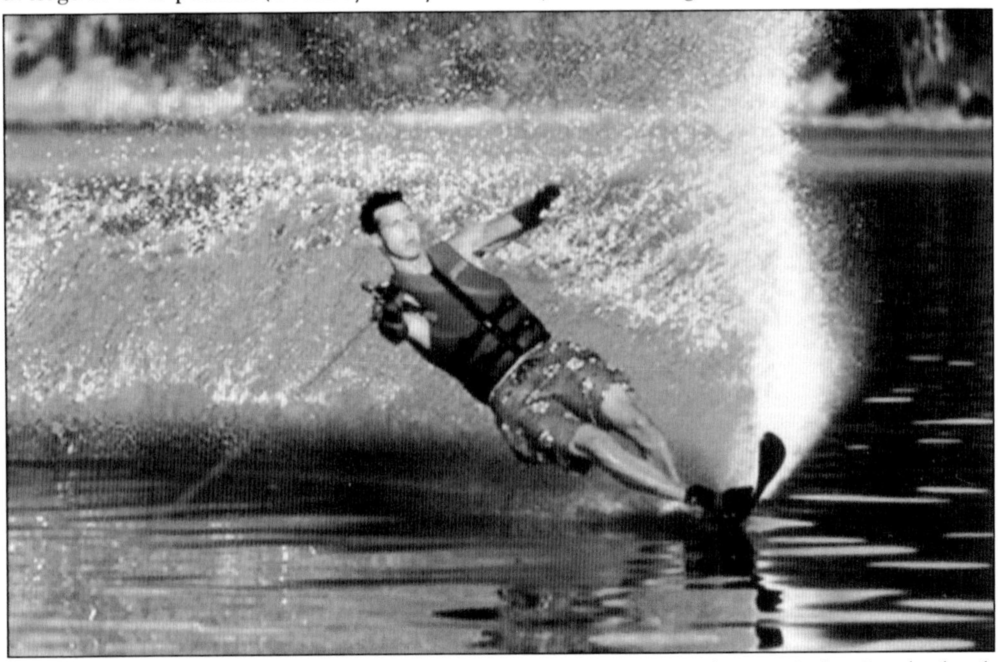

Despite lowered water levels, water-skiing remains an important draw to Lake Cumberland. Lined with trees and rocky cliffs, the water of Lake Cumberland is protected from wind, which keeps waves and ripples to a minimum. (Courtesy of Marge Bateman and Kentucky Department of Travel.)

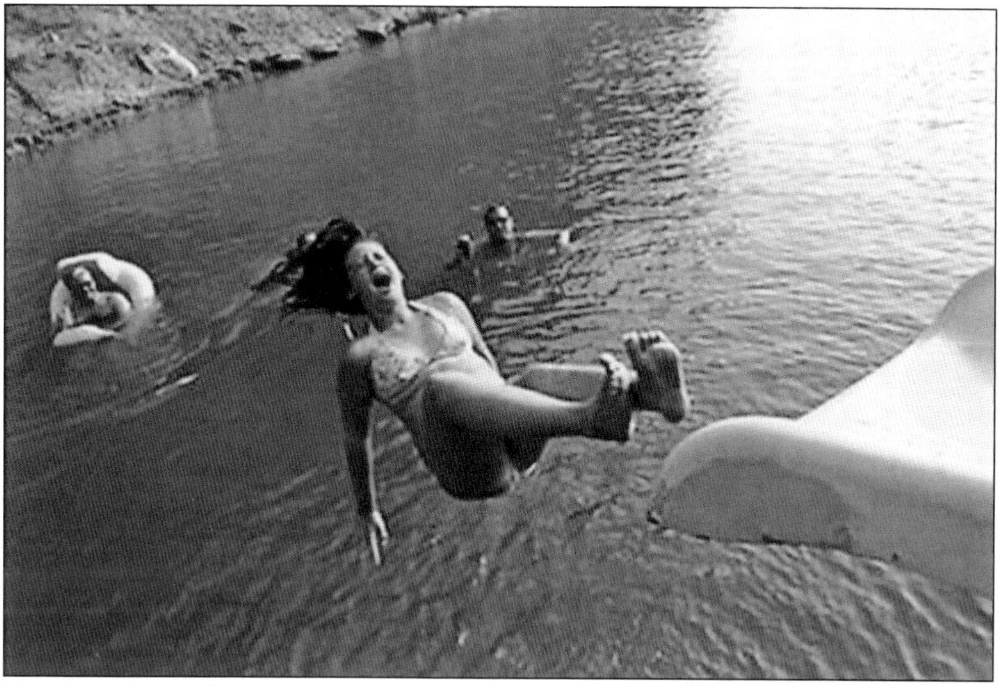

Many houseboats offer a large slide located on the rear of the boat. After sliders climb a ladder to the top of the boat, they are able to rush down into the water. In this photograph, an adventurous slider takes the plunge backward into Lake Cumberland. (Courtesy of the authors' collection.)

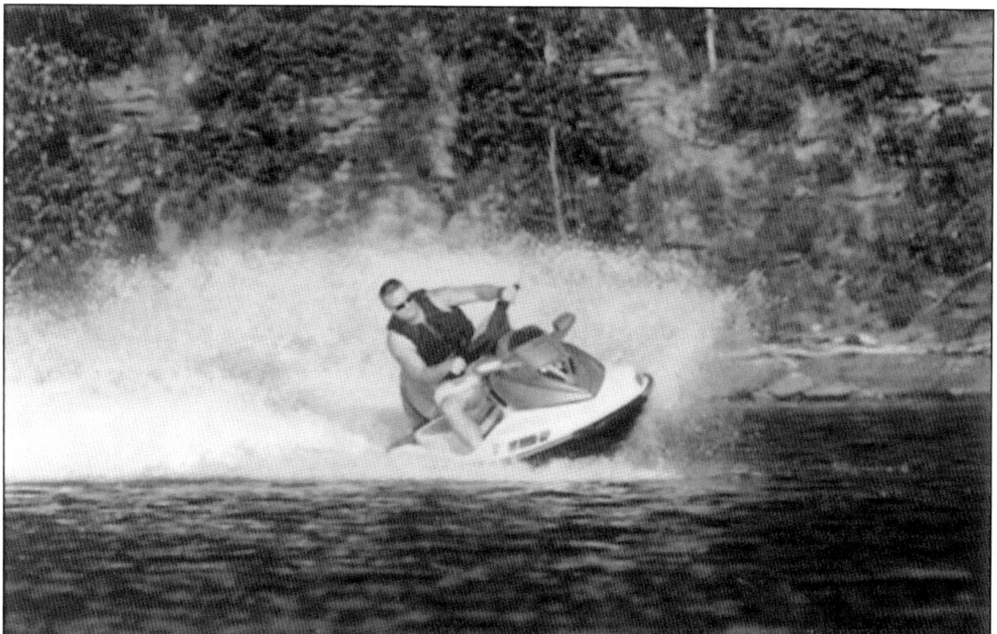

Jet-Skiing is tremendously popular on Lake Cumberland, as is water-skiing, knee boarding, and tubing. The first Jet Ski was marketed in 1973, although there was a workable personal watercraft available in the late 1960s. A Jet Ski uses an enclosed gas-powered motor to push water out in a jet stream. (Courtesy of Marge Bateman and Kentucky Department of Travel.)

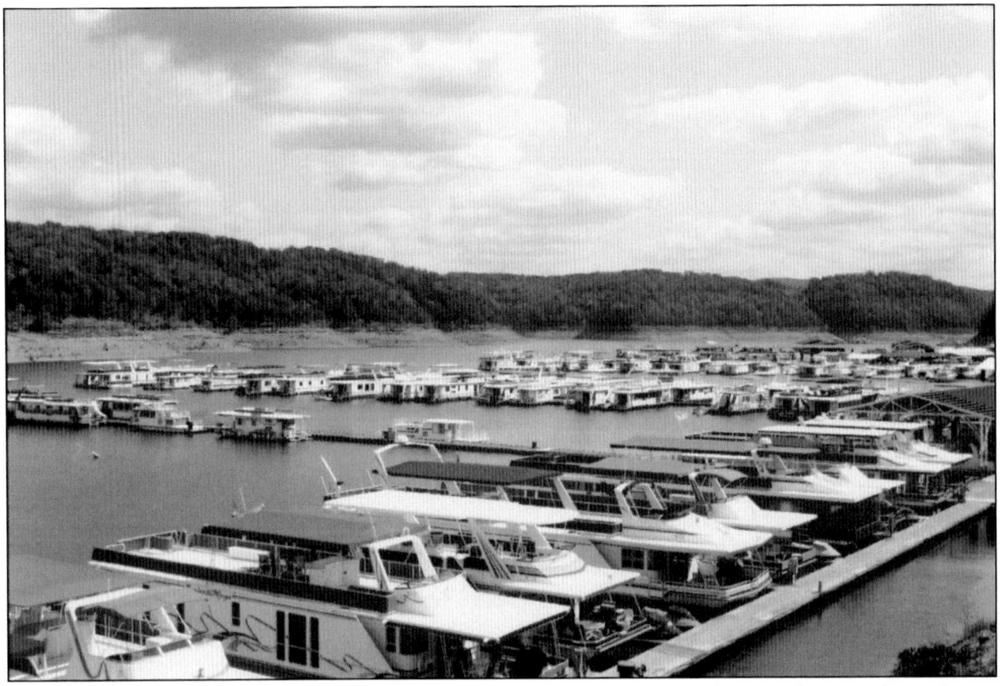

Grider Hill Dock offers 750 covered and uncovered boat slips. One thing is for sure: houseboats are here to stay. Lake Cumberland is known as the Houseboat Capital of the World. (Courtesy of Grider Hill Dock, Brian King, and Stacy Grafton.)

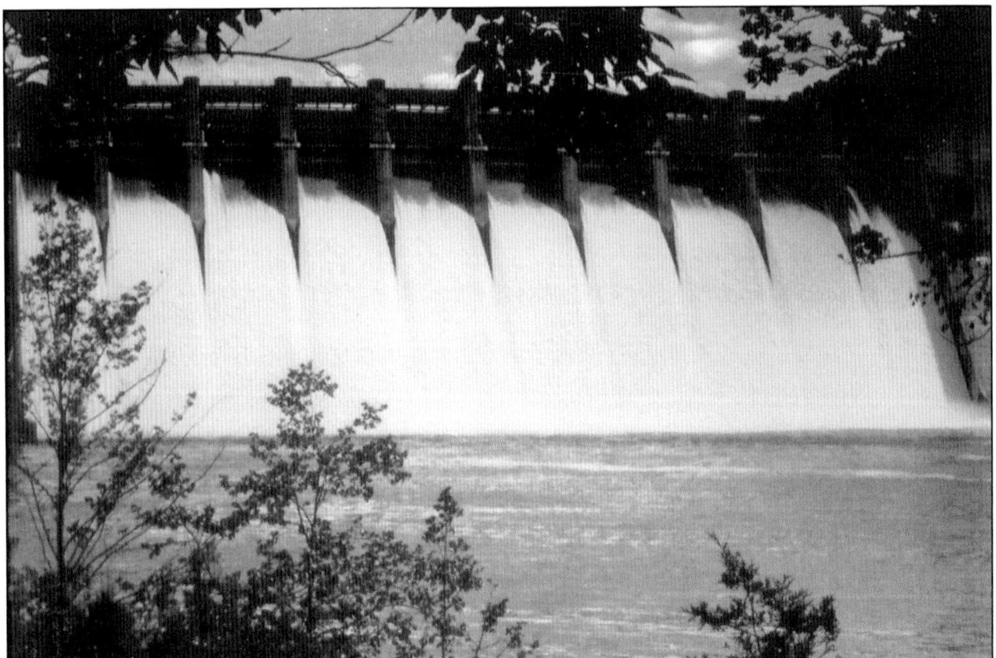

Repairs to Wolf Creek Dam are scheduled to be completed in 2012. At that time, the water will be elevated to past levels, and life on the lake will return to normal. (Courtesy of Carole Tupman.)

Even man's best friend enjoys Lake Cumberland. Lined with federally protected shores, this boating paradise is truly one of Kentucky's greatest all-sports lakes, with countless coves and inlets to explore and appreciate. (Courtesy of Cliff Steele.)

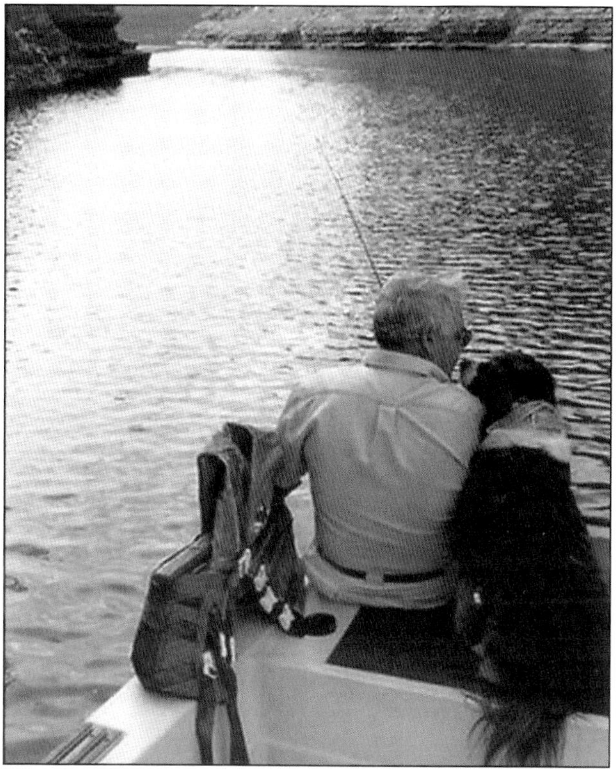

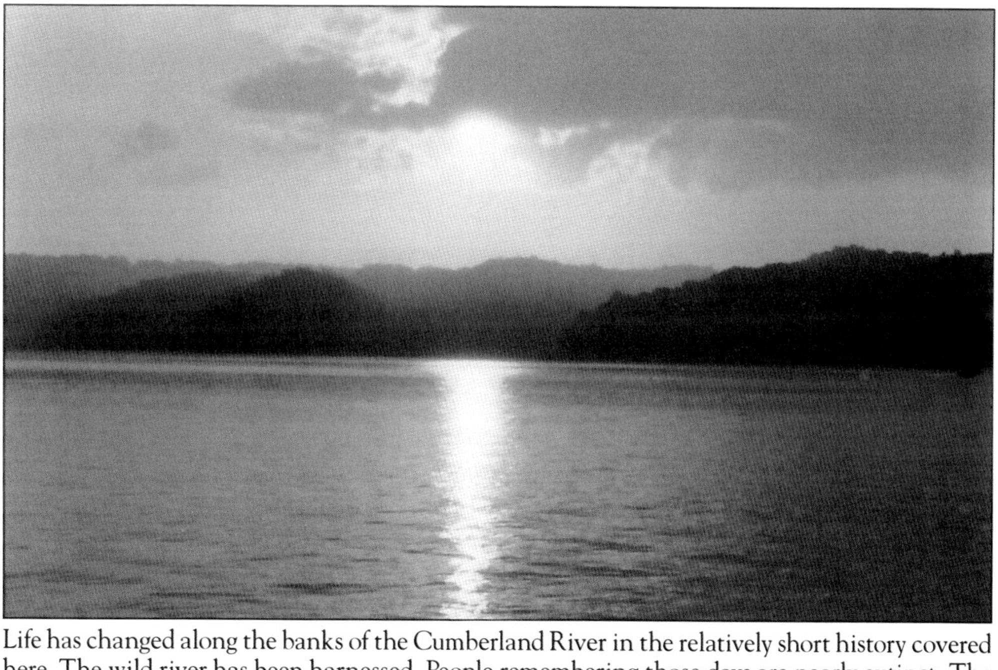

Life has changed along the banks of the Cumberland River in the relatively short history covered here. The wild river has been harnessed. People remembering those days are nearly extinct. The future is left with photographs and stories. But on a warm summer evening with gentle waves lapping at the shore and a full moon overhead, one can almost hear the voice of the Cumberland, still singing the song of the river. (Courtesy of Carole Tupman.)